FOR THE LOVE OF THE GAME

For the Love of the Game

*Amateur Sport in Small-Town
Ontario, 1838–1895*

NANCY B. BOUCHIER

McGill-Queen's University Press
Montreal & Kingston • London • Ithaca

Legal deposit first quarter 2003
Bibliothèque nationale du Québec

Printed in Canada on acid-free paper that is 100%
ancient forest free (100% post-consumer recycled),
processed chlorine free.

This book has been published with the help of a grant
from the Humanities and Social Sciences Federation of
Canada, using funds provided by the Social Sciences and
Humanities Research Council of Canada.

McGill-Queen's University Press acknowledges the
support of the Canada Council for the Arts for our
publishing program. We also acknowledge the financial
support of the Government of Canada through the Book
Publishing Industry Development Program (BPIDP) for
our publishing activities.

___

National Library of Canada Cataloguing in Publication

Bouchier, Nancy Barbara, 1958–
    For the love of the game : amateur sport in small-town
Ontario, 1838–1895 / Nancy B. Bouchier.

Includes bibliographical references and index.
ISBN 0-7735-2456-8
    1. Sports – Social aspects – Ontario – Ingersoll – History
– 19th century.   2. Sports – Social aspects – Ontario –
Woodstock – History – 19th century   3. Ingersoll (Ont.) –
Social life and customs – 19th century.   4. Woodstock
(Ont.) – Social life and customs – 19th century   I. Title.

GV585.3.O5B68 2003   306.4'83'0971346   C2002-903655-0

___

This book was typeset by True to Type in 10/12 Sabon

Contents

Tables, Maps, and Illustrations   vii

Acknowledgments   ix

Introduction   3

1   Tory Elites to Middle-Class Men: Changing Political, Economic, and Social Landscapes   9

2   The 24th of May is the Queen's Birthday: Civic Holidays, Locality, and Sport   31

3   From Holidays to Every Day: The Amateur Ascendancy in Local Sport   60

4   Cricket and Local Culture: From Centre Stage to the Margins   88

5   Baseball, Boosters, and the Amateur Not-for-Profit Approach to Community Sport   100

6   Lacrosse: Idealized Middle-Class Sport for Youth   117

7   A Respectable Man's World: Amateurism and Local Culture   131

Appendix: Notes on Methodology and Primary Sources   139

Notes   143

Bibliography   177

Index   203

Tables, Maps, and Illustrations

TABLES

1.1 Summary of urban growth and local services for Ingersoll and Woodstock, 1830–1901   147

1.2 Industrial employees and number of manufacturing establishments in Ingersoll and Woodstock, 1871–1891   148

1.3 Ingersoll and Woodstock census populations and the number of Ontario urban municipalities by population size, 1851–1901   148

1.4 Place of birth in percentage of total populations, Ingersoll and Woodstock inhabitants, 1851–1901   149

1.5 Per cent distribution of occupational breakdown, Ingersoll and Woodstock, 1851–1891   149

3.1 Per cent distribution of occupational breakdown, Ingersoll and Woodstock AAA executives and the local populations, 1884–1896   159

6.1 The number of senior and junior baseball and lacrosse clubs in Ingersoll and Woodstock, 1860–1889   173

MAPS

1 Geographic location of Ingersoll and Woodstock, Canada West/Ontario   19

2 Bird's-eye view of Ingersoll, 1885   26

3 Bird's-eye view of Woodstock, 1885   27

ILLUSTRATIONS

Ingersoll's Mammoth Cheese, 1866   20

Dundas Street, Woodstock, c. 1860s   21

Morrow Screw and Nut factory workers, Ingersoll, n.d.   23

W.A. Karn Drugstore, Woodstock, 1897   25

IAAA Dominion Day trades parade, Ingersoll, c. 1890s   39

Woodstock representative sports teams through time   41

Woodstock Cycle Club, c. 1885   43

Joseph Gibson and Ingersoll cyclists, n.d.   44

Lady cyclists on parade, Woodstock, 1897   45

Herb Clarke, Woodstock's famed amateur cyclist, c. 1888   68

Alby Robinson, Woodstock professional athlete, n.d.   85

The Young Canadians, Woodstock's Canadian Baseball
Champions, c. 1868   101

Boys' baseball team, Woodstock area, n.d.   111

Bain Factory Club first nine, Woodstock, 1898   113

Bain Factory Club members, 1896   115

Dufferin lacrosse club, Ingersoll, n.d.   124

Dominion Day lacrosse sketch, 1893   127

Acknowledgments

It has taken me quite a while – nearly half my lifetime at this point – to bring this project to closure after many interruptions and long times away from it. I am glad finally to see it done. I owe many people debts of gratitude for their help and support over the years. At the University of Western Ontario, George Emery, Don Morrow, and Bob Barney oversaw my training and eased my transition from physical education to history. I am fortunate to have studied with them. J.J. Talman responded to many questions along the way; for sure, Ontario history has lost much with his passing. My classmate and friend Chris Anstead gave cogent criticism and help with theory and data. He is a gem. My thanks for the useful suggestions of Fred Armstrong, Roger Hall, Susan Houston, and Sid Noel, who examined the dissertation upon which this book is based. Ken Cruikshank and Stephen Hardy gave invaluable critical feedback and encouragement for strengthening my argument and revising the manuscript. Mel Adelman, Peter Donnelly, Greg Gillespie, Colin Howell, Mary Keyes, Bruce Kidd, Alan Metcalfe, and Patricia Vertinsky each helped me at various points in the process. Thanks also to Marlene Cope, Deanna Goral, Marion Gerull, Ania Latoszek, Kim McNabb, Heidi Nash, Tina Parratt, and Ang Ross for their many kindnesses born of friendship. Rhoda Howard-Hassmann and Stefania Szlek Miller have shown me the true meaning of collegiality. Special thanks to Lesley Barry, who did a marvelous job of editing the manuscript, to Ruth Pincoe, for her great index, and to Joan McGilvray and Philip Cercone from McGill-Queen's, who helped to get the book into print. Over the years I have been helped tremendously at Western and in Oxford County by archivists, curators, librarians, and volunteers. I'd especially like to thank Mary Evans, herself forever a young spirit, who made research trips to Woodstock fun and interesting. Thanks also to Jill Jamieson, Shelia Johnson, Melanie Law,

Rosemary Lewis, Shirley Lovell, David Scholosser, and Walter Zimmerman, who all hunted down obscure materials that I needed. Finally, through the years my dad, Larry, has been a wonderful teacher for his children, his beloved grandchildren, and his students at Algonquin College. As a child I may not have listened to his stories with rapt attention – who really listens to their parents? – yet I have come to realize that from him I have learnt more about the importance of history, about being Canadian, and about academic life than from any other source. I am grateful for these gifts.

This research was originally assisted by a doctoral fellowship from the Social Sciences and Humanities Research Council of Canada. The Arts Research Board of McMaster University financed the indexing of the manuscript. Some of the material from chapters 1 and 4 has been reprinted, by permission, from "Aristocrats and their Noble Sport: Woodstock's Officers and Cricket During the Rebellion Era," *Canadian Journal of History of Sport* 20 (1) (1989):16–31. Revised from Don Morrow (comp.) 5*th* *Canadian Symposium on the History of Sport* (London: University of Western Ontario, 1988), 50–62; some material from chapter 1 has been reprinted, by permission, from "Strictly Honourable Races: Woodstock's Driving Park Association and Small Town Sporting Holidays," *Canadian Journal of History of Sport* 24 (1) (1993):29–51; some material from chapters 2 and 3 has been reprinted, by permission, from "'The 24th of May is the Queen's Birthday': Civic Holidays and Sport in Nineteenth Century Canadian Towns," *International Journal of History of Sport* 10 (2) (August 1993): 159–92; and some material from chapter 6 has been reprinted, by permission, from "Idealized Middle Class Sport: Lacrosse in Nineteenth Century Ontario Towns," *Journal of Canadian Studies* 29 (2) (Summer 1994):89–110.

FOR THE LOVE OF THE GAME

Introduction

Half a century ago, Marshall McLuhan surprised some listeners of the CBC's *Wednesday Night* radio program by stating, "baseball is culture." To many people, this idea was simply absurd. How could one of the greatest thinkers of the day think so highly of something so commonplace? Sports lovers, McLuhan mused, "would not thank anybody who told them that their eager spin through the daily sports page was a cultural activity of great value and significance to society."[1] As strange as this observation may have seemed to some at the time, it was and remains apt. Today, we live in McLuhan's global village, and Canadians cannot fail to notice the prominence and importance that sport takes in it, or the interdependence between sport – particularly professional sport – and the mass media.

McLuhan's observation, made in 1952, came on the heels of a crucial time in Canadian sport, a period when, according to Canadian historian Bruce Kidd, the corporate capitalist system of sport began its domination in a contested cultural terrain.[2] Epitomized by the NHL, it began its rise in the 1920s and 1930s – simultaneously a "golden age" for amateur sport in Ontario.[3] The professional model's intimate links to the media, particularly our state-run CBC, fueled its ascendancy in a continental mass culture. At the crux of this sport system lies something Kidd calls a great "cultural riddle"; that is, the ways in which athletes and their teams *represent* something for us. In effect, they have become surrogates for our various types of community. They represent things like our nation, a city or hometown, a school, or even a sexual-political stance. Few people were surprised when the Toronto Blue Jays' consecutive World Series victories in the early nineties were popularly hailed as saying something about us as a nation. In Hamilton, we believed that our Tiger Cat's 1999 CFL Grey Cup victory reaffirmed the greatness of our steel city. We had arrived, somehow. Yet in both cases, few of the players were even Canadians, yet alone *hometown guys*. Nevertheless, they were our representatives. Somewhere in time we developed the habit of casting athletes like our 2002 gold-medal winning men's and women's Olympic hockey teams into surrogate roles for our communal aspirations and glory-seeking.

The idea that sports teams represent something so permeates contemporary culture that we Canadians hardly notice it at all. It compels our reading of daily sports pages and finds expression in our language, dress, and mythology, among many other things. Yet this idea is not just part of the dominant corporate capitalist model of which McLuhan and Kidd spoke. It permeates *all* of our models of sport. Little leaguers and school boosters know this well, as do people competing in the Gay Games. You do not have to be a paid professional player or even the best athlete around to have your activities on the field or ice or court mean something to others. To borrow a good observation from historian Morris Mott, flawed games can still have splendid ceremonies.[4]

Ideologically shaped by amateur sports promoters in the last century, representative sport has distinct cultural baggage. It bears the stamp of fair play through "muscular Christianity," a kind of sporting approach to Christ's Sermon on the Mount neatly captured in what Gerald Redmond terms a popular yet glib phrase from the last century.[5] Embracing a durable essence of four characteristics – "manliness, morality, health, and patriotism" – muscular Christian sport is viewed as a means to the end of moral character building, not an end in itself.[6] Popular mid-nineteenth-century boys' novels, like Charles Kingsley's *Westward Ho!* (1855) and *Two Years Ago* (1857) and Thomas Hughes' *Tom Brown's Schooldays* (1857), spread this view to the reading public.[7] Muscular Christianity infused sport with a social reform agenda, heading off some of the ascetic pietist-influenced objections laid against the fun and frivolity typically associated with recreational pastimes. Playing field competition, in effect, became a testing ground for Christian action. This purposefulness carried with it the mark of rationality. In this way, the model of representative sport that emerged from the amateur sport movement was a model of rational recreation, designed to achieve some sort of socially constructive end.

This legacy lives on today. Many of us credit team sport participation, for example, with a capacity to build our moral character to good end. We believe that it teaches us larger life lessons about winning gracefully and losing with dignity. We believe that it helps us to vent anger and aggression, and teaches us how to cooperate with others under difficult circumstances. These are potent reasons why we have sports programs in our schools today. Little can shake these beliefs –

not even the unpleasant realities of sport as they are exposed by scandals surrounding doping and figure skating judging.

The Canadian connection to and fascination with representative sport dates from the mid-nineteenth century, when new transportation and communications links broke down the isolation of our early pioneering settlements. The development of what Stacy Lorenz terms "a world of sport," created by the mass media by the end of the century, transmitted important facts, ideas, and symbols about sport to places everywhere on the continent.[8] While early sport reporting lacks some of the colour and focus on personalities that we take for granted today, it does convey much information about our sporting past. It tells us who played, who won and lost, how they played, whether players and fans acted roughly or respectably, and the size of the audience. It also documents the work of early sports organizers as they created teams, challenged each other for matches, and structured competitive leagues. It captures their earnestness as well, revealing their rationale for promoting sport and the hopes that rested on the shoulders of the representative players who were hometown boys. What it doesn't do all that well is chronicle the activities and thoughts of those people who rejected respectable, representative sport – those on the social margins of the community who had their own vibrant alternative traditions, often linked with animal and blood sport. Bits of these traditions can be teased out from newspapers sources, but theirs is a story that remains to be written from richer sources like oral histories, court records, diaries, correspondence, and photographs.

While early newspaper reports provide much information about early representative sport, so too do the physical artifacts that remain standing today in many of our cities. The baseball diamonds, running tracks, arenas, and other sports facilities that dotted the urban landscape of almost every Canadian city, town, village, and hamlet by the end of the nineteenth century were the products of civic planning and entrepreneurial effort. Civic leaders and urban boosters pursued parks and sports facilities strategically as emblems of community progress and social order.[9] Organized sport became a means to bring notoriety to towns itching to make their mark in the evolving urban hierarchy.

Social reformers saw amateur team sports bearing the stamp of muscular Christianity and rational recreation as a way to project images of respectability to themselves and to those outside their towns. To them, sports could also deal with the ills that plagued urban life – keeping kids away from street corners while defining what it meant to be masculine or feminine, revitalizing the bodies of sedentary workers, and providing entertainment for city dwellers. Civic boosters believed that amateur sports could project images of social harmony and progress, and ambitious towns and cities throughout Canada earnestly carried on this social agenda. Yet historians consistently focus on representative sport in the nation's large cities, particularly looking at the professional sports that thrived in them, and overlook what went on in small cities, towns, and villages, where most nineteenth-century Canadians lived. This perpetuates an unproven assumption that what occurred in large cities set the tone and direction for urban life and the development of representative sport everywhere.

This book is about the roots of representative sport as they grew from the amateur sport movement, which sport historian Steve Pope rightly terms an "invented" athletic tradition.[10] In many ways, it provides a prelude to the story of the struggle for Canadian sport told by Bruce Kidd in his award-winning book of the same name, and a historic backdrop against which Marshall McLuhan's musings on the importance of sport to Canadian culture can be situated. It analyses civic holiday sport and three male amateur team sports – cricket, baseball, and lacrosse, the earliest summertime team sports to be organized locally – between 1838 and 1895 in two small towns in southwestern Ontario, Ingersoll and Woodstock, from the creation of the earliest sport club to the ascendancy of amateurism locally.

In the years after 1895, sport in the two towns began a new transition, away from an essentially Victorian discourse on respectability and rowdyism toward the general acceptance of commercialized forms of mass leisure. This led to new questions about the social value of sport in the cash nexus. My focus remains, however, on the development of amateurism before 1895, for reasons as practical as theoretical: the manuscript censuses that I rely upon so heavily are unavailable for the period past 1901, and the sporting world that had emerged by that time – including inter and intra city leagues for both males and females, as well as sports provided by churches, YMCAs and YWCAs, schools, and other organizations – is too large to be managed with the same sustained level of analysis. I will save that important work for someone else. As it stands, my book fits nicely with those of other Ontario historians – like Lynne Marks, Andrew Holman, and David Burley – who have written on related topics for the same time period. Their well-crafted and finely detailed books explore the shaping of class identities through religion, leisure pastimes, and work. To this literature I add my perspectives on amateur sport.

Generally this book is less about sports themselves (and few of them at that) than about social issues like class, gender, and community building. I am trying to get at the various cultural meanings associated with sport, rather than simply chronicling the history of particular sports. This can be found elsewhere: plenty of books document the past of big team sports like hockey, football, baseball, basketball, and rugby; small team and individual sports like curling, figure skating, skiing, tennis, wrestling, boxing, and trapshooting; outdoor/wilderness sports like fishing, hunting, mountain climbing, and sailing; and sporting competitions like the Olympic, Commonwealth, and Indigenous Games. The number of sports covered in such tomes grows yearly, offering tons of information about Canadian sport accomplishments and heroes, albeit sometimes without a critical gaze or broader social context. I aim to create something different – a social history about the ways in which one idea of sport became viewed by local social leaders in two places as *the* way to play – and to present my argument in a way that will appeal to a more broadly based readership than most academic sport history.

Although no single Canadian community represents a province or the nation, the focus upon two small towns broadens our perspective on Canada's sporting past. It captures and explores local contexts from which one brand of representative sport – the not-for-profit amateur model – grew. It also allows for individual level data for examining certain issues, such as class relationships in sport, with some precision.[11] This approach provides penetrating views into the social background of local amateur sport promoters and their connections to the ideology of middle-class respectability as they expressed it through local voluntary organizations and fraternal clubs, something typically overlooked in the historiography on English and Canadian sport.[12]

Comparing the two small towns shows the importance of local context in the rise of representative sport, while the period chosen shows the formative stages of this phenomenon that stand in contrast to the model of "ludic diffusion," from the metropolis to the hinterland, implicit in the works of many sport historians.[13] While developments elsewhere influenced what went on in Ingersoll and Woodstock, local inhabitants created their own meanings for the sports they experienced in their daily lives. I look at the ways in which their sport served as a surrogate for their various assumptions about community and how it was to be represented, connecting them to notions of the time about character building, muscular Christianity, and urban boosterism.

I examine these themes in six chapters, the first of which outlines the early settlement history of the towns and the social and cultural world of the old Tory elite – the "aristocrats" of Woodstock – and the emerging entrepreneurial and professional middle class that challenged their authority. In chapter 2 I use an idea from Clifford Geertz to show that we can understand civic celebrations as social texts from which we can read the story that a community is telling about itself. Changes in the sports found on civic holidays reveal the emerging discourses of rowdiness and respectability that accompanied the rise of local organized sport in the late nineteenth century. Chapter 3 focuses upon local amateur athletic associations, with their strict codes and regulations, formed by local members of a progressive, entrepreneurial middle class to organize and administer local sport both on the holidays and every day. The AAAs solidified the connection between teams and the towns, stimulating spirited sporting rivalries between Ingersoll, Woodstock, and other towns and cities throughout the province.

In the final three chapters I look at the three major summertime team sports found in the towns – cricket, baseball, and lacrosse – to elucidate social and class differences in local sporting culture. Local sport reformers who wanted to promote the idea of a democratic field of play saw cricket as an anachronistic sporting practice, firmly attached to the exclusivity of the old Tory elite. Baseball, popular among many segments of the local population, cut across lines of age, class, and ethnicity. Its creation by local urban boosters and sport promoters in the 1860s as the earliest representative inter urban sport and its later local development in the face of the rise of professional sport elsewhere reveals a vision of an ideal community where homegrown talent represented the best that the towns had to offer. In lacrosse, propagandists aimed to create a panacea for certain ills that plagued local society, providing a way to teach youth values necessary for upholding the dominant culture and succeeding in it. Tremendous player commitment to winning for their town sometimes stretched the limits of acceptable activity on the playing fields too far, shifting the emphasis from the process of character building to the goal of competitive victory.

Resistance to the new sporting culture emerged in a variety of ways in both towns, from those who were excluded from it, marginalised as spectators, or who remained allured by blood sports or professional events. Sometimes, paradoxically, the seeds of resistance came from within the ambitious middle-class group responsible for formulating local amateurism. Playing for the "love of the game" and "the honour of the town or city represented" were things that did not always fit comfortably together in Ingersoll and Woodstock.

ONE

Tory Elites to Middle-Class Men: Changing Political, Economic, and Social Landscapes

How much can places change in just a few generations? Apparently a lot, especially when you consider the story of the small, struggling subsistence communities in Oxford County's wilderness, born from the toil of political refugees and settlers and growing into complex urban and industrial centres connected to the outside world by railways, telegraphs, and telephones. Ingersoll and Woodstock underwent such transformations during the nineteenth century, and in the process both towns laid the foundations for vibrant amateur sporting cultures that had at their bases the ideas of middle-class respectability and representation.

Ontario historians have used the terms "Upper Canadian Tory elites" and "Victorian middle classes" to locate the old and new social orders that dominated the province in the early and then later decades of the nineteenth century. Tory elite members, men of English or Loyalist backgrounds, brought to the area wealth derived largely from inheritances, commissions in the magistracy and militia, patronage government positions, and land speculation. As historian David Mills shows, theirs was a paternal culture, marked by loyalty to the Crown and a view that they naturally belonged at the top of a social hierarchy.[1] Yet in time a rising group of middle-class professional and business people made their own impact upon the economy and politics of the province, ultimately changing, but not totally eradicating, the older group. The new group, with different sources of wealth and power, carried with it an emphasis on respectability and improvement, focusing its world-view upon accomplishment – political, economical, and social – achieved through personal initiative and merit.[2] The transition from one group to the other – keenly felt in Ingersoll and Woodstock – occurred on many fronts, through the political reforms of the late 1840s and through industrial development and the rise of a capitalist economy stimulated by railway communications. It also occurred through the creation of a distinctive middle-class social culture that burgeoned in the last few decades of the century. Organized representative sport grew from this culture.

Nestled in the fertile lands of southwestern Ontario, Ingersoll and Woodstock both lie in what was once the Brock District of the province. This area was relatively untouched by settlement until after the War of 1812, but then its close, easy proximity to the United States quickly made it ripe for development.[3] Settlers with an eye for good land loved the centrally situated region with its excellent soil and plentiful waters, supplied by the upper branch of the Thames River and its streams.[4] Building materials for local development came from the hardwood and softwood forests that covered the area's rolling hills. Two early primitive roads connected what would become Oxford County to the east and west. Travelers took them from Burlington Bay on Lake Ontario to Detroit, and also southwards to Lake Erie.

Ingersoll's early roots reach back to the late eighteenth century and the initiative of the enterprising family of Thomas Ingersoll.[5] In 1793, the wealthy promoter from Massachusetts, a veteran of the Revolutionary War, got a large land grant from Lieutenant Governor John Graves Simcoe's colonization program for Upper Canada.[6] It required Ingersoll, a somewhat moderate Tory, to settle forty families on the land and fulfill road-building requirements. He arrived to a largely uninhabited area, save for the small settlement of Beachville, which had a mill and post office.[7] Despite creating a small community, Ingersoll found his grant rescinded shortly after Simcoe's return to England. He petitioned the government in 1797 but failed to recoup his sizable losses. Frustrated by the experience and complaining about government anti-American sentiment, Ingersoll abandoned his fledgling settlement sometime in 1804–05 and moved to the Port Credit area.[8]

Soon after the War of 1812, two of Ingersoll's sons returned to the remnants of the pre-industrial, parochial, and subsistence settlement that their father had started. They named the place first Oxford-on-the-Thames, then Oxford Village, and finally Ingersoll. There husbands, wives, children, and other kin lived far from other households, working together to produce the necessities of life. Thomas Ingersoll's sons quickly capitalized on the potential of the area, venturing into small-scale commerce by harnessing the waterpower of a local stream for grist, carding, and sawmills. Soon a blacksmith shop, ashery, general store, post office, and distillery sprang up to serve the growing local population.[9] During the 1820s, the village had regular stage coaches and a log schoolhouse. As patrons of the local settlement, members of the Ingersoll family held important political powers granted through Tory connection, including the offices of postmaster and land registrar, as well as commissions in the local militia. By the mid–1830s improvements to the Old Stage Road cemented their village's increasing ties with its developing agricultural hinterland. This road bypassed neighbouring Woodstock, situated on the less frequently traveled Governor's Road.[10]

Informal and communal social institutions solidified and perpetuated the social identities of Ingersoll residents and area settlers. Despite road improvements, poor communications with the outside world kept people isolated from each other. In such a world, kinship and shared experiences promoted social bonding and the idea of neighbourhood. People looked forward to communal work bees, a long-lived and pragmatic approach to labour that, in the words of historian Catharine Anne Wilson, "operated much like a bank in which all made their deposits and were then entitled to make with withdrawals or acquire small loans."[11] A complex social phenomena, these cooperative work parties, helped along "by an abundance of good cheer," provided celebrations of strength for local males.[12] Area resident Alex Matheson Sutherland said of bees during the days of his youth, "Few thought of doing a work of any magnitude except by a Bee ... it was found that a lot of work was done quickly."[13] Although they played an important role in the farm economy, bees weren't all business, however; as Sutherland remembered – perhaps a bit too nostalgically – they brought people together, kept them neighbourly, cheerful, and unselfish, and "nearly always wound up with a dance."[14] As in other communities throughout the province, they also provided opportunities for sporting contests, as when barn-raising teams tried to out-build their opponents, or when a game of baseball followed the day's work with a little more fun.[15]

Pioneering conditions in the isolated countryside also made Sabbath worship important for socializing and for religious observance. As early as 1828, before permanent churches were built, itinerant Methodist preachers arrived on horseback every fortnight. They preached wherever they could, at the local schoolhouse or in a barn, packed with people dressed in their Sunday best. These were special occasions, with people eager for the opportunity to speak to kin and neighbour.[16] When the noted observer of early Upper Canadian society, Mrs Anna Jameson, visited Oxford County in the 1830s, she recorded that people's Sabbath gossip revolved around the stuff of life, like news of marriages and births, letters from England, crops and clearings, lumber, the price of wheat, and the mending of roads that were "so execrably bad that no words can give you an idea of them."[17]

Bad roads and long traveling distances made any social gathering memorable, like the militia muster day celebrations held in Beachville on 4 June 1838. The small village, located between Ingersoll and Woodstock, celebrated the day with a baseball match that was recorded for posterity in a reminiscence of former resident Adam E. Ford.[18] Young men, whose ages ranged from fifteen to twenty-four years, played in the game, using rudimentary, locally made implements: the club (bat) was "made of the best cedar, blocked out with an ax and finished on a shaving horse." The ball, made by a local shoemaker, contained "double twisted woolen yarn covered with good, honest calfskin sewed with waxed ends."[19] The rules for the contest, resembling versions of baseball known to exist in Massachusetts, New York, and Philadelphia at the time, fit local conditions and were passed down through an oral tradition maintained by local old-timers.

The thirty or so wayside inns and taverns dotting the seventy miles of roads between Brantford and London provided social gathering sites for other types of contestation. Area watering holes gave people places to watch sporting amusements like cockfighting or express manly fun through wrestling and pugilism.[20] Horseracing, which local bylaws eventually banned within town limits, thrived in the taverns along the road connecting Ingersoll and Woodstock through Beachville.[21] The Innkeepers Purse event, a race for local horses created for the pleasure of inn and tavern patrons, lasted well into the mid-1860s.[22] Nevertheless, as local historian Brian Dawe shows, popular discourses on political reform held sway as perhaps the most hotly contested sport enjoyed by tavern patrons.[23] Over a pint of locally brewed ale, people gossiped about the chief issues of the day – the weather, harvest prospects, stories about their own and other people's lives, and the reforming of local politics.

While some settlers had arrived earlier, the founding of the Town Plot, later to be called Woodstock, occurred in the 1830s a dozen miles to the northeast of Ingersoll on the Governor's Road. Its origins had much to do with Ingersoll's growth and prosperity and the political posturing of Oxford County inhabitants who met at area taverns. John Graves Simcoe had identified the site in 1783 in his provincial scheme as an ideal location for settlement, far from the border between Upper Canada and the newly formed United States of America. Yet the actual plans were not put into effect until the politically turbulent 1830s, when a popularly led political reform movement aimed to break the oligarchical power of the province's Tory elite.[24] The reform politics of non-Loyalist settlers in the region, particularly in the Quaker settlement at Norwich and also in the Brantford and London areas, prompted the government to take action. Hoping to stop the spread of reform ideas, Lieutenant Governor Sir John Colborne adopted a defensive strategy.[25] He induced the "right sort of man" – British immigrants loyal to the Crown and supporters of the provincial Tory elite – to settle in the politically troubled regions of the province.[26] In doing so, he sought to create a network of communities of cooperative men who could exert considerable influence in local and regional affairs. Coercion and example rather than cannonballs aimed to maintain Tory hegemony.

To this end, provincial government authorities persuaded a group of retired British naval and military officers to settle the Woodstock townsite in the troubled Blandford Township. This began in 1831–32 when two Englishmen – a retired army colonel, Alexander Whalley Light, and a retired naval captain, Philip Graham – came to the area. Yet the real impetus for the settlement began when naval Captain Andrew Drew arrived in York, the provincial capital, acting as the agent for the naval Vice Admiral Henry Vansittart of Bishum Abbey in Berkshire, England. Vansittart, the fifth son of a long-standing English parliamentarian, wanted to establish a landed estate in Upper Canada and secure a prosperous future for his own younger sons.[27] Excited by the prospect of his heading a quasi-military settlement of half-pay officers in the troubled area, government authorities in York successfully courted Vansittart through Drew.[28] As hoped, other retired officers followed.[29]

This settlement pattern, found in other places in the province like Richmond and Glengarry County, resulted in a strong military and naval presence in Woodstock, although technically it was not a garrison. Militarily, Woodstock's retired officers ranked with the best that many colonial garrisons had to offer. They included retired army lieutenants, captains, and a colonel, as well as navy captains, a commander, and vice admiral. These ranks automatically entitled their holders to sizable land grants from the government.[30] Military pensions and family money helped stimulate a local economy, encouraging a market for the agricultural products of area farmers. The officers purchased the goods and services of local skilled artisans and labourers, who "gathered the shekels that they scattered."[31] Their social, financial, and educational backgrounds set a high tone for Woodstock's social elite. The inclusion of family and newly found friends in the highest social and political echelons of the province fortified their numbers.[32]

Some males in this small clique bore impressive letters of introduction that would ease their access to colonial political and social networks and provide shortcuts through an otherwise inflexible government bureaucracy. In an age of unreformed politics plum appointments like the local magistracy could be obtained in this way.[33] They encouraged patronage as part of the natural order of things, and contested challenges against it. Concerned that the local postmastership might be granted to an American rather than a British settler, for example, Colonel Light appealed to the Upper Canada government to keep things in house, so to speak. Presuming to speak for his social group, he declared simply, "We abhor Yankees."[34] The government rewarded such sentiments and appeals to British connection, and within months of their arrival in 1833 a handful of officers dominated the local magistracy.[35] With its designation as the district town in 1839, Woodstock's elite gained control of the district political organization, administration, and justice. By 1847, other facets of administrative control had fallen under their purview: Oxford's land registry office moved from Ingersoll to Woodstock and with it moved Registrar Colonel James Ingersoll, a wealthy son of that village's founder.[36]

Largely homogenous as a group of military men, Woodstock's elite nevertheless had personal differences between them, like the varying degrees of social and political clout held by certain individuals. Not everyone was as politically well-connected as Vice Admiral Vansittart, although some men did come close, like Peter Boyle de Blaquiere, appointed county warden in 1842. His membership in Toronto's Upper Canada Club helped forge a strong link between Tory elite groups in the Brock District with their counterparts in the capital.[37] Eventually he would become the first chancellor of the University of Toronto. As well-off as they were, things did not always run smoothly between group members. Some, for example, just couldn't get along. Vansittart and Captain Andrew Drew apparently hated each other after a rupture between them, yet they managed to keep up a civil appearance. Others pushed matters a bit further. In keeping with their social pretensions, at least two men acted out their personal conflict on the dueling ground, through the stylized ritual that historian Cecilia Morgan argues "dictated that both masculine bravery and respectability be demonstrated publicly and physically."[38]

Infighting aside, many of the group's members held a conservative outlook, similar to other Tory elite groups in the province. They used their understanding of England's aristocracy as a reference for their own social activities, reinforcing their own elite status locally.[39] They believed themselves to be society's natural social leaders; as one turn-of-the-century writer remarked, they "held their heads high, thinking much of family, tolerant of the 'lower orders' and devoting much of their time to sport and amusement."[40] They spent their money "freely in the improvement of their estates and in the enjoyments of life."[41]

By doing so, they distinguished themselves from less well-off settlers in the area. Local people bowed their heads as their carriages passed and referred to them as the "aristocrats."

This elite's social traditions affirmed non-utilitarian attitudes toward life and leisure. Oxford County's earliest newspapers, published in Woodstock, advertised and reported on the group's various social activities. As a leisure class, the officers participated in lavish and conspicuous consumption and the formation of a local estate culture in the backwoods of Upper Canada.[42] The record of their fine homes, splendid libraries, servants, carriages emblazoned with heraldic shields, and stables of fine horses is impressive even today. Intermarriage, Anglo-ethnic bonding, Tory political leanings, and a common Church of England affiliation kept their small yet powerfully conservative social enclave tightly knit.

The officer elite and their families and friends brought the values of genteel English country life to Woodstock. With their wealth from old country estates and military pensions they possessed the resources to support their stylized social activities. They included only those whom they viewed to be their social peers, and used privately owned facilities and lands to ensure social segregation. Occasionally they entertained the highest society of the province, as in 1849, in the wake of the Montreal riots over the Rebellion Losses Bill, when Lord Elgin dropped in at the Vansittart estate on his way to London and received a cordial welcome.[43] Sometime later, Governor Sir Edmund Head visited his former college classmate Colonel Edmund Deedes, sitting in his conspicuously placed family pew during Sunday service at the front of St Paul's Anglican Church.[44]

The retired officers used their chosen leisure pursuits, such as riding to the hunt, steeplechasing, hunting parties, and cricket, to assert their social presence in Oxford County. In 1848 some of the officers held a banquet for John George Vansittart, the son of the vice admiral, who held the offices of district court clerk, magistrate, and surrogate court registrar. Speaking to his celebrators, Vansittart evoked their love of the sporting pastimes of England's gentry class, proposing a toast to "the pleasures of the race course, the cricket ground, and the stag hunt" to a room filled with cheers.[45]

The elite's lifestyle typically indulged in such pursuits, with crowds flocking in for their gala derby days.[46] Their exclusive annual steeplechase offered a princely sum of £53 to those the race committee allowed to compete.[47] Shortly after they settled in the Woodstock area, some of the officers formed one of the earliest and most noted cricket clubs in the colony. Local *Gazetteers* advertised it, along with things like the local subscription library (1835), agricultural society (1836), and subscription schoolhouse (1839), as a strong selling feature of the rapidly growing community.[48]

The Tory elite's very presence and lifestyle, however, exacerbated the significant political and social tensions that helped bring them to Oxford County in the first place.[49] Their intransigence over land claims, religion, and political appointments provoked Oxford County's numerous and increasingly vocal settlers of more humble social origins, and local political reformers aimed to break their stranglehold on power. The elite generally played out their presumed superiority over the local populace with paternalistic civility, while many other settlers viewed the elite's status quo as obstructing their own political and social advancement.

The Duncombe revolt of 1837 implicated Woodstock's retired officers in the Upper Canadian rebellion. This badly planned and poorly executed insurrection in Oxford County, hastened by the false report of the success of William Lyon Mackenzie's rebel group, showed the severity of the political frictions that had arisen between area settlers and the local elite.[50] Some time before, in the midst of mounting local reform agitation, concerned Woodstonians, led by members of the officer group, sent the lieutenant governor a pledge of their loyalty, promising to "make any sacrifice should the urgency of the case demand it, to preserve inviolate the Constitution."[51] During the rebellion crisis, they kept their word. Woodstock's half-pay officers jumped into the fray, with Colonel Alexander Whalley Light drawing up an elaborate plan, complete with fortifications for the defense of the town, and other officers leading armed forces to combat the insurrections. Light, along with Captain Phillip Graham and Peter Boyle de Blaquiere, headed locally raised contingents of government supporters. Captain Andrew Drew oversaw the cutting out and burning of the rebel supply ship, the *Caroline*, in American waters at Niagara Falls – one of the most spectacular incidents in the rebellion, which severely affected Anglo-American relations.

That the officers used St Paul's Church to imprison their captured rebels seems hardly surprising.[52] This Anglican church building symbolized what the elite stood for, being endowed through the notorious clergy reserves. The Reverend William Bettridge's personal appeal to his former commandant, the lieutenant governor of Upper Canada, Sir John Colborne, helped the church endowment.[53] Known as a religiously intolerant man, Bettridge apparently took to conducting the mass in militarist fashion while considering members of the Church of Scotland not worthy of clergy reserve monies. This understandably did not sit well with those of different denominational backgrounds among the area's sizable population of Scots and Americans. Bettridge's parish, a matrix of the elite's social power, used pew seating to mark the hierarchy of local social rank, with only certain families getting closer to God in the expensive seats closest to the altar.[54]

During the 1840s and 1850s, changes in politics and society undermined the Tory elite throughout the province. In Woodstock, the process was hastened by county reorganization in 1841 and by what became known as the "tombstone affair" in 1845.[55] As historian Christopher Anstead shows, this bizarre dispute erupted over the wording of an epitaph for a woman interred at St Paul's Church.[56] It pitted steadfast champions of the elite, notably Reverend Bettridge and Captain Philip Graham, against three local political reformers – middle-class men on the make. In the process, William Wilson, a boot and saddle manufacturer, T.S. Shenston, a harness maker and later publisher, and James Kintrea, a local painter and grocer, garnered the support of many disaffected residents.

The affair developed into a huge fracas, involving a gravestone, body snatching, arrests, and public cries against the magistracy system, yet it sprang from a strangely small and delicate matter. Wilson, a grieving husband, wanted to honour his wife, who had died in childbirth, with a suitable epitaph for her tombstone. Bettridge objected to the epitaph and the affair went on from there. Local public opinion, seeing Wilson set against the intransigence of Bettridge and Graham, went against the old order. The sour taste left by how the old guard handled the affair – including arresting Wilson and his two comrades and parading them in chains down the main street on the Sabbath for all to see – worked to lead local moderate reformers away from the extreme members of the elite.[57] By 1849, when the provincial Baldwin Act heralded a new era of responsible government and municipal reform, the fate of Tory hegemony in Oxford County was sealed. In the first Woodstock village election in 1851, local voters empowered five middle-class men – one of whom was Wilson – with the running of local democratic government.[58] None had been a member of the old Tory elite.

Demographic and social changes also led to the dissipation of the elite. Several of its leading members, old men by the 1850s, died, taking with them the stricter, more harsh vestiges of their high Tory political and social culture. Some remaining members of the elite felt the pinch of military pension purse tightening and left the area for England and other places in the empire to try their luck again. While the social experiment of transplanting a landed gentry to the backwoods frontier of Oxford County generally petered out, some members remained in the new political era to forge new political and social alliances.[59] Admiral Vansittart's son John George, Colonel Alexander Whalley Light, and James Barwick shifted their sights and energies toward local

improvement, particularly local railway development,[60] and thereby
allied themselves with former political foes like reformer Francis
Hincks, the great railway promoter who rose to become premier of
Canada West in 1852.[61] The Woodstonian elite thus stepped outside
their 'squire and parson' idea of society and stimulated a loose rapprochement with the province's rising group of urban mercantile men,
the very sort of people whom the more rabid Tories shut out in the
tombstone affair. Their new allies came from an emerging social order
who possessed sources of wealth and power that the old Tory elite did
not monopolize.[62]

Woodstock's emerging social order, reflected the *Globe* in 1878, consisted of a group in stark contrast to the old elite, "a race of thrifty,
industrious, money-getting men, with ideas more in unison with the
place and time."[63] These merchants, bureaucrats, and business and
professional men possessed skills and services demanded by the population of the rapidly growing town. Efficiency, morality, self-
improvement, merit through personal initiative and achievement,
neighbourhood, and the purposive use of spare time preoccupied them
as issues of lavish conspicuous consumption and the formation of an
estate culture formation based upon Tory exclusivity had preoccupied
the old elite. These new concerns became the hallmarks of a rising
middle-class culture in the heady days of late nineteenth-century
urban and industrial expansion. Civic voluntarism and urban boosterism gave middle-class men opportunities to connect their economic
and social interests in an emerging culture.[64] This would be the fertile
grounds from which organized amateur sport and local representative
teams arose.

   In Ingersoll and Woodstock, as in urban places throughout the
province, the arrival of the railway signaled the beginnings of this
new era of growth, development, and social change.[65] Access to rail
lines made or broke many nineteenth-century communities and stimulated rapid and profound changes everywhere in the province,
changes that had taken centuries to occur in Europe.[66] In 1853 local
capitalists succeeded in getting both Ingersoll and Woodstock access
to the Great Western Railway (GWR) line, connecting them to provincial and continental export networks by rail and water and opening
them to distant markets and the easy flow of goods, services, people,
and ideas. Within five years, the GWR network linked both towns to
Toronto, Hamilton, Niagara, London, Sarnia, and Windsor and to
the Great Lakes ports. Ingersoll and Woodstock grew dynamically
with these channels for commerce and communication. Local
capitalists, eager to take advantage of economies of large-scale

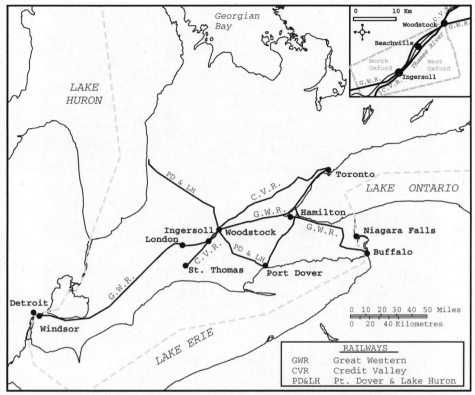

Map 1 Geographic location of Ingersoll and Woodstock in southwestern Ontario, along with some of their railway connections to other places in nineteenth-century Canada West/Ontario. (Rick Hamilton)

production, sought to develop propelling industries, integrating their factory products into the provincial, national, and international marketplaces.

The industrial success of both towns depended upon railway lines. Local businesspeople, industrialists, and area farmers in both Ingersoll and Woodstock pursued railway development aggressively to break the GWR's monopoly and lower the costs of transporting local goods.[67] Town councillors and local boards of trade devised ways to make their towns more attractive for railway and industrial development. In the 1850s, Ingersoll's several foundries, like the Eastwood, Noxon, and Brown firms, produced agricultural tools for local and distant markets, while the town became the centre of factory cheese production and marketing for Oxford County.[68] In 1866 James Harris's cheese company used some thirty-five tons of milk to make a Mammoth Cheese,

Ingersoll's Mammoth Cheese at Congress Springs, Saratoga, NY, 1866. Local
cheese manufacturers James Harris and Company created this 7,000-pound
cheese as an advertising gimmick. It traveled in its huge custom-made crate
to fairs in Toronto; Saratoga, New York; and London, England. Harris's old
estate, located along Highway 401, has been transformed into the popular
Elm Hurst Inn. (Courtesy of the Ingersoll Cheese Factory Museum)

a strange but effective advertising gimmick for Ingersoll cheese. The
three-foot high monstrous cheese wheel measured nearly seven feet
around and weighed some seven thousand pounds. Shown everywhere,
it traveled in its huge custom-made crate to fairs in Toronto; Saratoga,
New York; and London, England.

Railways ensured that the Mammoth Cheese and other agricultural
products got to places faraway. Lumber and wheat went from Ingersoll
to Britain, Europe, and the U.S. During the Civil War, the town's factories benefitted from war-ravaged markets requiring ammunition,
flour, and meat products. By 1870, Ingersoll had a slight edge on its
rival Woodstock. Its industries had more capital investment, more people employed, more horsepower used, more raw materials consumed,

Dundas Street, Woodstock, c. 1860s. A glimpse of the main drag of this ambitious but rustic Ontario town around the time that its Young Canadians baseball team began to put the place on the province's sporting map. (Courtesy of the National Archives of Canada, c8607)

and more goods produced.[69] Among the top forty-five industrial work-forces in urban Ontario at the time, Ingersoll ranked sixteenth to Woodstock's twenty-first place position.[70]

Yet after a devastating fire in 1872 gutted its downtown core and the economic depression of the later 1870s badly hurt the town and its cheese industry, Ingersoll's industrial and economic boom busted and Woodstock took the lead.[71] Woodstock managed to fare better during the depression overall, in part because the town succeeded in getting a second railway line, breaking the Great Western Railway's monopoly and creating cheaper freight rates. In 1876, the Port Dover and Lake Erie Railway connected Woodstock directly to Lake Erie, giving it a decided advantage over its rival.[72] By the end of the decade, a second rail line, the Credit Valley line, came to Ingersoll via Toronto and St Thomas; however, it also went through Woodstock.

Lagging behind Woodstock became Ingersoll's industrial fate. In 1901 Woodstock became a small city, while Ingersoll remained a town. Nevertheless, the two places occupied the same niche in the province's evolving urban hierarchy: by the end of the century, both belonged to the one-quarter or so middle-sized Ontario urban communities whose populations ranged from 2,500 to 10,000 people.[73] Both places grew dramatically during the late nineteenth century, quadrupling in population number while the rest of Oxford County stagnated and eventually declined. For both, the growth came in spurts. Between 1861 and 1871 Ingersoll's population grew twice as rapidly as did Woodstock's. A decade later, however, Woodstock's population took off. By the turn of the century, nearly nine thousand people lived there, nearly twice as many as in Ingersoll. Most of these people came from Anglo-Saxon backgrounds, born in Canada or England. Of those born in other places, Ingersoll had more Irish- and American-born people, while Woodstock had more Scottish-born people.[74] In 1901, roughly three-quarters of each town's population were Canadian-born. Local people of English, Irish, and Scottish descent could find at least a half dozen fraternal orders and voluntary associations to celebrate and perpetuate their ethnic culture.[75]

Occupational identities are another way of understanding the composition of local populations. While manuscript census records are problematic sources of information, since they under-reported itinerant workers and people who did not own property, they are useful if used cautiously. For example, they provide snapshots of the more stable element of the town population, even if only at ten-year intervals, giving clues about local men's occupational and social backgrounds. Local census records show that from the 1870s on, nearly three out of every four males working in the towns over the age of fifteen worked in jobs requiring skilled and unskilled manual labour.[76] We can only guess at just how many more were itinerant workers who came and left the towns between the censuses.

Local interest in securing and sustaining industrial development resulted from the view that industrial prosperity was connected with local prosperity overall. Successful factories meant a successful town. Ingersoll's and Woodstock's factories competed for survival against those from the larger centres of Toronto, Hamilton, and London, places that encroached upon local markets and dealt a deathblow when local industries could not compete. To counter this phenomenon, prominent local merchants and industrial capitalists in both towns – Ingersoll in 1874 and Woodstock in 1877 – formed boards of trade to stimulate the local economy and promote town business interests.[77] Working with local government, they stimulated manufacturing by handing out sizable cash bonuses and tax incentives to new local industries. Ingersoll bylaws show the liberal cash bonuses given to the Morrow Screw Company, the Hault Furniture Company, the Evans Brothers and Littler piano factories, with some new factories getting a

Morrow Screw and Nut factory workers, Ingersoll, n.d. A liberal cash bonus helped lure this factory to Ingersoll, but life was by no means easy for workers in this and other area factories. In 1888, the industrial inspector for the western district lamented that workers spent their time in poorly ventilated, inadequately heated work sites, in jobs that afforded them little time to rest. (Courtesy of the Ingersoll Cheese Factory Museum)

bounty of $175 a head for every newly employed man.[78] Woodstock's bonuses prompted the Thomas Organ Factory and the Stewart Stove Company to relocate their Hamilton shops in town.[79] Municipal bonuses became a double-edged sword, since industries could also be lost through the practice. Some nine years after its establishment in 1881, for example, one of Woodstock's largest and most successful manufacturing firms, the Bain Wagon Company, left town for opportunities in nearby Brantford. There it resided for six years before the Woodstonians managed to woo the factory back.

The men who worked in local factories often had unenviable lives. In 1884, "An Employee" outlined reasons why local industrialists and entrepreneurs ought to support civic holidays and early closings, writing in the *Chronicle*, "The labouring classes – to which your correspondent belongs – have few hours for recreation, their days being passed in close foundries ... and in other equally health-destroying and tiresome strife for existence." Holidays and early closings "would be recouped by increased zeal on the part of their workmen."[80] Local industrialists typically agreed with this reasoning. They allowed workers to take shorter lunch hours during the week for Saturday afternoons off in the summer. This popular practice raised the time workers spent on the job beyond the sixty hours per week limited by law. Yet while it gave them increased leisure time, it also intensified their daily labour, robbed them of needed rest intervals, and predisposed them to job-related injury caused by fatigue. In 1888, the industrial inspector for the province's western district lamented that workers in his jurisdiction spent their time in poorly ventilated, inadequately heated work sites, in jobs that afforded them little time to rest.[81] In fact, factory inspection reports and local newspaper accounts show accident-ridden work sites. Ingersoll's Ellis Furniture Company, the Noxon Brothers Agricultural Works, and Woodstock's Karn Organ and Bain Wagon factories posed many dangers to anyone even slightly fatigued, with their large machines, belts, pulleys, flywheels, gears, and huge saw blades. At the Noxon factory alone between 1895 and 1899, one worker died, one lost an arm, and one had an iron pin rammed through his hand.[82]

Few workers could escape the hazards of the industrial workplace. In 1888, Woodstonian George Page lost three fingers to a buzz-planer at Karn's Organ Factory. Nobody made much of the incident, presumably because it was commonplace.[83] Five years later, an accident took the life of William Chipperfield, a star player on the factory's semi-professional baseball team.[84] While the twenty-one-year-old's parents, five siblings, fans, and fellow workers mourned his death, nothing really changed the poor working conditions that caused it. Strangely enough, Chipperfield can be considered to have been one of the factory's more fortunate workers, since he could take afternoons off work to attend team practices; few others had such luxury in the heat of the summer, when grime and dust stuck to their sweaty bodies as they toiled in poorly ventilated workrooms. Unlike Chipperfield, who got a bit of extra money for playing baseball, many local factory workers could barely eke out a living. Few had much money for spending after they took care of the high cost of living, particularly if they had dependents.[85]

Yet despite this dismal situation, labour agitation, although known to both communities, occurred only sporadically and on a small scale. Ingersoll's branch of the Knights of Labor, Lynne Marks points out, was not terribly active on the strike front, leading the Ingersoll *Sun* to once claim that "fortunately this town has been pretty free from troubles of that kind."[86] The Noxon firm, for example, had sixty years of strike- and union-free business, with a workforce that in 1879 took a

W.A. Karn Drugstore, Woodstock, 1897. WAAA founder, local cycle club president, and Woodstock businessman, W.A. Karn shows off the clerks and customers of his respectable, well-maintained Dundas Street drugstore. (*Sentinel-Review*, The Garden of Ontario Special Edition, May 1897)

15 per cent cut in pay when the firm faced financial difficulty.[87] In 1881 navvies working on the local segment of the CVR struck for higher pay, but most probably weren't local men. Woodstock's *Sentinel* made similar claims about that town's relatively problem-free labour situation. There in September 1896 and June 1899, local CPR operators and GTR employees struck in a line-wide action. In July 1899, workers at Karn's Organ Factory struck for a half-day off so they could vote, a short-lived and quickly resolved affair when the owner gave in to their demand. In 1906 a writer in the *Sentinel* boasted about the town's fine labour record, arguing "there is very little floating population which gives the city a stability which is often lacking in larger centres ... a surprisingly large percentage of the working men in the city [are found] in the home-owning class."[88] It was easy to consider outsiders the cause of labour problems, as when railway navvies spent their payday in a drunken and disorderly "little picnic among themselves."[89] Rightly or wrongly, social critics pointed an accusing finger at itinerant workers as one of the roots of labour trouble and what little work-related social unrest they had.

As Ontario historians Lynne Marks and Christopher Anstead show in their studies of the towns, people in all segments of local society in

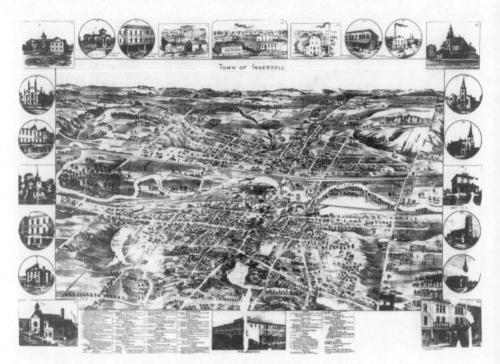

Map 2 Bird's-eye view of Ingersoll, 1885, highlighting churches, notable businesses, and civic buildings. The depiction of busy factory smokestacks belching out their waste into the air signified the town's industrial prosperity. (Courtesy of the National Archives of Canada, NMC 22392)

Ingersoll and Woodstock articulated concern over issues of social rootedness and responsibility – issues of respectability, in the language of the times. Nearly every group in town had their own version of what respectability meant. Working-class Protestant church organizations like the Salvation Army, the Knights of Labor, working and middle-class temperance organizations, fraternal orders, secret societies, and other voluntary organizations each cultivated their own version of respectability.[90] Clearly, it had a complex and changing cultural value over time. However, as Anstead suggests, "its essence proved durable: a respectable male individual had to be industrious, sober, religious, compassionate, morally upright and responsible for his own welfare and that of his family."[91] Respectability found a nurturing home in Ingersoll and Woodstock's middle-class culture, with professionals, merchants, businesspeople, and store and office clerks

WOODSTOCK.

Map 3 Bird's-eye view of Woodstock, 1885, highlighting local churches, factories, and the homes of factory owners like D.W. Karn. Notice the location of the WAAA track and playing field just under the title in the centre of the diagram. (Courtesy of the National Archives of Canada, NMC 22896)

making it a social crusade locally. While members of this group comprised a small proportion of each town's local workforce, they had access to tremendous economic, social, and political resources. In 1851, they accounted for only one-fifth of local workforces, rising to roughly one-quarter by 1891. In those forty years much had changed, with industry in both towns becoming more complex and local industrialists, businesspeople, and board of trades working to integrate the local economies into broader regional and provincial economies. Fraternal organizations, sports clubs, and other voluntary agencies also connected the local scene to a larger evolving provincial middle-class culture.

Local middle-class men ensured that their voices mattered locally. According to J.M.S. Careless, the middle classes "stretched multiple social networks out from metropolis to hinterland," relying upon "social relationships of mutual confidence" to accomplish this task.[92] Beyond their involvement in local government, they created high profile roles for themselves in the community through fraternal and voluntary societies that expressed their 'sense of duty' and played a large role in community life.[93] These organizations sponsored public events like concerts, lectures, plays, and performances.[94] They also offered many other things, but chiefly some sort of welfare protection. Friendly societies, like the Independent Orders of Odd Fellows and Foresters, provided members with sick pay and funeral costs, giving members and their families an economic buffer against hard times in an age otherwise lacking social safety nets.[95] Temperance orders such as the Royal Arcanum and the Independent Order of Good Templars aimed to rid the community of the evils of alcohol consumption, which destroyed the lives of drinkers and their families.[96] The Ancient Order of United Workmen and the Order of Fraternal Guardians gave insurance benefits that did not come with employee pay packets. Ethnic associations, like the Order of Scottish Clans and the Sons of England, provided social venues for people bound by ethnic or religious identities. Some societies, like the Ancient Free and Accepted Masons, and the Royal Arch Masons, kept their activities shrouded in a secrecy that has only recently been broken.[97] Christopher Anstead argues that the idea of respectability flowed through all of these groups: "men from the 'Victorian middle class' forged the lodge into an instrument for creating and managing cultural consent ... [their] benefits allowed members to protect themselves and their families from, or take advantage of, changing structural conditions. Individuals also joined secret societies because membership confirmed their respectable status."[98]

The search for respectability also influenced how local urban boosters in Ingersoll and Woodstock promoted their towns. Middle-class civic leaders used a variety of venues for promotional purposes, to highlight the work of local urban reform movements, industrial manufacturing, social agencies, and sports clubs.[99] They used whatever they could to present and celebrate images of the respectability that could be found in their town and its people. Gazetteers, directories, and newspaper special editions, for example, painted rosy portraits of the towns.[100] Marked by exuberance and optimism, they advertised all that could be considered to be good about the places, offering personal histories of leading citizens aligned with the booster cause – civic officials, industrialists, and prominent merchants – and focusing upon industry, business and consumer interests, neighbourhood, and public morality. Newspapers labeled local building developments as a sign of community progress and provided photographic evidence of the town's imposing public buildings, shops, and stately homes.[101] These, along with the town's sports and other facilities graced the pages of special editions. Such preening could be found everywhere throughout the province during the railway years, and Ingersoll and Woodstock each had their own stylistic flare. Woodstonians, for example, puffed themselves up by giving themselves new, meaningful monikers for their hometown. At first, they hailed Woodstock as the "Aristocratic Town," harkening back to its early history to reveal pretensions of grandeur. Later, as a market centre for Oxford County's agricultural produce, boosters called Woodstock the "Garden of Ontario." Finally, in 1901, when it achieved city status, it became the "Industrial City."[102] Ingersoll's leaders also advertised themselves and their town aggressively. They had done this early on, in the 1860s, with the Mammoth Cheese, memorialized by local poet James McIntyre in his particularly cheesy poem "Ode to a Mammoth Cheese."[103]

Civic leaders in Ingersoll and Woodstock designed parklands to cater to the recreational needs of their citizens, spaces designed to show off their town's progressivism. Although both communities always had some sort of parkland, the shape and function of parks changed through time as the towns grew in physical size and population. Very early on Ingersoll and Woodstock's inhabitants, for example, used commons' lands as pastures for their livestock.[104] Anyone who wanted to play sport there had to first deal with horses, cattle, sheep, and the mess they left behind. In 1879, Woodstock's newspaper editor gleefully reminded people, "Don't forget the park tonight. The cows will be turned out for a few hours to make room for the people."[105] Eventually, playing in cow dung just wouldn't do.[106] Medical and popular concerns over public health and pestilence prompted new land management practices, to be suggested by Ingersoll's public health officer, who oversaw community hygiene.[107] Urban rivalry and boosterism also hastened the transition of the commons lands when their agricultural use, once considered a community asset, increasingly became a social embarrassment – a sign of backwardness. In 1875, the *Chronicle* appealed to Ingersoll town pride because Woodstock had gained an edge in parks development. It asked: "is it to be said that Ingersoll cannot afford a place of recreation of honest pleasure for its citizens, young and old? ... We think not."[108] Public parks and the towns' boulevards, with their trees, shrubs, and flowers, were to be places filled with happy townspeople playing during their leisure time. Redesigned for active and passive recreation, public parks became the site for civic holiday celebrations and the home of organized, representative sport. They possessed all the necessary accoutrements: playing fields, stands for spectators, refreshment booths, and bandstands. By the end of the century, local people had many recreational opportunities at their doorsteps. With early closing bylaws in place, Ingersoll's park, "the liveliest place in town," provided what civic leaders believed was a respectable alternative to the street corners and taverns where devotees of rougher and rowdy entertainments lingered.[109]

TWO

The 24th of May is
the Queen's Birthday:
Civic Holidays, Locality, and Sport

Civic celebrations, with their parades, speeches, and sporting events,
are a rich social environment for studying the transformation of local
sport and society in Ingersoll and Woodstock. Yet, while cultural
anthropologists and social historians have long focused on such socially significant events, historians of sport have for some reason largely
ignored them.[1] This is unfortunate, since the holidays gave townspeople rare opportunities for leisure pursuits not bound by the structure of
their workaday lives. Among the earliest forums for inter urban sport
competition, holidays fueled the rise of representative team sport.[2] A
potent vehicle for displaying the respectable ideology, civic holidays
provided urban boosters with ripe opportunities to promote their community. To borrow insights from cultural anthropologist Clifford
Geertz, the holidays reveal stories that local urban boosters and sport
reformers wanted to tell about themselves and their world to an audience whose identities we will never really know.[3] Since community
members organized holidays for themselves and for visitors to their
town they provide a type of public manifesto, or declaration, with verbal and ritual texts that have been used by historians to study issues of
public space and rituals of collective behaviour in places like Halifax,
Saint John, and Toronto.

Before Confederation, many places throughout the province had the
24th of May, Queen Victoria's birthday, as their premier annual social
event.[4] After its designation as a statutory holiday in 1845, Ingersoll
and Woodstock citizens petitioned their local governments annually
for a day off work. Community members volunteered to work on
organizing committees for holiday planning and advertised the bill of
fare on broadsheets.[5] These committees involved the most socially
prominent and active men in town. They sat on local government and

ran the local voluntary and fraternal associations that played such an important role in community life and public entertainment. The social backgrounds of the forty Ingersoll men who organized civic holidays between 1850 and 1869 show them to be middle aged, Canadian-born, Protestant, and married. No unskilled workers could be found in this group – despite their large numbers in the local population – that canvassed local inhabitants for money to defray holiday costs. By assuming organizational and financial responsibility, middle-class committee members used the holiday events in paternalistic fashion to infuse the holiday events with their own version of social order. By doing so, they also reinforced their appearance as leaders of local society and politics. Many of them dipped into their own pockets to help with financing something that would be rewarded if local people and their consumer dollars remained in town, "ultimately to the benefit of every merchant and citizen."[6] By design the holidays transcended everyday life, with banners, garlands, and flags hanging from lampposts and buildings to transform the atmosphere of the towns.

Between 1850 and Confederation, holiday scenarios on the 24th of May in Ingersoll went something like this, weather permitting. Local residents awoke at sunrise to the crack of gun and cannon fire. Mustered militia volunteers fired the traditional *feu de joie* rifle salute, reminding people of all that they had to be thankful for and heralding the beginning of the town's special day. Townspeople dressed in their Sunday best or "holiday fixings," eager not to miss any part of the celebrations. Oxford County's rural dwellers drove into town in flower-decorated wagons. Children ran through the streets, chanting little ditties like, "The 24th of May is the Queen's birthday, if you don't give us a holiday we will all run away!"[7] The day's events filled the town's streets, playing fields, and banquet halls. In the early morning, something like a Mardi Gras went on at the market square. "Callathumpians," people in grotesque clown costumes, paraded by, banging on pots and pans, playing tin-horns, and rattling cow bells. This motley crowd reveled in the rude and risqué. The local press described their appearance as "most grotesque." Some walked on their hands while others rode on horses of almost every conceivable colour, size, and age. Others rode backwards, wearing masks, huge tin spurs, or strange, ludicrous coats with huge buttons. At eleven o'clock the town band met visiting excursionists at the railway station. From there they trekked down to the town hall for the noontime salute and speeches from the mayor and visiting dignitaries. Next began the noontime parade, with its bands, calliopes, volunteer firefighters, and uniformed paraders marching in military style to the town park. People flocked to the flag- and bunting-draped streets and hung out of second and third storey windows to witness the spectacle. Mothers, wives, daughters, sisters, and sweethearts cheered their men parading by. At the park activity abounded. Sunday schools held picnics, young lovers courted, and people indulged in treats like lemonade, strawberries, and ice cream.

The real attractions at the park were the games and sport activities that offered playful diversion for everyone: they included everything from fat men's races to greased pig chases, from slippery pole climbs to sack and three-legged running races. Some watched the activity from the sidelines, sitting on the grass or on hastily erected spectator stands. Others paid admission money to drive their handsome carriages into the park to witness the spectacles in style and comfort. Throughout the afternoon, the local constabulary scrutinized the crowd for pickpockets and other undesirables. They ignored genteel beer drinking, but tossed drunkards into the slammer. Following the afternoon events, people picnicked at the park or retired to their homes for special family suppers. A few chosen ones – visiting dignitaries, town councillors, and committee members and their families – dined in flag-draped banquet halls. At seven or eight in the evening, the town hall became the site of theatrical performances, concerts, *tableaux vivants*, and lectures. Then the excursionists began their train journey home. By late evening the celebration ended as it had begun, with local people massed in the streets. They flocked to see fireworks illuminate the sky with fire and sound. They ended the holiday around midnight, parading home in a torchlight procession.

A first glance of the above scenario leaves a general impression of fun and frivolity, consensus, shared pride, and patriotism. Yet certain antagonisms marked the holiday parades. Ingersoll and Woodstock holidays celebrated between 1850 and the decade or so after Confederation reveal rowdy and irreverent traditions that opposed the new, respectable ideals devised by holiday organizers, ideals fueled by concern for social order and the cultivation of urban pride.[8] In her work on nineteenth-century parades and power, historian Susan Davis distinguishes between respectable ceremonies and rowdy rituals, the former being privileged modes of communication of dominant classes and the latter the activities of un-empowered groups.[9] Respectable styles sought to set standards for private and public behaviours through the social hierarchy, and rowdy ones opposed them.

The callathumpian parades held in the early morning, for example, reveal some social tensions present in the communities.[10] Grotesque but comical figures of unusual proportion, callathumpians subverted normal social order.[11] Their outrageous and "rather pecoolear" costumes emphasized irrationality in an otherwise orderly world.[12] So did their exaggerated movements and dubious means of transportation, by walking on their hands or riding on an ass backwards. When Woodstock's callathumpians paraded through town "with tremendous eclat," the "usual accompaniment of admiring boys and small dogs" followed them.[13] Using masks, costumes, and caricature, they dealt with issues of social and moral concern with some degree of anonymity. Initially, organizing committees appear not to have organized these parades. Occurring before excursion trains bearing visitors pulled into town and during the hours when the holiday committee and others were busily preparing for day's official events, like the noontime ceremony and parade, callathumpian parades were creations of and for the segment of the local population that was not included in the more formal and socially select organized events.[14] Did women participate, as Bonnie Huskins has documented they did in Victorian Saint John and Halifax?[15] Females could easily subvert gender order, and other types of order, in this topsy-turvy world of disguise and buffoonery, and enjoy a rare opportunity to step onto the public stage. Unfortunately, we can only guess at whether this happened in Ingersoll and Woodstock, since no local records describe such a thing.

Callathumpian processions like those in Ingersoll and Woodstock have a lengthy history in antirespectable tradition in Canadian popular culture.[16] Historian Bryan Palmer suggests that, as a traditional form of revelry, they are associated with the genre of public performance that included charivaris.[17] As political commentaries, their content aimed for the enjoyment of a distinctly local audience, with insider's jokes that outsiders may have found baffling. Clearly, judging by how the local press treated them, not everyone found the parades to their liking. One commentator remarked, "ragged little urchins may be attractive to some people but there are many others who would rather have something better, a fine-looking body like our firemen, for instance."[18] Many others, including local civic leaders, sympathized with this viewpoint. They made no bones about connecting the masquerading callathumpians with the culprits of holiday disorder, associating them with the drunkenness, sabotage, and pranks endemic on the holidays.[19]

In 1862, Ingersoll's millpond became the scene of an ingenious holiday prank, carried out by unknown parties on an unsuspecting community. Reports of strange things happening there in the weeks leading up to the Queen's Birthday led to rumours about a mysterious "pond monster." Curious residents checked the place out, trying to catch sight of whatever lurked beneath the water. For sure, something was there, bobbing around the water's surface, making rumbling noises and emitting a real stench. What was it? As early local historian James Sinclair recounts, thousands of gullible souls thronged to the draining of the millpond on the Queen's Birthday, only to find themselves the victims of a great hoax. "This strange creature which had caused so much excitement and enquiry was not a crocodile, a turtle, a young whale or an alligator, but merely a calf skin stuffed with hay and loaded with bricks to keep it under water. On hearing of this a great din of shouting, cursing, singing, yelling and roars of laughter arose from the multitude, and all pressed even closer to get a good view of the object. Afterwards the skin was dragged through the streets by a number of little boys to the evident satisfaction of an admiring crowd."[20] Strange, but good fun.

By the 1880s, civic organizers in Ingersoll and Woodstock were striving to transform the parades from their silly, risqué, and rowdy activities into respectable representations of a proud and self-conscious urban community happily taking centre stage. Historians Craig Heron and Steve Penfold document similar transformations of this parade genre in other places throughout the province, in Ottawa, Toronto, Hamilton, and Chatham. They argue that "carnivalesque parading, stripped of its political bite, could fit comfortably into quite respectable public events, even those organized or sanctioned by prominent citizens and civic leaders."[21]

As the new parades were moved from the margins to the centre of public display, many strands of traditional culture were removed from them and replaced by middle-class symbols. As part of organizing the callathumpian parades, Ingersoll and Woodstock's holiday committees appointed judges to award prizes for the best floats and costumes. This and especially the new practice of publishing the names of paraders in the newspapers violated the anonymity through disguise that characterized early parades.[22] Of one reformed parade in 1880 a writer in the *Sentinel* observed: "while the privileges of unrestraint were enjoyed to the full there was very little evidence of a desire to abuse them," suggesting that parade organizers had co-opted the genre for a new social agenda.[23] Turn-of-the-century holiday-goers would indeed find the parades transformed. When, in 1901, people in the new city of Woodstock held a huge party for themselves, the proud mayor boasted that their callathumpian parade "was in harmony with such an auspicious occasion."[24]

The social commentary presented in the reformed parades sometimes presented a much sharper criticism than before, but the parades were sanctioned by those in power, likely because of their content and conformity to what civic leaders believed to be in the best interests of the community. In 1888, the *Sentinel* praised Woodstock's new callathumpians, describing them as "caricatures of social and political events that engage the attention and excite the interest."[25] They were described as standing in stark contrast to what had been eliminated – the "coarse and meaningless, though laughable, exhibitions of tomfoolery of no particular type." One parade-group lampooned certain civic leaders, aiming squarely at a political question of the day – the gas light company. Another float depicted members of the town council deviously encircled by the "gas company ogre," who attempted to secure control of the town's electric light. This caricature cut to the quick a significant local issue for local homeowners. So did a mockery of the Scott Act temperance legislation, with a bottle of booze fashioned from a threshing machine boiler surrounded by a group of tipplers. Other times, parade floats caricatured respectable community members of the propertied middle class, such as local bank clerks loafing after work and local gossips having a tea party, while fire department and squabbling schoolboard members received similar attention. Local parades even harkened back to earlier processional styles, like floats for the "Ingersoll Branch of the Whitecaps" and the "Cut knife Creek Artillery Brigade," which played upon the whitecapping and militia burlesque styles historically related to the callathumpian tradition. For a town with a sizable black population, paraders in the "Model Barber Shop" and the "Darky Town Fire Brigade" floats reveal tense local race relations glossed over by white community members in the guise of humour.[26]

Reformed parades became an important part of the noontime holiday processions. Organizing committees consciously arranged them, intending to present a model of respectability and an order of place in the towns.[27] Their routes went through the areas where middle-class men did their business: down the main thoroughfare, around the market square, and through the commercial district to the town park – the site of holiday games. Noontime parades gave a distinct and selective version of local social relations, which, like the social backgrounds of organizing committee members, did not represent all social classes. By their exclusivity, they symbolically confirmed the emerging social order and used male bodies to do so. Like the industrial capitalist system, they excluded workers, women, and children while highlighting middle-class men and their achievements. They stressed what middle-class myth-makers believed were the positive aspects of the town, like the local voluntary orders. Noontime parades were also intended to thrive upon and feed urban pride, especially that of respectable middle-class property holders, giving townspeople another opportunity to express their boosterism. "Our wide awake village," wrote one commentator describing Ingersoll's 1861 Queen's Birthday celebrations, "has been noted alike for its loyalty, ability and enterprise in every department of business. We will match it against any town of its 'inches.'" The key ingredients of success, the paper forwarded, lay in the town's middle-class population's "pushing men, its comely matrons, charming widows, blooming lasses, nice young men, and pretty babies."[28]

On the 24th of May 1889, four thousand people followed Ingersoll's noontime parade to the town's new park, Victoria Park, to witness the christening of the new public recreational space.[29] In his address Mayor Thomas Brown, owner of the town's large tannery works, commended the town's progress and boasted of its many merits. He praised the transportation and communication innovations that, during his own lifetime, had stimulated the town's urban and industrial growth. With its new park, he ventured ambitiously, little Ingersoll now occupied a noteworthy place in Ontario's urban landscape. Crowds cheered as Brown broke a bottle of wine on the wheel of a fine carriage. Ingersoll's town band then led the masses in a rousing chorus of the national anthem and in three cheers for Queen Victoria, the mayor, and the town council. The ceremony, begun with an allusion to the past, ended with Ingersoll's (notoriously bad) cheese poet, James McIntyre, capturing the excitement of the holiday for posterity:

... In future years it will be famed
The day whereon the Park was named,
With its boundary great extended
And nature's charms sweetly blended.

Full worthy of the poet's theme
Is hill and dale, and wood and stream,
And glittering spires, and busy town.
Where mansions do each mount top crown.

... Young men and maids, and fine old dames
Will gather on the banks of Thames
And though we have a tug-of-war
'Twill leave no wound or deadly scar.[30]

The imagery in McIntyre's poem, such as the reference to mansions on the crown, speaks to the ideal community envisioned by the poet and other middle-class holiday organizers. McIntyre, a socially prominent entrepreneur, owned a thriving furniture-making and undertaking business on King Street. Well-known in local fraternal and voluntary circles, he belonged to a handful of associations, sitting on the boards of the IOOF and Sons of Scotland and belonging to the local Masonic

order for more than forty years. He even helped organize the town's
civic holiday in 1880. In his poem, McIntyre suggests sport gives successful men like himself healthy battlefields for the same competitive
energies that have made them and their town so successful. Noontime
parade routes did not pass by the hills, dales, and streams evoked in
McIntyre's nature-filled rendering of the place. Instead, they went
through the busy town, where local entrepreneurs, professionals, and
politicians did their business. They didn't happen through the streets
passing by the town's many factories, where most local men laboured.

From the 1850s through to the late 1870s noontime parades highlighted the towns' preeminent voluntary organizations, the firefighters
and militiamen who protected the community in the era of few local
services. In their studies of Ingersoll and Woodstock, historians Lynne
Marks and Christopher Anstead each suggest that workingmen flocked
to local firefighting and militia units. In them they created a world of
camaraderie, masculine strength, and bravery, blending rough and
respectable cultures.[31] Before the Great War, argues Anstead, some
four-fifths of Oxford County's peacetime militia members were workingmen, with slightly more unskilled than skilled ones.[32] Heavy educational and financial requirements kept them out of leadership positions
in the officers' corps, but even so, Anstead contends, with its middle-
class leadership and its overall success in "reinforcing 'common sense'
values" appropriate to the dominant order, workers still found a place
to express their working-class identities in an atmosphere of strong
camaraderie.[33] Holiday parades, an important facet of this militia culture, provided a way for workingmen to display themselves in the public arena. Their ceremonial uniforms and military skill delighted audiences as they paraded by.

Firefighters in their fancy uniforms also strutted their stuff in holiday
parades, showing off drills and routines and gleaming firefighting equipment.[34] Occasionally they would wait for the holiday to set a derelict
building ablaze and then control its burning for local amusement.
Protecting the urban landscape from devastating fires was a deadly serious business, yet as Lynne Marks shows, firefighters sometimes wanted in discipline and lacked respect for their officers, attitudes that
lagged behind presumed community behavioural standards.[35] However, given the opportunity to display themselves in public, firefighters
towed the respectable line with their own flare. In 1878, Woodstock's
firefighters marched down Dundas Street under a banner that read,
"All work and no play makes Jack a dull boy," suggesting that for the
men involved, fighting fires was fun and excitement-filled.[36] Other
banners, like "Flame Fighters of Ontario – a Unit in Danger for the
Benefit of our People," reflected the serious side of their work and

IAAA Dominion Day trades parade, Ingersoll, c. 1890s. Trades processions gave respectable representations of what holiday organizers and industrial capitalists believed were the healthy and harmonious relationships between the town and industry. Yet they represented only the largest and most prosperous local industries and typically involved only the smallest and most economically secure segments of local labour. (Courtesy of the Ingersoll Cheese Factory Museum)

community dependence upon it. In 1872 Ingersoll townspeople learnt this lesson all too well as they helplessly watched their downtown core burn to the ground, despite the fire brigade's noble efforts.[37]

Throughout the century, other types of voluntary associations negotiated their way onto the holiday parade scene. By the early 1880s, secret societies and social clubs marched in the noontime parades. Many groups, including the Foresters, Oddfellows, Templars, and the Caledonians, held local holiday demonstrations along with their brethren from out of town. By the decade's end, local industrial workers also marched alongside these groups on the Queen's Birthday and Dominion Day holidays. The parades on these days were not quite the craftsmen's spectacles that Labour Day was to become in other places, but they nevertheless celebrated the workers who sustained the local industrial production fueling the town's economy. Trades processions gave respectable representations of what holiday organizers and industrial capitalists believed were the healthy and harmonious relationships between the town and industry. Civic pride and pride in local industry went hand in hand. The parades provided unique opportunities for advertising the town and its industrial establishments: Ingersoll and Woodstock's parades featured local manufacturers and their workers. Yet they represented only the largest and most prosperous local industries, and involved only the smallest and most economically secure segments of local labour.

In 1887, Ingersoll's Queen's Birthday holiday attracted four thousand people. There townspeople and their visitors witnessed what was really only the rosy side of the story of the relations between the town, its industrialists, and its workers at a time when the country's labour problem was being investigated by a royal commission.[38] Mayor Buchanan, a local agricultural tool manufacturer, along with eight civic officials mounted on horseback, marshaled a parade celebrating local factories. Workers in the firms of the town's chief employers – the Noxon Brothers and the Buchanan Company agricultural tool firms, the Mitchell Carriage Company, and J.L. Grant's Pork Packing and Cheese Exporting Company – comprised a huge number of the town's male workforce. The Noxon Brothers produced by far the largest display.[39] Four- and six-in-hand drafts drew six floats carrying artisans working. Twelve men from the moulding shop cast commemorative medals of the day's event and handed them out to the eager crowd.[40] Other floats included men from the wood shop, eight from the vice room, blacksmiths, and painters, each performing some aspect of their job for all to see. Jumbo, the well-known company draft horse, trudged along, drawing the latest model of the Noxon Elevated Steel Binder. His motto, "Only Fun for Jumbo," suggested that the new machine would be "mere child's play for this noble brute."[41] Noxon must have been pleased with the effectiveness of the advertising. A year later, when sixty-six local men purchased Noxon light steel binders, their names could be found listed in the town's newspaper coverage of Dominion Day events.[42]

On Dominion Day 1887, Ingersoll's Knights of Labor assembly held a grand demonstration celebrating organized labour while presenting another symbolic articulation of the underlying social order. The ideal of mutualism – harmonious relations between labour and capital – led the day.[43] Heralded by the Mount Elgin Brass Band, the parade began with carriages filled with visiting dignitaries from the Woodstock and St Thomas Knights of Labor assemblies. Then came the carriage of Ingersoll's mayor and his guests, followed by others filled with local

1. Young Canadian B.B. Team; 2. Atlantic B.B. Team; 3. Active B.B. Team; 4. Beaver Lacrosse Team; 5. Woodstock Hockey Club; 6. Bain B.B. Club; 7. Hay & Co. B.B. Club.

Woodstock representative sports teams through time. Local boosters published this montage of Woodstock sports team photographs in 1901 in a souvenir album chronicling Woodstock's rise to city status. (Courtesy of the Woodstock Museum)

assembly officials. Marchers from London, Woodstock, St Thomas, and Ingersoll assemblies took up the rear. After the procession to the town park the noontime speech from the mayor commended the excellent relations between local labour and capital. "What we here see before us," he proclaimed, "tells a story of peace, prosperity, and happiness among all classes of people. Here we have no strikes to cause disorder, no trouble among races, but we assemble as one people serving the Queen and one God."[44] Woodstock's K of L representative, a Mr Gribble, outlined the philosophy of the Knights while denouncing the opinion, apparently held by many, that they incited workers' strikes. In reality, he argued, they aimed to prevent them. Local industrialists sitting on the holiday organizing committee likely found these words to be sweet music to their ears.

Sporting parades that featured hometown teams and their visiting rivals also pleased the organizing committee and the growing numbers of sports fans who viewed local teams as hometown ambas-

Woodstock Cycle Club, c. 1885. When the cycling craze hit the town, penny-farthing bicycle parades became an extraordinary and popular type of parade. Club members in their military garb ran over rough, unpaved streets while singing choruses and performing precision drills. (Courtesy of the Woodstock Museum)

sadors. From the mid–1860s on, organized team sport competition took hold of the public's imagination and emerged as a mainstay of local recreation, entertainment, and urban boosterism. Sports teams assumed an honoured place in the orderly noontime parades, reflecting their increasing importance to community life. Interwoven into the fabric of civic holiday celebrations, sports parades and team victories became an ideal means with which to boost people's pride in their hometown. Team names, like the Woodstocks, emphasized a team's ties to the town. Sports fields became surrogate battlegrounds for all sorts of rivalries and, as suggested in the words of Ingersoll poet James McIntyre, of battles that left "no wound or deadly scar."[45]

Baseball first found its way into the holiday parade agenda as inter urban matches commenced in the mid–1860s. Ball teams and their fans congregated at the train station in the early morning to meet their competition and its entourage as it arrived. Brass bands paraded the uniformed teams and their fans to the market square for an official wel-

come and pep rally. The more important the game, the bigger the crowd. Then it was on to the game site. When in 1866 Woodstock's hometown baseball team, the Young Canadians, hosted Dundas's Mechanics, some fifteen hundred spectators, nearly half of all Woodstonians, watched the lively competition at the town park.[46] Two years later, some three thousand followed the Young Canadians and their visitors, Ingersoll's Victorias, as they paraded to the park. There they competed for the Silver Ball, the coveted emblem of the Canadian baseball championship.[47]

In the 1880s, when the cycling craze hit the towns, penny-farthing bicycle parades became by far the most extraordinary and popular type of parade genre.[48] When Woodstock held the Canadian Wheelmen's Association's annual meet in 1885, local people welcomed cyclists from the prestigious Montreal and Toronto clubs and from smaller clubs from Stratford, Belleville, Brampton, Brantford, and Ottawa, who arrived by train. The busy scene at the station, blanketed in billows of dark smoke, had cyclists disembarking from the train with their wheels in tow as throngs of people crowded around cheering. Order emerged somehow through the chaos as the cyclists lined up in their formations and then paraded from the station to the market square for a rally led by civic and sporting officials. Then it was down the main thoroughfare and on to the town park, with the cyclists

Joseph Gibson and Ingersoll cyclists, n.d. Ingersoll's longtime grocer and postmaster, Gibson had a reputation as a staunch temperance man. He played for the local Victorias team that wrested the Silver Ball baseball championship from Woodstock's Young Canadians in 1868. An avid cricket, baseball, and curling man, his passion for sport remained throughout his life. (Courtesy of the Ingersoll Cheese Factory Museum)

running over rough, unpaved streets while singing choruses and performing precision drills. Led by captains, lieutenants, and buglers, they wore expensive outfits of dark waistcoats, puttees, and little rifleman's caps, finery that cost upwards of $30.[49] Whistles, medals, and ribbons heightened the military effect. These tokens of identity unified the cyclists, distancing them from the others who stood by, taking in the unusual scene. Imagine the fun spectators had watching the officious men riding the big cycles accidentally crashing into each other – an image very different from the disorder that characterized earlier callathumpian parades.

By the turn of the century, when safety bicycles provided for female emancipation everywhere that one could afford such a contraption, local female cyclists joined the community's respectable parade genre. As members of the Karn Organ Factory Cycle Club, they rode through the streets upon two-wheeled safety bicycles with their low, nicely designed frames that, because of their evenly sized wheels, gave a more comfortable ride than the penny-farthings. Judging by their numbers, the women of the Karn club were the wives, sweethearts, daughters, and sisters of Karn employees, not factory workers themselves. Their male counterparts in the club were a relatively privileged lot, working

Lady cyclists on parade, Woodstock, 1897.
This rare photo shows females on two-
wheeled safety bicycles playing a prominent
role in a holiday parade as members of the
Karn Organ Factory Cycle Club. They
performed precision drills while wearing
long skirts with hemlines that were easily
destroyed by bicycle chains. (*Sentinel-
Review*, The Garden of Ontario Special
Edition, May 1897)

for the town's largest employer. Employees pooled together their
resources to purchase cycles – costing anywhere from $30 to $100
apiece – for club use, something that most working people could simply not afford to buy on their own. Only certain types of workers at
the organ factory – those with specific skills, like organ tuners, case
makers, and finishers – had salaries that afforded much surplus
income, that is, if they didn't have dependents to support.[50] The high
cost of a bicycle would have been well beyond the reach of organ pol-
ishers, at the lowest end of the factory's salary scale. How much club
members paid to belong is unknown, as is whether Karn helped the

club along financially to lessen the effects of idleness upon his work-force.[51]

During civic holidays, the members of the clubs followed the town band down the main street, performing careful drill routines. They paraded for an audience that may have already caught a glimpse of the clubs and their mixed membership going through town during their evening rambles. The clubs gave women the freedom to get about in town and through the neighbouring countryside chaperoned only by club leaders and friends. The sight of women – young and old alike – cavorting about so freely shocked some people. In 1889, Kit Coleman, the first women's page editor of the Toronto *Mail*, wrote, "No girl over 39 should be allowed to wheel. It is immoral. Unfortunately it is the old girls who are the ardent wheelers. They love to cavort and careen above the spokes, twirling and twisting in a manner that must remind them of long dead dancing days. They have descended from the shelves in myriads and in the burst of Indian summer are disporting themselves on the highways and byways."[52] While lady cyclists may have been seen daily by some, the sight of women holding any place, yet alone a prominent one, in public parades was still uncommon.

Did any of the women ride while corseted? Some may have, but it must have made straddling a bicycle strange and most uncomfortable for them as they concentrated on drill routines. Even so, constraints both self-imposed and required by the club tempered such a move as abandoning the corset. Club social sensibilities compelled women to wear respectable, appropriate clothing to avoid charges of immorality. None of the Karn factory club members wore the type of military garb seen on the Woodstock Amateur Athletic Association's old penny-farthing contingent. While men wore everyday wear – trousers, jackets and caps, the club's women wore fashionably feminine outfits that protected their modesty – hats, blouses, and ankle-length skirts. No one really pushed the boundaries of dress sensibility too far by wearing bloomers, that era's symbol of female physical emancipation. Bicycle chains probably ruined many a hemline.

Cycle parades in Ingersoll and Woodstock reflected at first the novelty, and then the increasing importance of bicycles to local culture. Great levelers, bicycles captured local people's imagination, providing a form of recreation, a means of transportation, and a social activity for males and females alike. Like other types of sport-related parades, bicycle parades changed, ebbed, and flowed in the last decades of the century. Yet while the form of sport parades changed through time, some type of sport was *always* to be found during Ingersoll and Woodstock holidays. Sport parades mark the importance given to sport in the civic life of both towns.

Initially, holiday sports were comprised of local, communal activities that accentuated fun and frivolity and were deeply rooted in local tradition. Between 1850 and the late 1860s, however, their focus and structure shifted, as social tensions surfaced around those traditional sporting activities that had strong elements of disorder and ritual inversion, the same ingredients seen in early callathumpian parades. By Confederation, reformers perceived these activities if not as an actual source of social disorder then as being socially useless. From the late 1860s until the early 1880s, holiday sports organizers began shedding the informal local focus of holiday sport for organized activities run by the towns' newly formed clubs. Driving park associations, for example, organized holiday turf (horseracing) events, and Caledonian Societies ran holiday Highland (Scottish track and field) games. As competition stretched out beyond local boundaries, the sports of this era, like respectable noontime parades, emphasized rational and respectable elements at the expense of earlier traditions.

Local sporting excellence and innovation gave townspeople a convenient means to elevate their sense of self-worth while deriding opponents from other towns – key ingredients in urban boosterism. Ingersoll and Woodstock townspeople used their holiday sports attractions as another area of competition in their ideological battle over who had the most forward-looking town – and by implication, which would be the town of the future. The *Sentinel*, advertising Woodstock's expanded agenda for sports on the 1874 Dominion Day celebrations, poked fun at Ingersoll's sporting traditions, ridiculing the town's ability to keep abreast of the changing times. It implied that Ingersoll was a backward place with downright primitive holiday sports, "possibly a greased pig worrying for the delectation of our friends ... who are extremely partial to that sort of 'intellectual' recreation."[53] This direct jab was made by a town that prided itself on its commitment to organized, rational sport and the notion that town victories came from team victories. The press encouraged townspeople aspiring to true glory to "forsake their own hamlet on the day in question for the bill of fare to be provided in the county town and the chief town of the county." Of course, that would be Woodstock. In 1887, the *Sentinel* wrote caustically, "it will do our rustic neighbors good to come to town on the 24th, while Woodstock citizens would probably enjoy a glimpse of rural life [in Ingersoll] on Dominion day."[54] Sometimes decidedly poisoned verbal battles surfaced, as when the *Sentinel* defended its town's approach to sport against the "slurs of the Ingersoll mudslinger."[55] Stuck with living in a small town, underdogs to the larger centres of Toronto, Hamilton, and London, urban boosters in Ingersoll and Woodstock found their niche in each other's company.

This gave meaning to their battles in their quest for urban identity, battles most visible during civic holidays.

Before Confederation, Ingersoll and Woodstock's civic holiday sports were consistent with what sport historians Melvin Adelman and Allen Guttmann have termed "pre modern" types of sport.[56] Informally organized and meaningful only locally, the events had simple, unwritten rules. Few things distinguished the players from the spectators, since anyone in the crowd (that is, people of the right gender) could step up to the starting line to compete in an event. The rules were informed by local custom and tradition: old-timers, like 'Old' Ned Dolson from Beachville, who had learnt local variations of age-old games in their youth, passed them down to subsequent generations.[57] Men, women, and children paid token amounts to compete during holiday games for the list of prizes, usually small sums of money. Broadsheets plastered all through the town invited all to come and join in the fun. However, one's age and gender limited participation. Girls' races, boys' races, and races for single and married women prevented males and females from competing against each other when biologically based physical attributes of size, strength, and speed, as well as cultural constraints associated with appropriate gender behaviour, were at issue. People raced against each other, not the clock, and whoever crossed the finish line first took the victory. Newspapers sometimes recorded event outcomes, things to be spun into tales of obstacles and prowess that meant something to local people who knew well the cast of characters involved. Running races, jumping and throwing events, the precursors of modern track and field events, could be found interspersed among pre-modern games of disorder and ritual inversion. The latter accentuated chance, hazard, and sheer fun for everyone involved, participants and spectators alike.[58]

The hilarious games of inversion and disorder pitted people against obstacles designed to wreak total havoc. Silliness ruled the day. Tied up in a large sack with only their heads protruding, contestants in the sack race struggled to stay upright as they hopped along the racecourse. People on the sidelines cheered them on, enjoying the bizarre image as the competitors, faces strained in effort, huffed and puffed their way to the finish line. In the three-legged event, racers coordinated their bound legs while waving their free arms to avoid tripping; bickering, uncooperative pairs tumbled to the ground, much to the crowd's delight. In the wheelbarrow race, blindfolded racers pushed wooden wheelbarrows, crashing into each other as they tried to manoeuvre their way around the fallen bodies in their path to victory.[59] Blindfolded racers laughed and squealed in delight as they chased a bell-ringer, who wove a path skillfully through the mêlée, dodging and ducking eager hands that grasped for the bell. Other squeals came from a greased pig as eager pursuers stumbled through the mud to yank its tail. When caught by some fleet-footed individual, the pig became a prize destined for the victor's supper table. Spectators also enjoyed the hilarity of watching Ingersoll's pole-vaulters as they tried to jump over the mill stream. They usually ended short of their mark, scrambling out of the water, their hair dripping wet and their clothes covered with pond scum. 'Oohs' and 'aahs' accompanied the contest for the fattest baby as proud parents preened over little ones. The participants in the fat mens' race, by contrast, good-naturedly let themselves be the objects of hilarity and derision. A reporter in 1865 asked:

Reader did you ever behold a number of 'phat' men running for dear life? If you did not, a scene was missed that was well worth seeing. Several of the weighty men of the neighborhood ... from 220 lbs and upwards, contested for the honors, and the race was an exciting one. Fat, fat, nothing but fat! Such Herculean efforts – such puffing and blowing – locomotives on a small scale as fast as their powers of locomotion would permit. The condition of the 'phat' men after the race must have been anything but comfortable to themselves, and as they stood surrounded by their admiring friends, their looks conveyed the emphatic rebuke of bullfrogs to the mischievous urchins who threw stones at them – 'what is sport to you is death to us!'[60]

Not everyone enjoyed the fun of traditional games of disorder and ritual inversion, however, or felt that they were important to community-building or town identity. To those earnest souls concerned about disorder in urban society, traditional games became a vexing issue. The social and moral imperative of sport engaged sport reformers keenly in the era of rational recreation. They viewed games of disorder sceptically, precisely because of their frivolous nature.[61] How could obese men huffing and puffing or greasy pigs darting about be of any merit to local society? How could they develop the moral character of participants or spectators? The rational approach to recreation demanded that physical activities prepare people, especially young people, to meet the physical and moral demands for success in an industrial-capitalist economy.[62] Hard work and diligence, not silliness and laughter, should win the day. Social and sports reformers did not see luck, chance, or frivolity as parts of the equation for success.

Nor did this view have room for activities tainted by any hint of moral vice. Thus some activities that had the guise of scientific rationalism – like horseracing – still posed problems for sport reformers. Many people of the day found horseracing to be the most problematic traditional holiday sport. Ever since its original settlement by half-pay British officers in the late 1830s, Woodstock had prided itself as a horse town. An integral part of the social lives of the local leisure class of retired military officers, equine sport possessed its own lengthy tradition and system of ideological sanctioning long before it arrived in Oxford County.[63] The officers' horse events, which included annual steeplechases and fox hunts, bore decidedly elevated social tones that distinguished their group activities from those of other people residing in the area.[64] In their carefully circumscribed paternalistic social world, the officers' interest in horses maintained a gentility rendering it above reproach. However, the people's equine sport differed vastly, particularly horseracing, as it was linked to tavern culture, a highly contested social terrain.[65] Ontario historian Edwin Guillet describes the popular styles of horseracing as events that "commonly resulted in fights and brawls; while in all parts of the province gambling and drunkenness were characteristic of such sporting activities. There were races of all varieties and conditions, but they were usually restricted to native horses, which the meets aided greatly in developing."[66]

As early as 1845 someone writing in the Woodstock *Herald*, a local paper expressing a moderate Tory view, expressed certain concerns condemning popular versions of horseraces. With some disgust the writer pointed out that horseracing's association with vice actually made it appealing to some people. "No argument of a feather's weight can be adduced in its favor," the writer forwarded, "As an amusement it is not worth half a game of marbles, blind man's bluff, or pitch and toss; and were it not for its numerous train of attendant moral evils, it would not be worthwhile for the press to bestow a paragraph on such trumpery. Improving the breed of horses indeed!"[67] From Christian church pulpits came sermons decrying the immorality and intemperance thought to be associated with popular versions of horseracing. This wasn't just a moral issue, however, since innocent pedestrians could get hurt and property could be damaged by people who took to racing down local streets. But moral reasoning lay just below the surface, since local bylaws prohibited immoderate driving on local streets, gambling, and charivaris all with the same stroke of the pen.[68] As a cultural form, certain people viewed horseracing indeed to be in dubious company.

Given this state of affairs, it appears odd that early Ingersoll and Woodstock civic holidays featured horse races. Yet, the rationale of horse breeding supported the sport. Canadian sport historian Alan Metcalfe suggests that by Confederation, most areas included horseracing in their Queen's Birthday celebrations. Canadians everywhere needed well-bred horses for agricultural work and for transportation.[69] A horse had to be a kind of multi-purpose vehicle: it had to be strong enough to draw a good load, travel at a good pace, and avoid physical injury. Careful breeding ensured these qualities. Horse-races provided a cost-effective and entertaining way to test horseflesh, and agricultural associations and fairs supported horseracing for breeding and entertainment purposes.[70] Their holiday races typically involved flat, trotting, and paced races.[71] Any available broad, clear track of land, like the gravel road running through Beachville between Ingersoll and Woodstock, provided a passable racecourse.[72] In the winter, tracks lay on Ingersoll's ice-covered pond and along snow-covered flats of the Thames river.[73] Events such as the Innkeepers Purse, held during the spring and fall months, gave local people an opportunity to test the capacity of their horses while giving folks in the area some lively entertainment and opportunities to win sums of money.[74] Local historian William Perkins Bull, writing on early horse promoters in Peel County, observed that tavern and innkeepers had the racecourses end at their door – not bad for business.[75]

More than any other sport that found its way into community celebrations, horseracing cut to the quick of pressing social and moral issues, revealing, as Mike Huggins demonstrates, tensions between middle-class visions of civilization and moral improvement on the one hand and economic and social self-interest on the other.[76] Horseracing possessed rowdiness quite distinct from traditional events such as games of ritual inversion. Seen by some as cruel to animals, by others simply as an avenue for betting, gambling, and event-fixing, social reformers were generally sceptical of horseracing and its indelible ties to the cash nexus.[77] To them it undermined and often disrupted social order. In 1871, Woodstock saw the creation of a local Driving Park Association, which was intended to elevate the moral tone of horse-races by bureaucratizing, rationalizing, and systematizing turf events. It wanted to produce "strictly honorable races," similar to what was going on in a loosely connected network of associations throughout the province.[78] A joint-stock venture, the Woodstock association aimed to organize and foster local horseracing along "legitimate lines." Apparently not incorporated, it likely attempted to ensure exclusivity and protect members from legal liability.[79] Promoting turf events while providing entertainment facilities for the town would make its park "a pleasant resort for driving, riding, ball games, etc."[80]

The Driving Park Association's executive included fourteen of the town's most socially prominent and active middle-class leaders. Three-quarters of them held an office in local government, among them past or future reeves and mayors. Five belonged to the local board of trade. Their involvement in local voluntary and fraternal organizations was impressive. Nine sat on sports club executive bodies, six doing so for three or more different local sports. Seven governed local fraternal orders, sitting on the executives of the local International Order of Odd Fellows, the Ancient Free and Accepted Masons, the Royal Arcanum, and the Ancient Order of United Workmen. With most belonging to at least three different fraternal bodies, associational leadership in the town apparently had an overlapping nature.

Among the area turf promoters who benefitted from the Driving Park Association's work are three notable names in Canada's early turf history – Charles Boyle, John Forbes, and T.C. Patteson. Boyle, an ardent sport promoter, lived at the east end of town, where he ran the Firs Stables. Like his son, 'Klondike Joe' Boyle, who is remembered in Canadian sport lore for taking his hockey team from the Klondike to Montreal by dogsled and train to compete in the 1903 Stanley Cup, Charles Boyle is well remembered in Canadian horseracing circles. The turf historian E.K. Dodds considers Boyle to be the dean of thoroughbred horse trainers in nineteenth-century Canada, responsible for training horses for notables names such as Patteson and Seagram.[81] John Forbes, his partner and sometime owner of Woodstock's Caister House hotel and livery stable, had a reputation throughout North America for training winners. His horses captured the likes of the New York Ladies Handicap, the Belmont Stakes, and the Queen's Plate.[82] According to Dodds, Forbes held a reputation above reproach among the Canadian turf fraternity, so much so that no one thought to accuse Forbes of being in a conflict of interest when he set odds on races in which his own horses ran.[83] Matters played out slightly differently on the local scene, with amateur sport leaders speaking out against his involvement with the betting community. His habit of holding the stakes for professional sports matches ruffled feathers among amateur sports promoters. T.C. Patteson, the Eton and Oxford graduate who was the sometime editor of Toronto's *Mail*, postmaster of Toronto, and a founder of the Ontario Jockey Club, spent his summers at Eastwood, the old Vansittart estate, which he had purchased to be near his horses at Boyle's stables.[84] These three men extended Woodstock horse interests and the town's reputation in horse circles well beyond local boundaries and connected the town to provincial and national sporting networks.

Under the Driving Park Association's leadership Woodstock became known in horse circles as the Newmarket of Canada, with its "strictly honorable races."[85] The *Canadian Gentleman's Journal and Sporting Times,* reporting on turf activities in Woodstock and other places, took pride in its editorial conviction (though not its practice) never to report upon "scandals, criminal records, and everything else to deprave the taste or shock the sensibilities of our readers."[86] In 1876, it identified Woodstock as "one of our leading towns," a place regarded highly in respectable sporting circles.[87] The Driving Park Association's resolution to forbid driving on the Sabbath and its prohibition against liquor worked to give the organization and its races an air of propriety and decorum.[88] Those who violated these rules faced the stiff hand of the law, meted out by constables hired to maintain order at park turf events.[89]

Throughout the 1870s, the association took advantage of citizens' days off by holding their annual spring races on the Queen's Birthday and Dominion Day holidays. Using the holiday venue to promote horse interests, and encouraging inter urban competition broadened the local focus of the town's holiday activities. The association's purses offered sizable rewards to induce competitors, and by 1874 Canadian horses vied for an astronomical $200 prize. Admission to the park cost the hefty sum of fifty cents, while grandstand seats cost fifty cents more. Those who did not wish to mingle with the masses could watch the action from their carriages a dollar and a half. When Woodstock held the Queen's Plate in 1875, the town became part of the history of a long-lived and prestigious Canadian sporting tradition, one limited to Toronto's Woodbine Race Track after 1882.[90]

As leaders in local finance and politics, the executives of Woodstock's driving park wanted to advance the cause of the turf while enhancing the reputation of the town. Their scientific approach to horse breeding and strict rules for riders and spectators made the turf appear implicitly rational. The local press hailed this intent, calling association members "the town's best and most prominent men who would tolerate nothing but strictly honorable races," with meets conducted "in an irreproachable manner."[91] Yet judging by the association's repeated efforts to clean up the environment of horseracing, they apparently could not sever all rowdyism associated with the sport. For example, although signs reminded spectators that obscene language was not allowed at the park, frequent newspaper reports show many people ignored park rules.[92]

The issue of wagering, as betting or gambling, also plagued the association, although the *Canadian Gentleman's Journal and Sporting Times* supported the association's approach to legitimizing its version of horseracing. In 1875 it argued the case that the science of horseracing required betting, an innocent and healthy thing. To appeal to the logic of respectable businesspeople, it likened betting on the horses to investing venture capital in wheat. Scientific principles informed the actions of men who staked their money on horses, just like those who invested in the stock exchange. This differentiated bettors from gamblers, who staked their money on chance and "the hazards of the die." The code of gentlemanliness informed the actions of honest bettors:

[G]ambling and betting are very distinct things. Although he who gambles must bet, it does not follow that he who bets must gamble ... The gambling spirit is altogether opposite to that of manly honest betting. The object of the gambler is not to support his convictions, for he generally has none, but to gain an advantage. Therefore he always wishes to bet upon a sure thing, while the true sportsmen prefers to risk his money upon the certainty of his own judgement. No gentleman would bet upon a race which he knew was to be sold ... but such a secret knowledge of what is to come is precisely what the gambler needs. He cares nothing for the fight, but only for the spoil afterward. It is not his to have fair play, for in that case he would be a little wiser than the rest of the world. Everyone should remember that gambling is a business, and those who profess it do not intend to lose if they can prevent it.[93]

Yet, as with rowdyism, the need for repeated proclamations about the respectability and innocence of the sport indicates that alternative beliefs and practices lingered, and indeed, sport reformers never totally shook the deeply rooted associations with gambling and alcohol from the sport, despite their efforts. Because of this persistence, horse enthusiasts seeking respectability frequently denied any connection between the turf and social vice. Turf reformers sought out gentlemanly fair play from all concerned, and the acceptance of this idea established in their eyes the thin line between what they would and would not condone. But it was like new bottles for old wine – the same old thing just packaged slightly differently. As William Perkins Bull humorously put it, "For a time [the Puritan Conscience] was salved by calling the trotting races 'trials of speed' and at least one clergy man of Peel [County] is known to have hung over the rail in joyous enthusiasm, convinced that he was not watching a horse race – but something entirely different – though with the same effect."[94]

As historians Doug Brown and Greg Waters each show, attempts to rationalize horseracing – again and again – produced a social and moral quagmire.[95] Never above reproach (indeed subjected to a royal commission inquiry in 1920), horseracing could hardly be seen to celebrate and articulate a town's feeling of collective identity when the social and moral issues surrounding it consistently split rather than unified the community.[96] Moreover, as inter urban horseracing competition grew and became organized into circuits, it typically involved non-local people.[97] Horseracing declined as a civic holiday sport just as other sports – notably amateur team sports moulded in the fashion of muscular Christianity – became popular locally. Apparently, the impeccable social standing and high intentions of Driving Park Association executives did not ensure that townspeople would embrace their sport as part of their holiday venue. Though the subject of reform through the associations, horseracing never quite made it. Those turf reformers who wished to use it to project their version of reality had a difficult time of it. Horses could not display human moral character – the respectable qualities of character urban boosters wished to project. While they attempted to control the sport suitably, driving park reformers did not eschew the essentially commercial nature of horseracing, nor perhaps could they do so, since betting remains an indelible part of the sport today. Ultimately, while turf promoters withdrew from the holiday, their sport nevertheless remained a permanent fixture of agricultural fairs, where horse breeding fit in more easily.[98]

Sport promoters involved with Caledonian (Scottish Highland) Games also had a short-lived and problematic association with local civic holiday celebrations. With so many Protestant Highlanders in the Zorra area, Oxford County had a Caledonian Society early, in 1848. By the mid–1870s Ingersoll boasted its own society. Promoting Scottish culture and holiday games, it aimed "to perpetuate ... some of the pluck and pith [and] muscular strength and dexterity of Auld Scotia's sons."[99] Like other holiday organizers, solidly respectable middle-class men made up the twenty executives of Ingersoll's society between 1880 and 1885. Their local activities numbered them, or were to number them, in a handful of the most active men in the town's social and political life. In their thirties and forties, these were Canadian-born married men, although a few had come to Canada in their youth with their parents from England and Scotland.

The Caledonian Society's executive, like other promoters of organized sport, used their games as a vehicle to cultivate other ends. Their particular approach blended the ancient notion of *mens sana in corpore sano* (sound mind in a healthy body) with a sense of nationalism. "This Society," wrote the *Chronicle* in 1882, "true to the history of the dear old land from which it takes its name, believes that a well developed muscle and a sound physique are elements of national greatness ... if Canada is to take a front rank place among the nations, her sons must have not only sound minds, but sound minds in sound bodies. A nation of weaklings and dyspeptics must necessarily degenerate."[100] Noble sentiments, yet Caledonian events held an individual – rather than team – orientation, stressing physical skills over social ones, while organized team sports were seen as testing socially acquired qualities, the hallmark of the muscular Christian approach to sport. As Morris Mott points out, "A good baseball team reflected the vitality and the ideals of a whole community to a degree a good shot-putter did not."[101] This difference became significant in the local acceptance of Caledonian Games on the holiday agenda in Ingersoll and Woodstock, although not in other places like Glengarry, where the connection between civic pride and ethnicity was more deeply entangled, making the local meanings of Caledonian contests different.[102] Perhaps more importantly to the situations in Ingersoll and Woodstock, amateur sports teams were filled with hometown boys, youth, and young men; Caledonian athletes – usually grown men – typically came from other places, and were perceived to have no stake in the town's welfare or moral progress.[103]

The Ingersoll Caledonian Society's first holiday games, held on Dominion Day 1876, provided a fare of running races, throwing events, and tugs-of-war that was familiar to most local inhabitants. Within a few years, however, the focus shifted to Scottish spectator-oriented cultural extravaganzas, with athletes and officials in Scottish garb and events designed to draw in participants from places far away.[104] Between 1881 and 1885, the society ran the town's Queen's Birthday holiday, employing a professional sport promoter, A.G. Hodge, proprietor of Toronto's St James Hotel and sometime president of the North American United Caledonian Association, to manage the event.[105] Broadsheets and newspapers highlighted the prizes, which in 1882 included prize monies amounting to a staggering $1,000.[106] Hometown boys were displaced by athletic specialists from other small places throughout southwestern Ontario like Embro, Kincardine, Zorra, Nissouri, and Lucknow, as well as ones from big cities like Montreal, Kingston, Toronto, Hamilton, London, and Buffalo. Since they weren't representing their place of origin, these athletes were likely enticed by prize money and the opportunity to compete against the best around, not urban pride. Hodge, an astute sport entrepreneur, ran the proceedings with an "iron hand," pushing everything "forward like clockwork – no lagging behind under any pretense."[107] He and the society cultivated a particularly Scottish flavour for the celebrations, offering prizes of ten and fifteen dollars for events like the Best Dressed Highland Piper. At night people paid from fifty to seventy-five cents to attend the society's Grand Scottish Concert, which in 1884 featured New York's Mrs Jessie Robertson, "the Queen of Scottish, English, and Irish songs," and Miss Ryckham, Hamilton's "charming soprano."[108] Members from other Scottish societies attended the event, such as, in 1881, Evans McColl, the great Scottish bard from Kingston and Captain W. Ormie McRobie of the New York Scotsman.[109]

The Caledonian sporting spectacles may have been superb, but while local Caledonian executives themselves upheld a philosophy of manly and respectable sport, they encountered problems everywhere. They found it hard enough getting local people to behave in desirable ways – how could they keep 'foreigners' accountable to local social conventions? The behaviour of transient Caledonian athletes became a matter of public concern in Ingersoll, Woodstock, and elsewhere throughout the province. More than that, with their popular rise, the Caledonian Games undermined the flexible and communal nature of holiday sport. Most townspeople had little, if any, chance of ever winning an event, even if they knew how to toss a caber, throw a hammer, or play the bagpipes. Displaced by talented athletic specialists like Cornwall's Roderick "Big Rory" McLennan, who trained year round in the hopes of winning substantial cash prizes, locals felt like outsiders on their home turf.[110] Why bother setting yourself up to getting humiliated on the track? The prowess of the Caledonians may have resulted in high quality sporting spectacles, "veritable Olympiads in caliber of participants and performances," but mass community participation fell by the wayside in the process.[111]

In 1936, Woodstonian runner Alby Robinson, describing the thrill-seeking lifestyle he had lived as a professional traveling athlete during his youth in the 1880s, revealed the darker side of local sporting culture. For him and others like him, the romance of adventure "formed an almost irresistible magnet for those men of wit and virile bodies." Of his experiences, Robinson recalled that "the most enthralling stories which can be told relate naturally to ... those community competitions where runners under false names trimmed the backers of some local celebrity or where one or a number of men imported sprinters to take the money of such local bettors as were not 'in the know.'"[112] Itinerant athletes like Robinson found small-town Caledonian competitions to be full of opportunity to "beguile the credulous and gullible" and bilk townspeople of their money. Small towns like Ingersoll and Woodstock, Robinson continued, were "vulnerable spots of such innocents. Herein lay ample play for their energies and enterprise in 'framing' up those that pitted home products, heroes of their local people and an imported gentleman who bore anyone else's rather than his own name ... to them the ends justified the means."[113]

Towns offering huge prizes for competitions became easy prey for athletic con games. Eventually, however, local townspeople got wise and turned against the Caledonian Games. This happened in Ingersoll and Woodstock, as in other places throughout the province. In the nearby small town of St Mary's, for example, the issue of public celebrations held as private enterprises for Caledonian backers became a cause célèbre. In 1886 its *Journal-Argus* argued that "Public celebrations ought never to get into the hands of private individuals because private entrepreneurs cheat townspeople through misleading advertising and shady practises." Citizens' committees, it claimed, should be responsible for the community holiday, since local people knew best how to take care of their own: "When money making becomes a consideration the admission fee is such as to prevent a poor man from taking his family, then the general holiday character of the day is lost, it becomes the speculator's, not the citizen's day."[114]

Ingersoll inhabitants shared these sentiments. Complaining about what amounted to the expropriation of the town holiday by foreign cultural and commercial interests, the *Chronicle* noted in May 1884 that "a glance at the prizes will show that a larger population were carried off by a few professionals."[115] Many townspeople took offense at the non-local and particularly ethnic nature of the games, with some taunting the Caledonians for "appropriating the day for their own self-engrandizement" at the expense of the participation and enjoyment of townspeople.[116] In October 1883, the *Chronicle* reported something that the *Scottish American Journal* itself was beginning to concede: "the shade of novelty has passed away from Scottish games ... the public are tired of being treated year after year to the inevitable hammers, cabers, stones, sword dances, highland flings, and so forth."[117] Over the next two years, civic leaders searched to establish new sporting traditions to make the Queen's Birthday and Dominion Day events more locally meaningful and more in line with community interests, talents, and social concerns. They aimed to address a local desire for community-based rational recreation. They also wanted to project respectable representations through sport to boost townspeople's morale and the reputation of the town. For them, Caledonian Games just did not fit the bill.

As the next chapter shows, in 1884 Woodstock came upon one such alternative – respectable amateur representative sport – that, in turn, heavily influenced Ingersoll's holiday sport and the progress of sport in both to the towns. Indeed, the amateur movement influenced *all* organized sport in Canada until the Great War.[118] Woodstock sportsmen founded the Woodstock Amateur Athletic Association (WAAA) to regulate amateur athletics in that town, and, more importantly, to satisfy local demands for a community-based and town council-sanctioned organization to provide sporting and social entertainments for the Queen's Birthday and Dominion Day holidays. When Woodstock began promoting its holiday amateur competition, Ingersoll's Caledonian Society increasingly found their games under intense local fire. In May 1884, the *Chronicle* wrote: "the Society, if they wish to keep up their representation, will no doubt see the advisability of getting up something in the way of novelties next year and encouraging amateur athletics."[119] By adopting locally based amateur competition, local sport reformers felt that they could kill two birds with one stone. Amateur codes would subvert the under-the-table payments, event fixing, and gambling endemic in holiday sport. They would also highlight the physical and moral qualities of townspeople, evidence of their town's overall greatness.

The Ingersoll Caledonian Society attempted to continue its Scottish games as next door the Woodstonians offered a holiday agenda of amateur events, but townspeople voted with their feet and their dollars, abandoning the town to attend the WAAA's rival games. This left the Ingersoll Caledonians shouldering a costly deficit, which they attempted to recoup from their hesitant town council.[120] Though they did eventually get reimbursed, the battle was not easy. Had the Caledonian executives not been men of considerable local prominence (many themselves sometime town councillors) they likely would have fared much worse. The *Chronicle* lamented the situation, claiming it "a pity" that the games were not to go on. Careful to separate the intent of the society executives from the activities of non-local entrepreneurs and their traveling athletes, the paper defended the society. It had tried its best but failed: because of them townspeople got first class amusement at a low price. But this entertainment had been problematic: "barring their being rather inclined to pay bit prices to professionals rather than to encourage amateurs by cups, medals, etc., of less value ... the members have spared neither time nor expense, and sometimes against very great difficulties and with begrudging aid from the general public."[121] A clear lesson came from Ingersoll's Caledonian Games experience: people considered the town's holiday to be sacred territory. Holiday management and participation needed to be a local affair to be successful.

THREE

From Holidays to Every Day: The Amateur Ascendancy in Local Sport

In 1884, Woodstonian sport reformers adopted an ingenious way to project respectability and boost urban pride during local civic holidays. They took a strategy taken at the time by other Canadian towns with great pretensions but limited resources.[1] Led by members of the Beaver lacrosse club, along with the local baseball and bicycle clubs, they created a local multi-sport regulatory agency, the Woodstock Amateur Athletic Association, known popularly as the WAAA, to encourage and regulate all athletics for the town. As a not-for-profit community organization it would provide sporting and social entertainment for the town's two big civic holidays, the Queen's Birthday and Dominion Day.[2] Wanting "to encourage strictly amateur athletics in every legitimate way," it had moral objectives that were rooted deeply in social reform, urban boosterism, and the quest for respectability. The WAAA aimed "to supply the young men and boys of the town with the means of innocent and health giving recreation, and the public with attractive amusements."[3] By the end of the century, the WAAA would be responsible for having created clubs for snowshoeing, tobogganing, shooting, bowling, and lawn bowls, among other activities. With local government support, it managed all civic holiday celebration events in ways that predecessors like the Woodstock Driving Park Association had not.[4] "We hope to see every resident of the town become a member of it and extend encouragement to legitimate athletic sports and innocent means of recreation," said the WAAA.

In founding Woodstock's Amateur Athletic Association local moral entrepreneurs connected the town with a larger reform movement that was sweeping urban Canada during the late nineteenth century.[5] This movement originated with the formation in 1881 of the Montreal Amateur Athletic Association (MAAA) by certain members of

Montreal's white, English-speaking elite. The MAAA emerged at the helm of what became the most influential, prestigious, and powerful sport movement in nineteenth-century Canada. The AAAs in Woodstock and, from 1889, Ingersoll, and associations in Charlottetown, Moncton, Quebec City, Toronto, Hamilton, St Catharines, and places as far away as Dawson City in the Yukon Territory, modelled themselves upon the MAAA.[6] Connections between the AAAs and local town councils, with their concerns for urban boosterism, may be implicit in this modelling. Many associations, including the MAAA, the Abegweit Amateur Athletic Association of Prince Edward Island, and the Athletic Association de St Roche de Quebec, had strong connections to local civic government and boards of trade. As in Woodstock and Ingersoll, AAA-run sports events highlighted local civic holiday celebrations in places as diverse as Dawson City, Charlottetown, and Montreal.[7] Promoting tourism, the MAAA ran Montreal's annual Winter Carnival,[8] while the QAAA and the Association Athletique de St Roche de Quebec ran the one in Quebec City.[9] Whether the QAAA's connections to that city's chamber of commerce happened by design, as in Ingersoll and Woodstock, is not known.[10] Regardless, town sanctioning of amateur sport clubs for the running of local civic holiday events is an important key to how the amateur movement diffused throughout urban Canada outside of educational institutions.

The close popular connections between amateurism and a town's moral health fueled the fires of urban rivalry between urban boosters in Ingersoll and Woodstock. They caused particular friction between sport reformers in the two towns during in the mid to late 1880s, when the WAAA and the Ingersoll Caledonian Society competed for the patronage and dollars of Oxford County's holiday-goers. By 1889 Ingersoll's holiday organizers relented and adopted the AAA holiday strategy, likely fed up with dwindling attendance numbers and the mockery meted out by their neighbours. Ingersoll did not have its own amateur athletic association, prodded the Woodstock press, "for the same reason, we suppose, that Robinson Crusoe didn't wear a dress suit on the island. He hadn't the material to make it out of!"[11]

Townspeople from other places scoffed at such lofty attitudes. Reporters from nearby towns, bemused onlookers of Woodstock and Ingersoll's posturing battle, poked fun at the earnestness of the WAAA's approach, since Woodstock held a notorious reputation in the province as a haven for gambling men. Turf historian E.K. Dodds remarks about this reputation that "there was no game from pitch and toss to parlour croquet that they wouldn't play and bet on. Woodstock could a little more than hold its own with any other 'burg in Canada at pigeon shooting, foot racing, trotting, running, or any other game that might be proposed."[12] To knock the Woodstonians off their high horse, a Stratford *Herald* reporter wrote with glee that John Forbes wanted to sponsor a sparring match on the Queen's Birthday.[13] The report itself was a well-placed jab at Woodstonian puffery, since local holiday planners never sanctioned such an event for their town's respectable holiday. To them Forbes promoted questionable sporting activities, to say the least. Two years earlier, he had sponsored A.G. Hodge, who was then managing Ingersoll's Caledonian Games, to run Woodstock's Caledonian Games during the Dominion Day holiday, but the event did not go off well at all. As we saw in the previous chapter, the experience helped cement local people's desire for public institutions – not private individuals – to manage the town's holiday.

Carefully crafted arrows were shot by local newspapers between the towns, aiming at what amateur sport was *not*. Sport reformers who promoted the local AAA agenda sought to suppress those sports that drew their ire, particularly the bare-knuckled, eye-gouging kind of sparring most popularly associated with the tavern culture of working people. Even sparring under a respectable guise did not fare well locally. In 1881 Woodstock's mayor refused to let an exhibition of "scientific" sparring occur at the town hall. John Forbes promoted and initially backed the event, but a public outcry against it prevented the event from happening.[14] Civic leaders sanctioned fighters – though not fights – only in certain circumstances, as happened in the mid–1880s when the town council allowed an inspirational talk to be given in the town hall before a reform-minded audience. The speaker, a former prize fighter and reformed drunk, spoke about the evils of his former lifestyle.[15]

John Forbes had amassed his considerable fortune through what some local observers saw as morally dubious activities, including horseracing and pool setting for sports betting. Renowned in Canadian betting circles, he had organized the $4,000 McIvor race in 1881.[16] Some time later, he backed Woodstonian Alby Robinson against any half-miler in America for an astronomical $5,000.[17] Itinerant athletes knew well that Forbes would back them financially and give them food and lodging at his Commercial Hotel when they visited Woodstock to compete. He was clearly a man in the know who kept con men like Robinson in business.[18] Outraged by his activities, WAAA executives distanced themselves from him: "Mr. Forbes will have nothing to do with the games of the Queen's birthday ... and there will be no sparring. The games are under the direction of the Amateur Athletic Association, and are likely to be the most interesting ever held in the county."[19]

When not defending itself in this way, before 1889 the Woodstock AAA and the local press carried on their own attack against Ingersoll and its unreformed holiday sport. By touting its amateurism as the only legitimate sporting form, the WAAA tried to undermine publicly the otherwise honourable intentions of the executives of Ingersoll's Caledonian Society. From its outset, the executives of the society had upheld the cultivation of respectability and manliness as part of their mandate – goals not far afield from those of the WAAA. However, in practice, their plan failed, partly because of the ethnic flavour of the Caledonian Games. Certainly the hiring of A.G. Hodge to run their 1882 Dominion Day's events undermined the society's respectable ideals in local eyes.[20] As we have seen, many local people considered the itinerant professionals whom Hodge attracted to the games to be con men. Having games designed to attract non-local competitors and making the athletes unaccountable to anyone or anything did little to help matters, and nor did the local Caledonian Society seem able to end the abuses: like the public, it had no real way of gauging whether the events held under their auspices were real or fixed.[21] In the end, stunts and hoaxes aimed at conning the public undermined the livelihood of itinerant athletes as people became wise to them and word spread through the sporting circles of the province.

Locally run AAAs had what they believed to be a nobler vision for sport with a membership that carried personal stakes in the well-being of local society.[22] The WAAA, and later the IAAA, relied on the Montreal-based Amateur Athletic Association of Canada (AAA of C), created in 1884, to decide who could compete in track and field competition. It determined that eligible athletes included "one who has never competed for a money prize or a staked bet, or with or against any professional for any prize, or who has never taught, pursued or assisted in the practice of athletic exercises as a means of obtaining a livelihood."[23] Associated AAAs throughout Canada carefully monitored their system by barring professional athletes from sporting competitions, except for "open" events for recognized professionals to compete in. Still, in these instances, the professionals competed only among themselves, as in a one-mile championship race in the Canadian Wheelmen's Association races held by the WAAA in 1885. Amateurs daring to compete in such matches lost their amateur status.[24]

The AAA of C's definition of an amateur aimed to exclude those men who made their livelihood through sport, yet amateur restrictions, if interpreted literally and really enforced locally, would have limited the participation of any soul who had competed in holiday events in years gone by and been awarded a small sum of cash. Ultimately, amateur rules that were aimed to squelch goings-on that sports reformers deemed unsavoury created a barrier between themselves and others. Local AAAS required that athletes live up to a certain moral code, wishing them to be responsible and respectable representatives of their town, accountable to the locally run clubs that certified their amateur status. Local AAAS "carded" amateur athletes, giving them little cards as proof of their status – a practice that continues today. They also created symbolic prizes – with cups, medals, trophies, and small tokens awarded in lieu of cash – in the hopes of avoiding the issue of money entirely. Whether the WAAA came closer to the ideal of respectability that they and the Caledonian Society executives upheld in common is in some senses irrelevant, since their very claim to do so went far in local eyes. People believed amateurs to be somehow more 'pure,' and local sport reformers worked hard to undermine the credibility of those who did not share their own particular vision. In doing so, they eliminated from public holidays sports they considered unworthy of public sanctioning. They carried on their agenda with an air of moral superiority, claiming: "We are sorry for the man who would not prefer these beautiful trophies for a few dollars in cash."[25]

Historian Melvin Adelman, in writing on the rise of modern sport in New York City, argues that the amateur movement had a basically anti-modern nature.[26] In many ways this is true, especially if the movement's idealism is considered, but at the same time amateurism paradoxically had some of the "means-ends" characteristics that Adelman states are the hallmark of modern sport. For example, Woodstock's strict amateur rules regulating competitions worked to decrease opportunities to fix races. Con men like Alby Robinson had little chance to ply their trade on amateur fields since local clubs and the AAA of C kept track of where, when, and how athletes competed.[27] Their closed system of competition, practically speaking, gave spectators some assurances that what they were watching was not a hoax or deception. While not entirely a foolproof system, the local public accountability of AAA leaders counted for much, with the town's most noted citizens putting their reputations on the line. In 1887, out of 250 applications for AAA membership submitted in Toronto, amateur organizers granted only 180. The Toronto association decided "not to pass anybody for the present who is not already a member of an amateur club or who is known to somebody of whom they have personal knowledge."[28] Intending to keep everything above suspicion, the association found it "preferable to err on the side of strictness rather than take in any of the doubtful element."[29] Thus, if people laid money down on amateur races, they could do so with some confidence. They hoped to lay their money on their ability to judge the athlete's skill, not the athlete's ability to deceive them. AAA leaders used this situation and their own connections in the community to their advantage. Of course, if people bet – something considerable evidence suggests actually happened, even among AAA members – they contravened both the rules and the spirit of the AAAs. Nevertheless, newspapers reported on the betting at nearly every holiday meet. In reality, many people had become just too suspicious to lay their money down on any but the *bona fide* amateur. In 1888, local professional Billy Boyd found no backers for a match race against the infamous duo of Quirk and Anderson. The *Sentinel* explained the situation: "there is that which still lingers around professional sporting, which makes a person feel doubtful even if he does get a right tip."[30]

Sport reformers in Ingersoll increasingly saw things Woodstock's way after 1886 and ended up embracing the AAA solution to holiday management. Led by the town's Dufferin amateur lacrosse club, several local amateur clubs in various sports investigated the merits of forming their own multi-sport association. After negotiating access to a suitable playing field, in 1889 they founded the Ingersoll Amateur Athletic Association (IAAA).[31] This umbrella organization involved the town's baseball, lacrosse, cycling, and tennis clubs. From that time until well past the turn of the century, the WAAA and the IAAA became sister institutions, bound to common causes – middle-class respectability and town success through amateur sport. A sense of accommodation and support buffered the often vitriolic rivalry between people in the two places. The AAAs extended the class interests of amateur organizers, equated with their towns' interests, beyond town boundaries. Holiday organizing committees now became AAA committees and sport reformers in both towns laid aside their petty disputes, ending their competition for holiday-goers. Combining efforts, they took turns holding holiday celebrations: Woodstock became the county's home of the Queen's Birthday, while Ingersoll held Dominion Day gatherings.[32] Their work together went beyond holiday management as they did things like raising money to improve the Beachville road linking the two towns so that AAA cyclists could go on their evening rambles with ease and relative comfort.[33] Each town also sent its finest athletes and officials – timers, scorers, and referees – to the other's events, with both reaping financial rewards as the size of their holiday crowds grew by thousands. Perhaps more important, the amateur movement gave middle-class leaders in the two towns a united front in the larger cause of respectability – both a product and hallmark of their emerging middle-class world-view.

Under AAA management, civic holidays in Ingersoll and Woodstock became sporting celebrations. During the Woodstock AAA's first

Queen's Birthday holiday, sport could be found in all parts of the day's celebration, from sunrise to sunset. The evening entertainment in the packed town hall featured a concert and the performance of a *tableau*, "The Athletic Sports of Canada."[34] The local press commended the day's events for their high social tone: "A finer assemblage of people was never seen in Woodstock," wrote the *Sentinel*, "no drunkenness or rudeness was anywhere to be seen. Not a single row or unpleasantness occurred during the day. We are glad to say that intoxicating liquors could not be had at the booths. The feeling of the association on this point is, we believe, the feeling of all the best elements of the community."[35] That first AAA-run holiday began auspiciously, with the amateur band leading the London Alerts and the Woodstocks baseball teams from the railway station to Central Park for their matches. Just after one o'clock, a second procession left the market square, marshaled by the town's two largest industrial manufacturers, Messrs Karn and Hay, representing the Woodstock bicycle club. The uniformed sport teams marched behind them, including the Beaver lacrosse club, their visitors, the Paris Brants, and the two baseball clubs. Bicyclists from throughout the province – London, St Thomas, Simcoe, Stratford, Brantford, Hamilton, Toronto, and Berlin – took up the rear. Four to five thousand people lined the streets to witness the parade to the WAAA grounds, where amateur athletes from all over faced stiff competition for cups and medals.

The AAAs of Ingersoll and Woodstock controlled the local holiday sports more closely than had been the case in times past, when anyone in town could walk up to the starting line, pay their nominal entrance fee, run a race, and collect a small cash prize. Ironically, the amateur approach worked to narrow townspeople's involvement in the games significantly, because the races and other events included only *bona fide* amateur athletes and not everyone in town had the financial and social resources to belong to a club or local association. The amateur approach stood in sharp contrast with informal and communal approaches to the holidays. Consider, for example, the WAAA's farmers' race in 1891, where competitors paid the hefty sum of one dollar to compete under rules that, by earlier standards, bordered on the absurd. Only farmers and farmers' sons over twenty-one years who had never won an open race could compete. They had to reside in Oxford County for a year before the event and furnish proof about their eligibility to the satisfaction of event organizers.[36] Even the schoolboys' race had strict and exclusive rules. Only boys younger than thirteen who had never won an open race and could furnish a certificate verifying their age and school attendance signed by their teacher could compete.[37] Events for females, a long-time part of holiday activities, quite simply disappeared, since the AAAs, like the AAA of C, excluded females entirely from the amateur movement of the day.[38]

Local amateur sport thus consisted of a distinctly male world, with competition confined to AAA-approved sports. Unlike the variety of games of inversion and ritual disorder that characterized early civic holiday activities, AAA sports involved only certain regulated track and field events. Traditional events held on makeshift playing spaces became obsolete: the slippery pigs, greased poles, and bell and horse races of the former era disappeared from sports fields, just as females had done. Standardized track events like the 220-yard hurdles and 100-yard and one-quarter mile races required regulation-sized running tracks. This standardization, more than local in scope, imbued local contests with non-local meanings. The keeping of records and quantifying of event results changed many things. Amateur officials used clocks to carefully time running races, recording and then analysing performance data. The statistical records, published in newspapers and AAA of C track guidebooks, set standards for new sporting achievements, allowing people to compare local results against national and international records. Stories about the fame and prowess of athletes doubtlessly still lived in local lore, yet the oral tradition, with the flexibility that spinners of tall tales had relied upon, stood now against new hard evidence that had a split-second precision formerly unimaginable.

So, while local amateur athletics were intended to keep holiday events locally focused, AAA-run holiday games in Ingersoll and Woodstock relegated local people to the spectator stands and created a tremendous gap between townspeople and amateur athletes. Requiring athletes to be *bona fide* amateurs and making club membership a requisite for amateur status created an athletic aristocracy that performed during civic holiday celebrations for others who paid money to watch them perform. Yet when fans sat cheering in the stands, especially in amateur team sports like baseball and lacrosse, they cheered for *their* town's representatives on the field. Amateur promoters and town officials carefully laid the seeds of the connection between the AAA and town identity. When a local athlete like Woodstonian Herb Clarke competed against Canada's finest cyclists on the WAAA cycle track in 1888, Woodstonians everywhere took pride in his winning the Canadian half-mile cycle championship. They considered him to be their own since he represented *their* institution.[39] This hometown boy, son of a local grocer, had risen through the ranks of local amateur sport. He had been weaned on amateur sport at an early age, cutting his teeth playing for the town's junior lacrosse team, the Otters, then graduating to the town's senior

Herb Clarke, Woodstock's famed amateur cyclist, c.
1888, shown with his high wheels and awards for amateur competition. In 1888 he won the Canadian half-
mile cycle championship at a meet hosted in Woodstock. The son of a local grocer, this gifted athlete had
risen through the ranks of local sport, playing for the
town's junior lacrosse team, the Otters, then graduating
to the town's senior club, the Beavers. (Courtesy of the
Woodstock Museum)

club, the Beavers. In 1884, at age eighteen, he helped create the
WAAA.

Like Clarke, other organizers of the IAAA and WAAA had their names
placed squarely in the town's historical record, making it possible to
reveal something about the nature of this group. Ingersoll and Woodstock AAA holiday organizing committees between 1884 and 1896
include civic leaders and prominent local men whose names were
found on local buildings, store fronts, street signs, town council rolls,

and lists of sport club and fraternal order executives. Data collected on 103 AAA executives from Ingersoll and Woodstock reveal that these men had strong demographic similarities. Their network, like their associations, was male: they presumably never prohibited females through rules and regulations, since social and cultural constraints had already done that work.[40] Their social class and ethno-religious background also unified them, being overwhelmingly middle-aged, Canadian-born, and Protestant. Their occupational characteristics are striking when compared with local male workforces. Working people – particularly unskilled workers – could not be found among AAA organizers.[41] This characteristic alone differentiated them sharply from others in town, since the numbers of unskilled workers captured on local manuscript censuses accounted for roughly one out of every four men employed locally.

Other elements show those who governed local AAA executives to be a socially cohesive group. Fraternal and voluntary organizations, and the activities that went on inside their lodges, offer another glimpse into the world-view of amateur sport reformers. As historian Christopher Anstead shows of fraternal life in Ingersoll and Woodstock, in both lodge and club, members experienced respectable and exclusively male environments. He argues that ritual, literature, and other aspects of these cultures emphasized thrift, self-responsibility, sobriety, honesty, compassion, personal and sexual morality, and support for the dominant religion. Voluntary associations gave their members opportunities to shape the idea of respectability and keep behaviour in check. Their public activities, such as sponsoring lectures, plays, and public demonstrations, spread their conception of respectability through the wider community.[42] Board of trade and, to a lesser extent, town council involvement showed commitment to entrepreneurial capitalism and provided alternate venues for middle-class respectability. These associations of businessmen, industrialists, and professionals boosted local economic development and their economic self-interest through supporting local industrial growth.

Prominent Woodstonians – men well experienced in sport and civic life – figure among the fifteen who first organized the WAAA. A glimpse into the lives of a few of them shows their great interconnectedness. One WAAA founder, A.S. Ball, for example, followed the civic and professional footsteps of his father, a noted local barrister of Loyalist descent. A.S. Ball began his career living in his father's Vansittart Street home and working out of his Hunter Street office near the courthouse; by his retirement, he had been the town's police magistrate for nearly three decades. Born in the early 1850s into a family of some means, he lived in the right place and time, being among the first generation of local children raised in a place connected to the outside world by the railway. During his childhood years his hometown began emerging as a place of competitive zeal, shedding its early paternal and parochial settlement roots under the leadership of enterprising middle-class men elected to local office in the era of reformed politics. When organized teams became all the rage locally, he and his playmates would find Woodstock a town of promising avenues for sporting greatness for athletically ambitious young males.

A.S. Ball took advantage of these sporting opportunities, and created new ones for others in his community. His involvement in sport lasted his lifetime, although its pattern changed as the years went by.[43] When he was ten, his town's baseball team, the Young Canadians, put Woodstock on the province's sporting map by creating and winning the coveted Silver Ball award, emblem of the Canadian baseball championship. In his late teens and early twenties, Ball spent his own joyous hours running around local playing fields, under the watchful eye of early amateur sports promoters. Considered a leader, he captained the Beaver lacrosse club and helped direct the Atlantics baseball club. In his late twenties and early thirties, while securing a place as a local lawyer, he slowed the pace of his physical activities, playing tennis, refereeing amateur lacrosse matches and holiday running races, and acting as corresponding secretary for the town's curling club. He helped create the WAAA in 1884 while in his early thirties, and at middle age, married with a handful of children of his own, he pursued a rich fraternal life, filled with social and civic activity. He rose to the rank of captain and became the quartermaster of the Strathallan Company of the Oxford Rifles, and was made an honorary major at his retirement.[44] Living in the well-to-do Light Street neighbourhood near the town park, he and his family lived a comfortable life. His wife donated his old suits to be cut up and sewn into quilts for raffles to raise money for a local chapter of the temperance cause.[45] A member of the organizing committee for the Woodstock Old Boys 1901 Reunion, Ball lived to see a second reunion during Canada's fiftieth birthday celebrations, when he was himself hitting eighty years old.[46] He kept other ties to Woodstock's old boys, sitting on the executive boards of many local voluntary organizations, including the Ancient Free and Accepted Masons, the Ancient Order of United Workmen, the Order of Scottish Clans, and the Royal Arcanum.

Other WAAA founders in Ball's social milieu shared his fraternal and voluntary persuasions. Dr A. Beverly Welford, a physician and graduate of Trinity College who became Ball's brother-in-law, also lived in the Light Street neighbourhood and held an impressive array of offices in local voluntary and fraternal orders. He, too, became a member of the 1901 organizing committee for the Woodstock Old Boys Reunion, and attended the reunion when it met again in 1927. As a young man he helped govern the Woodstock bicycle club, and held the presidency of the local Otters (junior) and Beavers (senior) lacrosse clubs. Appointed surgeon to the Grand Trunk Railway, Welford examined medical candidates for the College of Physicians and Surgeons. He brought his medical expertise to his involvement in local insurance-based friendly societies, being a physician and board member for the Independent Order of Foresters, and sitting on the local board of the Canadian Order of Foresters.

Around the block from Welford's house lived another WAAA founder, W.A. Karn, whose extended family could be found all over Oxford County. Not to be confused with another prominent sport-promoting Karn, D.W. Karn of organ factory fame (a survivor of the famous St George railway accident in 1889), W.A. Karn worked as the town's druggist. Belonging to the Ontario College of Pharmacy, he ran a Dundas Street drugstore that served for many years as a local landmark. Karn loved cycling, being a first lieutenant of the Woodstock bicycle club and later president of the Canadian Wheelmen's Association, a position that placed him in the esteemed ranks of powerful amateur sports promoters from Montreal and Toronto. Sometimes he could be found marshalling the town's civic holiday parade while riding high atop his penny farthing cycle. A town councillor between 1885 and 1888, Karn kept active in local politics and fraternal life, being a board member in the Order of Fraternal Guardians and the Ancient Free and Accepted Masons.

The social and political backgrounds of the men who created the Ingersoll Amateur Athletic Association in 1889 reveal a strikingly similar portrait of noteworthy men in town. They were a potent minority from very comfortable middle-class households who were, or became, preeminent civic leaders. Joseph Gibson, Ingersoll's longtime grocer and postmaster, had a reputation as a staunch social reformer in the county. A self-made man, he carried his social passion and love of sport throughout his life. Born in England in 1842, Gibson arrived in Oxford County with his parents during the early 1850s and resided in Ingersoll until his death in 1920. The Dominion Alliance's *Pioneer* observed of his modest beginnings: "His educational advantages were limited, and to quote his own words, he had in youth only a common English education, and that rather 'common,' but his experiences emphasize the fact that some who have been denied the privileges of the schools make a success while the pampered sons of fortune fail. Rising above early disadvantages and under the stimulus of a splendid mother, he read extensively the best English literature, Macauley being his favorite author, and became one of the foremost orators of Canada. Probably no speaker has been listened from as many platforms and with greater delight."[47]

At the turn of the century, Gibson used his oratorical skills when he represented Canadian Methodists at the World Ecumenical Council of Methodism in London, England. Ironically, this staunch temperance advocate had political connections to the country's best known drunkard and another great Canadian orator, the first prime minister of Canada, Sir John A. Macdonald. Gibson, also a political Conservative, did not make it to office when running in the 1878 national election.

Gibson took up the prohibition cause at a young age, during the Dunkin Act campaign of the 1860s. Reports hint that he had an abusive father, which, if true, likely helped his temperance convictions along. An expert baseball pitcher, he captained the town's Victorias first nine. When they managed to wrestle the Silver Ball championship trophy away from Woodstock briefly in 1868, the joyous townspeople threw themselves a huge party, with libations flowing easily as people toasted their conquering heroes. Whether Gibson tried converting his teammates to the temperance cause is not known. To be sure, he never converted other well-known early baseball promoters in Ingersoll, owners of local hotels whose livelihoods rested with the other side of the liquor debate.[48] The love of sport at times creates odd bedfellows, while at other times creating a niche for those who are similarly inclined. Having learnt to love cricket in his youth in England, for example, Gibson must have been disappointed that the game never really gathered a following in Ingersoll. During summers spent at his cottage in the resort area of the Muskokas, he managed to play in matches against other vacationers, like those members of Toronto's monied elite visiting the Beaumaris Hotel, who presumably learnt to play at posh private schools. Well-remembered for his activism, Gibson "was as live and active in athletics as in debate."[49] His twenty-two years as a town councillor gave him many opportunities to display his debating skills. He sat often on holiday organizing committees, both as an executive member of the local Caledonian Society and as a founder of the IAAA. The president of a short-lived local cricket club, he also helped organize more popular sports, as with the Dufferin lacrosse and Victoria baseball clubs. Beyond this, Gibson also devoted himself to a varied fraternal life, being a Grand Master Workman of the Ancient Order of United Workmen, and sitting on the governing boards of local chapters of the International Order of Odd Fellows and the Ancient Free and Accepted Masons.

Through their AAAs, men like Ball, Welford, Karn, and Gibson worked on their lofty social agenda by overseeing community sport in

Ingersoll and Woodstock. They did so in ways preferred by middle-class sport reformers, and they used gentlemen's business clubs as a vehicle to institutionalize these preferences and articulate their underlying rationale.[50] They held a basic reform orientation in their desire to provide physical and mental culture through rational amusements for their members. To do so they prohibited all sorts of things – gambling, betting, lotteries, profane language, and alcohol – while expelling members who acted in a uncivilized way.[51] AAAs appeared to be democratic, implying that every community member who ascribed to the amateur code was welcome in the open contest of sport and life, yet the associations excluded many people by design. They didn't need to discriminate against working men overtly, since scheduling practices when factory workers couldn't attend and charging expensive membership, clothing, and equipment fees already prevented their participation.

The AAAs had a predominantly social orientation that encouraged sports playing for social ends, leaving the actual policing of amateur rules – granting or suspending amateur status – to the AAA of C, the national custodian of the amateur principle.[52] Yet despite the appearance that this national association ran the show, the local associations held considerable power. The 1885 annual report of the AAA of C, for example, shows that many smaller AAAs throughout the country did not join the national body. While the IAAA never formally affiliated, the WAAA did, although it took its sweet time.[53] When it finally submitted an application, the AAA of C eagerly received Woodstock, with one voter scribbling on the back of his ballot, "Glad you got Woodstock at last. We have been at them every year, but without avail, however, better late than never."[54] No coincidence, the WAAA's application had decidedly self-interested motives: the association's prized runner, Billy Farrell, the athletically gifted son of the proprietor of the local Caister House hotel, had lost his amateur status. To compete, Farrell needed reinstatement as an amateur, something done by the national association through its affiliated local agencies.[55] The WAAA ended up getting what it wanted by simply following what the national body told it to do – it got "a letter or two from some well known citizens of Woodstock recommending Farrell's reinstatement."[56] This approach equated Farrell's amateur status and the honour of the WAAA with the word of the town's elite and naturalized the group's power both inside and outside the town. Two years after Farrell's reinstatement, the WAAA let its AAA of C dues lapse into arrears.[57] Apparently, its affiliation with the national body happened only when needed.

Clearly, the idea of protecting local interests was a cornerstone of AAA life in Ingersoll and Woodstock. In the interests of middle-class cultural formation and expression, the associations aimed to create a rational and respectable environment for their members, much like what has been described in J.S. Gilkeson's work on the club ideal in middle-class Providence.[58] Strict rules carefully circumscribed member conduct. The local press reported the earnestness of the IAAA's approach – "any attempt at infraction of the law has been frowned upon by the members" – while commending Ingersoll's clubrooms as "capital place[s]" that provided "amusement and exercise for the young men of the town, separated from those pernicious influences which are too apt to surround places of recreation of this character."[59] How could local sport reformer and temperance devotee Joseph Gibson not have been pleased?

As an adjunct to controls on club behaviours, AAA organizers in Ingersoll and Woodstock carefully restricted the social background of people admitted to the club. This approach created an occupationally homogenous and, on the surface at least, an ideologically unified membership. Club constitutions required membership elections in which two nominators read out the candidate's name, occupation, and home address at an association meeting, making it clear to all who supported whom.[60] Voting took place by ballot. Three negative votes excluded the applicant. In his work on the rise of sport in New York City, Melvin Adelman points out that the nomination process in itself worked against "undesirables" gaining admission, so that voting was aimed at excluding candidates disliked by certain members for personal reasons.[61] To become a member, one needed to be respectable, with the right personal and professional connections. Those whose personal behaviour breached the codes of gentlemanly conduct outlined in club constitutions probably wouldn't ever get nominated, yet alone be admitted to the club.[62] AAA organizers assumed that people possessing certain occupations would necessarily be respectable. Staff members of Woodstock's chartered banks, for example, received automatic membership rights.[63] Thus long before the membership voted on any name, much social screening had already occurred in a self-conscious way. In 1894, the *Chronicle* hailed the IAAA as consisting of "the principal business and professional men of the town, as well as the young men who will, at no distant day, take the lead among our prominent public men."[64] By implication at the very least, workers wouldn't be considered suitable membership material. According to one proselytizer for the IAAA, the association's "first step backward" would "be indiscriminate admission to membership."[65] Sacrosanct male preserves, AAAs did not even bother excluding women; they simply did not exist, barring perhaps roles as cooks or housekeepers and the occasional guest at a lecture or concert.

Despite their status as local agencies authorized by local government, both the IAAA and the WAAA carried themselves off as private businessmen's clubs catering to the sporting and social pursuits of an exclusive clientele. They offered a place where members socialized in a decorous fashion. The associations praised themselves for their strictly regulated social environment, which fostered "a sense of self-respect springing from a consciousness of social equality [which] ... by its rules, demands acknowledgment." This, noted the *Chronicle*, was something new to Ingersoll's social scene: "taking our town for example, say twenty years ago or even less, the opportunities of spending an evening in social intercourse or health recreation were but few, and even then of a character surrounded by associations of doubtful benefit, if not positive danger to the average youth. At that time the bar room, or at best the sitting room of the hotel was the best he could do under the circumstances, aside from his own home."[66]

To provide the right sort of atmosphere, Ingersoll and Woodstock AAAs had elaborate clubrooms that, while less opulent than the MAAA rooms, offered the best to be found locally for their two hundred or so members. Impressive three-storey buildings near the towns' market square and business districts housed the best social and sporting facilities in Ingersoll and Woodstock. Both organizations had sought out the finest quarters, sometimes leaving places after the end of their lease in search of better rooms. The IAAA stayed in its first rooms, situated on the west side of Thames Street, for five years before moving to the Royal Hotel Block, which had commodious rooms "fitted up with a degree of comfort, convenience and elegance that would do credit to a city club of much more exalted pretension."[67] Woodstock's first clubrooms housed more than $2,000 worth of equipment and within two years the association expended another $8,000 on its new building and facilities.[68] The WAAA's final quarters were in the Muir Block, at the corner of Dundas and Perry streets in a building demolished during the spring of 1989. Both associations had their own bowling alley and gymnasium.

At their clubrooms IAAA and WAAA members pursued physical culture using state-of-the-art apparatus – parallel bars, vaulting horses, swinging ropes, mats, ladders, and Indian clubs. When needed for lectures and concerts the gymnasiums seated several hundred people. Club libraries and reading rooms offered members the luxury of reading Canadian and New York daily newspapers, as well as sporting magazines like the *New York Clipper* and *Sporting Life*. Games rooms offered billiards and pool tables, while club parlours had a piano for club sing-songs and tables for chess, checkers, and whist. Other rooms provided a quiet atmosphere for people to conduct business transactions. Full-time managers ran the club's day-to-day operations, taking care of the members in style and comfort and ensuring that only the right people ever crossed the club's threshold. Every year, Charles Pyne, the first manager of the WAAA, made sure that the local press remained on board with the AAA, treating "the employees of the *Sentinel-Review* office from the 'devil' down to cigars on Christmas eve. This is one at least of Charley's habits he need never swear off."[69] Of course, sport reformers normally aimed at eliminating bad habits, yet they used them when it suited themselves.

Although they did not assure an individual financial or social success, the AAAs provided their closed membership with access to an extensive business network that spanned well beyond local boundaries. Club policy dictated that upon furnishing the requisite proof, a warm welcome met visitors from other associations.[70] Local men whose business activities took them away from Ingersoll and Woodstock relied upon reciprocal courtesy from clubs in other places. Among the signatures recorded on the IAAA visitor's register are those of guests of Ingersoll's leading local businessmen who came from London (England), New York, Washington, Boston, Hartford, Chicago, Salt Lake City, and California, as well as from Canadian cities like Montreal, Toronto, Ottawa, Hamilton, London, and Winnipeg.[71] Businessmen hardly ever needed to leave the club: there they could strike a business deal or spend leisure time relaxing in preferred company.

The AAAs apparently covered all the bases in their cultivation of business connections, with the cigars that Pyne gave out a trademark of club life and a gift showing high esteem for its recipient.[72] Sport reformers hailed AAA rooms as wonderful places to get away from it all. There a man could "indulge in the luxury of a fragrant Havana without feeling that he is taking a liberty."[73] Wintertime smoking concerts in club rooms, attending a lecture or play together, or just resting in the club's all-male world forged social bonds between members. These bonds continued outside, as in 1894 when twenty-five IAAA members invested $100 apiece to form the Ingersoll Fish and Game Association.[74] They got the rights to use Marsden Pond as a fish nursery, and stocked it with 10,000 trout for their fishing pleasure.[75]

IAAA organizers proclaimed that "instead of being governed and controlled by a few," the IAAA was a town institution and not "the particular pet of a class."[76] Still, this rhetoric did not mean that the AAAs held no class interests. In their clubby and exclusive approach, they cultivated a model of behaviour they believed would be appropriate for middle-class community members. Clubrooms taught many social lessons, framed in the language of social reform through self-improvement.

Reporting on the association's growth, the *Chronicle* argued that the IAAA was "a social innovation of the most healthy kind that we are able to discern at a glance; begetting as it does a feeling of companionship and fraternity and breaking down that class distinction that formerly kept men isolated from each other."[77] Rejecting the old model of ascribed rather than earned status, as had been found in the old Tory elites, the associations espoused meritocractic principles. Even so, they distanced themselves from others in the community, rejecting any man who took money for sport and eschewing the sporting culture associated with taverns. In their world-view, neither held merit.

The AAAs appealed to the moral imperative of amateur sport and dissociated their recreational pursuits from supposed rowdy influences. In doing so, they garnered widespread support from the local Protestant clergy. In 1889, the names of at least four clergymen graced the IAAA's membership rolls; "No clergyman is out of place in lending encouragement to amateur athletic sports properly conducted," proclaimed the *Sentinel* approvingly.[78] AAA rules prohibiting idle diversions long discountenanced by clergymen helped shape this view.[79] In 1895, Ingersoll's Reverend Arthur Murphy of St James Anglican Church, himself a member of the IAAA, used the club's rooms to speak to his sporting brethren about "A Manly Man," a topic well suited to the venue. He called for club members to use amateur sport to cultivate the delicate balance between their physical, intellectual, and spiritual selves.[80]

Woodstock's Reverend Dr Farthing of old St Paul's Anglican Church, who later became the Bishop of Montreal, spoke to the WAAA membership, outlining the importance of amateur sport in the lives of Christian men and citing many reasons why local churches ought to sanction it. He viewed nothing to be "more conducive to the progress of a town either morally or physically" than the amateur sports and rational recreations promoted by AAAs.[81] Yet traces of the scepticism characteristic of pietist-ascetic opposition to sport nevertheless lingered in Farthing's message. His support of amateurism involved an apparent compromise, based upon his faith in the AAA to accomplish its stated objectives. He stated,

I want to say that I am quite certain that as long as the amateur athletic association maintains its present position it will be supported by everyone who believes that the physical culture and training of man is conductive to morality, if not also to spirituality. And while there might be a great deal of evil in connection with all athletic movements which it is almost impossible for any association to avoid, still at the same time if we withheld all countenance and support from everything because of its being abused our lives would be narrow and it would not be conducive to our own moral and physical culture, nor would it enable us to help our fellow man.[82]

Sport reformers believed that amateur sport helped all manner of fellow man, including the souls so limited that they turned to selling their athletic performances to get ahead in life. It could also help those who played sport in the shadow of the tavern, those who cheated in life, or who cheated simply to win a game. Perhaps these fellows would learn to view sporting victories not as an end in themselves, but as the means to some greater end, like Christian manliness.

Sport reformers praised the sense of camaraderie and appropriate social behaviour they believed club membership engendered, even holding these things up as a model for the rest of the community to emulate. In 1885, a staggering fraternal and community response happened when County Registrar Colonel James Ingersoll's thirty-three-year-old son, James Beverly, met an untimely and heroic death from injuries sustained while rescuing a young lady from the path of a runaway toboggan on the WAAA's slide. The tragedy struck during a WAAA nighttime toboggan party, a gala event entertaining club members and their visitors from neighbouring Ingersoll. Like many of his WAAA brethren, Beverly Ingersoll's personal history touched many facets of local Woodstock society. His schooldays at Toronto's prestigious Upper Canada College, where he learned to play cricket, moulded him into a young muscular Christian. He later spent his work hours in the registry office working alongside his father and his social hours engaged in an impressive array of voluntary and fraternal organizations. An avid sportsman throughout his short life, he helped govern the local Atlantic baseball club and captained and later acted as a director for the Beaver lacrosse club. People remembered the lieutenant and adjutant of the Strathallan Company of the 22nd Battalion of the Oxford Rifles militia to be "the Beau ideal of a military man, and one likely to gain rapid promotion."[83] A young member of the Oxford Lodge of the Ancient Free and Accepted Masons, a Masonic service was read at Ingersoll's graveside. The eulogy given paints him as the personification of the ideal muscular Christian: "It was a brave and gentle nature that passed away from earth ... a nature full of manliness, whose first duty was to be gentle and at the same time brave. In the fulfilment of the characteristics of that nature he met his death, and in the throes of agony never regretted the sacrifice he had made. Natures such as his are uncommon, and their rarity causes us to cherish them."[84]

Businesses closed shop in the afternoon so townspeople could attend the funeral at New St Paul's Anglican Church, and the large church was filled to capacity. Throngs of mourners lined the path from the church along Dundas and Riddell streets, paying their respects and catching a glimpse of the procession as it headed to the Episcopal Cemetery. They laid Ingersoll to rest in a spot neatly overlooking the grounds of his beloved WAAA grounds. Thirty riflemen from the Oxford Rifles led the procession, with the 22nd Battalion band behind playing the funeral dirge. Fraternal brethren then followed, with one hundred 100 WAAA men and 150 members of the Oxford and King Solomon Masonic lodges wearing association badges and mourning ribbons. Eighteen pallbearers, representing the WAAA, the Masons, and militia volunteers, escorted the coffin. In its reaction to Ingersoll's death, the town celebrated both his life and the principles upheld by men of his particular social milieu. Ingersoll's funeral, and the community's reaction to his death, reminded people how sport shaped a young man's moral character through good habit formation. It reaffirmed the importance of the lessons that were believed to be learnt by youth on local playing fields: "Known by everyone as a quiet, genial, uncomplaining, unostentatious gentleman, he was more particularly the fast warm hearted friend of the youth, indulging in their manly sports, and by his genial nature influencing them to acts of kindness."[85]

The AAAs received the sanction of civic leaders to create and project the images of respectability and honourable camaraderie epitomized in Beverly Ingersoll's funeral. Yet they provided only one vision of sport and society, one that evidence suggests many people resisted. Sometimes the resistance came out in overt acts of aggression; sometimes it came out in other, more subtle ways. The WAAA leadership, for example, took a rigid attitude toward the use of its athletic grounds, waging war against those who used its facilities without permission. The grounds, supposedly a public facility, were kept tightly controlled by the association, believing that through their exclusivity they acted in the public's interest. WAAA advertisements warned all that constables patrolling the park would arrest non-members: "Trespassers Beware. Complaints have been made of parties running horses and practising footraces on Sunday on the grounds of the AAA. Notice is hereby given that anybody who is found trespassing in the grounds, on any day of the week will be prosecuted, and that a constable will be there on Sundays to see the notice carried out."[86] By insisting on Sabbatarian observance, the WAAA showed its insensitivity to working-class leisure.[87] Sunday afternoons provided a cherished time for factory labourers to indulge in a little afternoon's sport, especially in the weeks before competition on a civic holiday.[88]

Nevertheless, the WAAA's repeated efforts suggest that it never quite achieved the exclusivity for which it longed.[89] It soon found out not

everyone shared its agenda. When able, the WAAA punished transgres-
sors swiftly and with an iron hand.[90] In November 1886, the club's
bowling alley pin boys, young Sampson and Jim Cromwell, pilfered
cigars from manager Pyne's office. The club had the boys summarily
arrested and sent to jail.[91] Saner minds might question the harshness of
the punishment meted out to little boys. A month later, something
referred simply as "a missile" came crashing through the WAAA window.[92] Even later, the club's dog, named Rowdy, was found poisoned
to death across the street from the clubrooms.[93] Association members
wondered about the strange occurrence, not knowing whether it was
willfully or accidentally done. "It is impossible to say," the local paper
commented, suggesting that the question of vengeance had crossed
their minds. During Woodstock's bicycle races, an unknown party
sawed the spokes of competitors' cycles in half.[94] Could this be the act
of a competitor trying to get an advantage? Or a disgruntled towns-
person trying to get even? Or was it an expensive but simply foolish
prank, aimed for the macabre delight of persons wanting a bit more
levity in the day's events at the expense of the poor rider?

Although the IAAA appears never to have been the target of such
overt acts, similar patterns occurred with Ingersoll's skating club. It
waged a decades-long battle to keep its rink off-limits to anyone save
its membership. Although the club felt badly about those people who
could not afford to join and participate in its skating carnivals, it made
no apologies for exclusiveness. About the "so cold and lonesome"
masses who enviously eyed the skaters from the sidelines, one commentator wrote: "I may observe that we shall feel no great anxiety
about the class who are accustomed to 'rough it,' but we recognize a
large number who are accustomed to comfortable homes, and it is for
them our hearts are moved. We should be very gratified were we able
to admit them to our rink free, but we could scarcely discriminate
between them and the miserable element which renders the scheme
impractical."[95] When, in March 1884, someone set the rink on fire and
burnt it the ground, the *Chronicle* fingered a gang of roughs as the culprits.[96] Whether this was the same rough bunch who some years earlier had frequented the abandoned Beehive Factory is unknown. That
place had been the site of many pedestrian contests for money,
described as a "resort of tramps and scene of low villainy."[97] While
local authorities had kept a close eye on the boarded-up facility, it, too,
mysteriously burnt to the ground.

These incidents clearly did not originate in the benign and civilized
world of gentlemen envisaged by middle-class sports clubs. Yet
whether resistance was particularly class-based cannot be determined
with any certainty. It likely involved some elements of class resistance,

plus some from within since, as sport sociologist Peter Donnelly argues, sport is a site for popular resistance.[98] Judging by sport reformers' exhortations, resistance came from a male, not female, group. Fanatic behaviour of spectators, encouraged by urban boosterism, undercut efforts to build a consensus of a more placid, respectable nature. Fans who would "howl like maniacs for their own team and act with little short of brutality toward their opponents" behaved undesirably.[99] Of course, fan rowdiness occurred mostly in the stands, rather than at the centre of public display, but it remained visible. Newspapers, forever an instrument of persuasion in the hegemonic process, admonished locals to treat visitors in a courteous and generous way. Obviously, at times the opposite happened.

The press, acting as a voice and conscience for the rational recreation movement, had its own inconsistencies. Newspaper employees knew well that their paper's owners and publishers belonged to local AAAs. G.F. Gurnett of the *Chronicle*, A.W. Francis of the *Times*, and Andrew Pattullo of the *Sentinel* all kept with the conventions of their social position, making their support of the AAAs well known and having their papers pay strong lip service to organized amateur athletics. To be sure, the success of the amateur movement locally depended upon the goodwill and support of local newspapers.

That is not to suggest that local papers did not carry contradictory messages at times. For example, while ardently supporting amateur sport, they also covered rowdy sports frequently, presumably because of their attractiveness to the reading public. In 1884 the *Sentinel* boasted about this strange situation, saying "Our readers will find a great deal of interesting local matter in our sports and pastimes column every week, besides the inlegitimate [sic] athletic circles outside. Read it!"[100] In 1892, the *Sentinel* reported that Woodstonian 'Billy' Boyd began racing operations in Mexico, with some glee about the danger involved: "Boyd and Coyne (of Chatham) are on a recent job they scooped up $30,000. Heretofore no professional runner has had the nerve enough to go down amongst the greasers, where life is held so cheaply, and work the game, so that Boyd and Coyne are reaping a harvest from the innocents. But it is a risky occupation."[101] The local press's extensive coverage of "inlegitimate" sport included covering illegal prizefighting, dogfighting, and cockfighting.[102] Tony Joyce, a historian of working-class sport in Toronto, points out that since the law forbade even the reporting of such activities, newspapermen wrote their coverage in a way that was "cryptically worded and shrouded in secrecy."[103] Two years before the passing of federal legislation against prizefighting, one outraged Woodstonian questioned the Toronto *Globe's* coverage of a prizefight at Long Point.[104] The *Globe*, the letter to the *Sentinel* argued, began with "two or three lines in which it is spoken of in terms of strong disapproval. All the rest, however, is devoted to a minute account of the [fight]." The writer continued:

Well, if the *Globe* is sincere in its condemnation of the fight, why, I ask, in the name of common sense, does it devote so much space to an account of that event? Does it believe that the reading of that article is fitted to benefit society? Baugh! The few words of condemnation are meant to please those who abhor what is brutal in men's actions. The long account of the fight is meant to please the ruffians, whether these be so openly, or only in heart. Among these, that issue would sell well ... Prize fighting is against Canadian law. The two black-guards who fought should have been punished. So too should their seconds. So too should the witnesses. Of course, newspaper correspondents who were present belong to the last named. Had those who employed these correspondents been punished – could that have been done, they would have got only what they deserved.[105]

Alternate sports and sports practices thus remained in the towns, ironically with some support among certain AAA members like local newspapermen and other leading citizens. No one apparently batted an eye when Woodstock's mayor, James Sutherland, held the $4,000 stakes for the famous McIvor race. As historian Timothy Bonney-James puts it, this situation involved "one of the most respected figures in the town actively endorsing the mixture of gambling, professionalism and sport that was supposedly anathema to all but social undesirables."[106] Some might call such supporters of unsavoury sports culture a group of 'fancy men,' a term identified by Tony Joyce as describing individuals from 'polite society' who attended sports events that "existed on the edge of or beyond the law's reach."[107] During the 1880s and 1890s, local officials attempted to stop the frequent cockfights that plagued the east end of the town, at Eastwood Hall, the place where a prizefight between Casey and Bittle had been fought.[108] This happened, strangely enough, at the old Vansittart estate owned by T.C. Patteson, the sometime owner of the Toronto *Mail* and president of the Ontario Jockey Club. Was Patteson himself a 'fancy man'? His name never seems to have found its way onto the local record book in this context, although if it had been those in power could have easily suppressed it, as happened in nearby Hamilton when men of high social standing were caught at a cockfight.[109] Woodstonian sport reformers hoped to squelch the cockfights and other unsavoury activities going on at East-wood by bringing attention to them. Woodstock's *Spirit of the Times* newspaper reprinted an article from the *Christian Advocate* for local benefit. It called cockfighting a "barbarous custom" that only "the debased of the human family engage in." From a Christian perspective, cockfighting numbered among the "pomps, shows, or exhibitions of this wicked world which is at amity with God."[110] Police magistrate and charter WAAA member A.S. Ball provided a concrete approach to the problem, instructing the local newspaper to publish the names of twenty-six offenders arrested at a cockfighting main.[111]

Ball's move doubtless embarrassed some of his brethren in the WAAA, since W. Henry Martin, Charley Pyne's successor as its manager, stands out among the names of the people arrested. A bicycle trainer of national renown, and the caretaker of the association's dog until it died, Martin apparently kept poisoned company himself. The incident situated him publicly with the very breed of men and with the very type of sport that the WAAA built its reputation upon castigating. Were these the sorts of bad habits that the *Sentinel* had teased Pyne about earlier?[112] Among those arrested alongside Martin were many workers whose names never graced the rolls of WAAA membership. They included a driver, cooper, finisher, and upholsterer from Hay's Furniture Factory, a local grocer, a barber, and bartenders from the Oxford, Central, and Royal Hotels, one of them being the father of Billy Farrell, the WAAA's prize runner. Martin's cockfighting companion Waites, a bartender from the Oxford Hotel, worked under Charley Pyne, who had left the WAAA to manage the hotel. Martin apparently suffered no repercussions: he held his management position at the WAAA for some sixteen years, and later ran an impressive bicycle business in town.

Perhaps little came from Martin's involvement in the cockfighting affair because, unlike the middle-class club gentleman-amateurs, he had never really been in a state of grace from the start. Although WAAA members may have liked him well enough personally, they may have seen him as a member of the service class, in the same way English gentlemen viewed cricket professionals, known popularly as "players." From the WAAA perspective, the very conditions of his appointment showed Martin to be neither a gentleman nor an amateur. By definition he couldn't have been a 'fancy man.' Perhaps, therefore, the association leadership did not expect him to be as pure as they hoped WAAA members would be. Members might even view Martin's behaviour and his links with the tavern-based gambling crowd as vindication of the AAA approach. After all, Martin earned his living through sport. From the amateur perspective, that alone was a strike against his moral character. Yet at the same time, the WAAA obviously relied heavily on Martin and men of his ilk for the successful running of the association. As one local historian recalled, before its final demise, the association's last clubrooms were situated above a barber shop well known as a place where local bettors could lay their money down.[113]

Many people found other ways to resist AAA organizers' attempts to control their behaviour while availing themselves of AAA holiday sport entertainment. This particularly troubled the WAAA, since freeloaders could see what went on at its athletic grounds from the hilltop Presbyterian and Episcopal cemeteries overlooking it. Rather than pay to watch the holiday sports, many people simply found a comfortable tombstone to sit on to watch the day's entertainment *gratis*. While the grounds of the WAAA prohibited betting, drinking, and the use of profane language, who but the dead could protest at the cemetery? Power relations clearly surrounded almost every aspect of the holidays. By refusing to enter the WAAA grounds, the cemetery hill-sitters denied the WAAA opportunities to carry out their social agenda. They seem to have garnered the best of both worlds. By sitting on the hill they tacitly refused to defer to the AAA's authority while enjoying an afternoon's competition. They did this on their own terms – socially segregated, yet among similarly inclined people. They also physically distanced themselves from, but remained visible to, outraged sport reformers. How could people sit on the graves of Woodstonians – like Beverly Ingersoll – to watch sport without paying their fair share for the entertainment? Officious appeals to honour and decency did not persuade the recalcitrants to behave as social reformers presumed respectable citizens should. Threats of publishing a list to castigate sneaks publicly in the same manner that A.S. Ball unmasked the cockfight supporters did not work. Nor did the "arrangements, at great expense, to have a special artist for the day ... to photograph those who take their position on the hill."[114]

In an unusual and candid recollection, local professional runner Alby Robinson described other ways in which people resisted the AAA agenda by betting on running races, much to the chagrin of sport reformers.[115] When fixed by racers and their backers, these events created an alternative to respectable sport. Robinson recalls: "Small or fair sized communities would be selected as the base of operations. One of them would approach a local town merchant, horseman, or farmer, who had been carefully selected for his discretion and importance, seeking employment. The employer would be told the honest story of his identity and accomplishments. He would don the garments of his employment and keep up his practice in concealment and to all intents and purposes become a native of the place."[116] From that vantage point, the runner would "command the attention and confidence of a following willing to lay bets that he could beat one or other of the speed-boys whom he had encountered." Occasionally Robinson worked with another runner in the know:

Alby Robinson, Woodstock professional athlete,
n.d. Notice Robinson's lack of award parapher-
nalia, in contrast to the Herb Clarke photograph.
In an unusually candid recollection published in
1936, the runner describes the thrill-seeking
lifestyle he had lived as a traveling athlete during
his youth in the 1880s. Such events, fixed by racers and their backers, created a long-lived alternative tradition to the 'respectable' sports events
forwarded by amateur promoters. (Courtesy of
the Woodstock Museum)

Sometimes there would be another top-notch pro, also come in to that or some
nearby community, town, or city. Usually the plan was for this other fellow to
settle himself under the same conditions of employment and compete in the
same events of local origin and by his showing ultimately attract the betting
element and supporters of this neighbouring place, with the final results of the

main matched races would be between these two good outside men who generally were the closest of pals, and to make the most of this termination in those neighbourhoods they seesawed their finishes by inches until the last available chances for betting faded away.[117]

Workers, too, carried on their own sporting traditions in ways that resisted amateur ideologues. While factory life provided them with few opportunities to engage in after-work leisure activities such as sport, workers played in ways of their own making. August civic holidays, for example, became *the* play day for working men throughout the 1880s and 1890s.[118] Typically they took their families out of town on excursions and celebrated the holidays in ways that continued social and sporting traditions long abandoned by middle-class sport reformers. Promptly after their local formation, the Ingersoll and Woodstock chapters of the Knights of Labor devoted their energies to workers' recreation by sponsoring factory holiday picnics with cheap excursion fares. These holidays began with an early morning parade from the Knights' lodge rooms to the railway station. There the excursionists climbed into trains taking them to lakeside resorts like Port Stanley and Port Dover. At the beach they swam, danced, and spent the afternoon enjoying holiday treats.[119] Sport highlighted the day's events with activities designed to be especially inclusive, some of which encouraged betting. There you could find greased pole climbs, tugs-of-war, catch-as-catch-can wrestling, dog races, and quoit matches – all in stark contrast to AAA holiday activities.

In his examination of sport and state control in mid to late nineteenth-century Toronto, Tony Joyce argues that people who sought recreation could choose from a range of alternatives. They could join socially sanctioned sports clubs, they could risk arrest and engage in illegal activities, or they could enjoy watching sport created for public consumption.[120] In Ingersoll and Woodstock all of these options could be found, especially in the culturally significant forum of civic holidays. Ironically, local people sometimes engaged in all three types of activities under the nose of amateur clubs, much to the chagrin of local sports reformers!

AAA efforts to define legitimate sport for others and to sublimate and make marginal alternate traditions remained subject to various forms of resistance. Clearly, not all sports fit the plans of amateur ideologues, since they chose representative team sport bearing the mark of the muscular Christian ethos to fulfill their purposes. Even so, as the next three chapters show, civic leaders and urban boosters only supported certain team sports: those shaped to seem accessible to all males in the community and which would focus upon local talent and local civic aspiration. Of the three team summer sports organized between the 1840s and 1870s – cricket, baseball, and lacrosse – amateur sport reformers chose only the latter two for their community agenda.

FOUR

Cricket and Local Culture: From Centre Stage to the Margins

In June 1840, a young Woodstock lad got together with some of his chums and skipped off for an afternoon's adventure to see what was going on at the estate of old Colonel Deedes, a retired officer of the Tory elite. They found his place nestled in the wilderness along the Thames River between Ingersoll and Woodstock on the Beachville Road. The lad recalled, "Henry Carroll and other boys were continually going into ecstasies over the wonderful things that were being done there."[1] He, too, had "caught the fever" and was "just dying to see it." Dressed up in a linen suit, starched collar, and blue ribbon tie, he and his chums checked the place out. There he found himself introduced to the Woodstock Cricket Club and the retired officers who were its members.

This initiation into cricket, the earliest summertime team sport known to be organized in Oxford County, and its genteel and esoteric world became indelibly etched upon the young lad's memory. He remembered particularly the larger-than-life figure of Colonel Deedes, who sat like "a sphinx" while watching the match. Sitting in awe nearby his host, the boy and Colonel Deedes silently followed the players in their white flannel suits, starched shirts, and little caps, running about the field, chasing after a small ball. Occasionally, someone commented upon the batsmen's hitting or plays made or fumbled by the fielders. Ever mindful of the need to be on his best behaviour, the lad enjoyed watching the match and observing the social niceties displayed by the gentlemen and ladies during its formal lunch and tea, careful himself not to break convention. He remarked years later that the day's events made him feel as if he were "attending church."

A certain ritual, solemn like the mass, characterized the games playing that went on at the old Woodstock Club on that day and many others. Like the mass, one could learn from it many of life's lessons, if one only paid attention to what was going on. In front of the lad lay many keys to success in the officer's social milieu. For example, he could learn from the men's deportment how one took the thrill of victory or the pain of defeat on playing fields, and in life. He learned how one acted in the presence of one's social superiors and in front of others, like servants. He found out how gentlemen and ladies behaved together in public. He also learned from the officers about the role of sport in the shaping of identity. The lesson was clear: by playing English sports like cricket, people could keep their connection to England alive, even if they lived far away from their homeland in a colonial frontier.[2] Neither the young lad nor old Colonel Deedes would have likely known how much their locality would change in the next few years to come.

From the time of its introduction to Canadian soil, the culture of cricket carried with it a vision for Englishmen and colonials alike of what it meant to be a gentleman. While addressing the first English touring eleven upon their return from Canada in 1859, a speaker at the Marylebone Cricket Club toyed with a cricket ball in his raised hand. He announced, "I have a little weapon of war to introduce to you."[3] After the laughter subsided, he continued, "cricket balls ... would do more for civilization and the cultivation of good feeling than all the cannon balls in the world." Cheering heartily, the men in the room, like many others of the day, believed cricket to be a handmaiden and goodwill cultural ambassador for Britain's empire.[4] English historian Keith A.P. Sandiford suggests that Englishmen glorified cricket, claiming it "a perfect system of ethics and morals which embodied all that was most noble in the Anglo-Saxon character. They prized it as a national symbol, perhaps because – so far as they could tell – it was an exclusively English creation unsullied by oriental or European influences."[5]

This portrait of the culture of cricket speaks well to Canada's early Tory elite enclaves, like Woodstock's retired officers. In the early history of Canada, cricket generally thrived in imperial garrison towns or places such as Woodstock that had retired officers making the power of the empire keenly felt locally.[6] The Woodstock elite established cricket in Oxford County in 1837–38, at the very time when rebelling reformers stood up against the officers and other Tory oligarchies throughout the province. Woodstock's club members used cricket to form a kind of cultural cement that reinforced their British connections. It also integrated them within the network of colonial Tory elites that spread throughout the province. Woodstock's 'aristocrats,' exceptional men in Oxford County's backwoods frontier, held a high culture approach to cricket in the years between the Upper Canadian Rebellion and the coming of the railway in 1853.

As was described in chapter 1, these Woodstonians and their peers emulated the social pursuits of England's landed aristocracy. They did so in a way that articulated their social superiority symbolically in what they believed to be a natural colonial hierarchy.[7] For them, cricket reinforced their allegiance with the ruling class of England. Writing in 1878 about "That Aristocratic Neighborhood of Woodstock," the *Globe* commented that the old elite "brought with them traditions better suited to an old and advanced state of civilization than to life in the Canadian backwoods. Though living among the other settlers they were not of them, and [they] formed an aristocratic clique into which outsiders were not admitted. Carriages emblazoned with heraldic bearings and attended by flunkeys in family livery were seen in the streets, which thus presented somewhat of the appearance of the streets of old-fashioned rural towns in England."[8] This small, powerful group bound itself together ethnically, through intermarriage, and through their common affiliation with the Church of England. Its members stressed the naturalness of social hierarchy, deference, and the maintenance of class distance through self-assertion. They ensured their social segregation from others by admitting only themselves and those whom they viewed to be their social peers into their activities. Among their many sporting pastimes – including riding to the hunt, steeplechasing, and shooting wild game – cricket provided opportunities to assert their presence and consolidate their high social position in the area.

Soon after they settled in Woodstock, this group established the Woodstock Cricket Club, one of the earliest in the colony. A hallmark of the high culture of the rapidly growing small community, it impressed Mrs Anna Jameson favourably when she visited the area.[9] The club's English-born and -bred members belonged to St Paul's Anglican Church.[10]

In 1838, Edmund Deedes, the retired colonel, donated land along the road to Beachville for the club's private use. Workers leveled, sodded, and fashioned the land into a well-manicured playing field with a high board fence and evergreens protecting it from the sun and wind and creating a sort of sanctuary from prying eyes, wandering cattle, and undesirables.[11] The club preserved social exclusivity in many ways, with guests watching matches comfortably from a spectator's stand, wearing genteel apparel that few in the Upper Canadian wilderness could afford. Players wore fashionable cricket costumes, while the game's official carried a cane and wore a tall hat and full-length coat.[12] Such finery stood out in Oxford County's backwoods frontier of the 1840s.

Clearly more than just a game to club members and their guests, cricket expressed the certain dignity that the officers, their families, and friends associated with their social station. In keeping with England's high culture tradition of the sport, the game depended upon the right social atmosphere.[13] Propriety and convention, particularly regarding appropriate behaviour, circumscribed club affairs. Ladies and gentlemen partook of the festivities and watched the game while sipping tea and resting comfortably in tent-covered stands. Cricket provided opportunities for children to learn the social niceties considered appropriate to their social station, with young boys wearing their finest clothes as they helped with the game and practised their throwing, batting, and fielding skills at the sidelines.

The game that they aspired to play held well-observed ritual elements. Custom dictated that players and their guests had a luncheon served to them during the match, and that a banquet and ball complete the day's events. Early in the fall of 1845, Woodstock's club members played against officers from London's garrison. They followed up the match with a ball at nearby Love's Hotel.[14] Two seasons later they played a two-day match in Hamilton, where the Woodstonians found their hosts to be "hospitable, good and true." Mr Peter Hamilton graced them with "a polite invitation to dinner at his picturesque villa overlooking the scene of the amusement."[15] They reciprocated a fortnight later with a return match in Woodstock. Afterwards, the Hamilton players and their entourage congregated at President Deedes' mansion, where "music stole over the senses and festive board was spread."[16]

The restrictions that shaped so profoundly the work and leisure patterns of other area inhabitants, people of more humble social origins, did not affect members of the Woodstock elite. Time constraints, for example, did not get in the way of their sport playing. If the second innings of a match could not be completed during daylight, game officials pulled the stumps and continued play the next day, in keeping with elite practice back in England among those who had the resources to spend their leisure time in high style. What some observers might view a stylistic obsession really expressed values shared by the English and colonial ruling classes.[17] Woodstock's elite had the financial and time resources to carry on in this way, competing in matches against players from other towns and cities at least a decade before the coming of the railway, when few but the very rich could afford the luxury of nonessential travel.[18] Their carriages tripped to Toronto, Guelph, Hamilton, and London, over the notoriously bad roads of the province. Making their way at roughly four to five miles an hour, the players needed to set aside several days just for their journey.[19] Their

fine horses and high quality carriages lessened some of its physical dis-
comforts, but as Mrs Anna Jameson observed, the roads in the area
were "execrably bad."[20] Only the supporters of this sporting culture
would willingly undertake such uncomfortable trips for the sake of a
game, an opportunity only for people of some affluence. Before the
mid–1850s, local papers, ranging from moderate to extreme Tory pub-
lications, reported on the cricket happenings of the Woodstock club,
painting a picture of an honourable sport that improved character and
men's physiques and drew Canadian colonists closer to England.[21]
They also highlighted the patron-client relationships that existed
between club members and the skilled artisan and trades communities,
whose goods and services the elite purchased. In 1849, the Snelgroves,
local English cabinetmakers, felt "deeply honoured" to present the
club with an elegant set of handcrafted stumps at a testimonial for the
retired officers.[22]

A few men from more modest social backgrounds occasionally
found their way onto the club's exclusive playing field. This emulated
the long-standing paternalism of England's county cricket tradition, in
which lords and masters played alongside men from lesser social
ranks.[23] In September 1845, R.W. Sawtell found himself invited to take
a place on the club's field when visiting his sister, a dressmaker
employed by Mrs Deedes. He remembered the event vividly when writing about it at the turn of the century, delighted that, in "being a cricketer, just from the old land," Deedes had invited him to join in the
fun.[24] Phillip's *Canadian Cricketer's Guide* commended this democra-
tizing feature of the English cricket tradition, claiming, "the ranks and
classes of society are natural, not artificial ... but nowhere are they less
marked than on the cricket field, where we waive for awhile all social
distinction."[25] Such sentiments encouraged people of differing social
classes to play alongside each other without any great threat to the
existing social order. Nevertheless, the egalitarianism intended on the
field existed only for "awhile." Social boundaries circumscribed social
interaction as clearly as the boundaries of the cricket field limited
play.[26] For example, club members treated their guests from more
humble backgrounds with paternalistic civility.[27] No one mistook
Sawtell's playing with them for his being their social equal. Even
among their own, club members found that propriety about deference
to social station ruled the day. On the matter the *Canadian Cricket
Field* declared, "the dignity of the situation" is undermined "by famil-
iarity on the cricket field."[28] In this observation, it reminded its readers that the relaxation of social constraints could only go so far.

By the early 1850s, as the social and political power of Woodstock's
Tory elite waned, so did the high culture formulation of local cricket.

The old guard of the province noted the rapprochement between those members who had not died or left town with the rising group of mercantile and professional men in the area, something the 1858 *Canadian Cricketer's Guide* called a "strange move." It seemed perplexed by how the "absorbing claims of railways and politics" led to the abandonment of the Woodstock club.[29] Locally, this ended an era for the elite style of cricket as played by the old colonial club. Throughout the colony, however, cricket play continued among the status elite and members of the province's rising middle class, even after the withdrawal of imperial troops.[30] Institutions such as Toronto's Upper Canada College that modeled themselves upon England's public schools used cricket build the character of the sons of the old elite as well as of the emerging middle class.[31] According to sport sociologist Richard Gruneau, they emphasized the idea that games built character in a way that accommodated declining aristocratic interests with those of the rising industrial bourgeoisie.[32] Schoolmasters believed that the initiative, self-reliance, discipline, loyalty, obedience, and fair play demanded by the sport affected in good ways other aspects of the schoolboys' daily lives. The sons of Ingersoll and Woodstock's most prosperous families attended schools like Upper Canada College and were exposed to cricket as part of their overall education.[33]

Authorities in the province's private schools viewed the sport as ideal for social indoctrination. According to historian David Brown, their approach to cricket engendered within the students an "association with British practice and ideal."[34] In a way, an appreciation for the sport of cricket became emblematic of one's having *arrived* in Canada. As early as 1836, the *Patriot* opined, "British feelings cannot flow into the breasts of our Canadian Boys through a more delightful or untainted channel than that of British sports. A Cricketer as a matter of course *detests democracy, & is staunch in his allegiance to his King.*"[35] Moreover, cricket matches between various private schools created bonds between elite groups throughout in the province. Three members of Woodstock's emerging elite – Fred McQueen, Warren Totten, and Walter Mills – attended Upper Canada College. After graduation, they played in the prestigious Gentlemen of the Province against UCC students, partly because of their skill at the game, but more importantly because of their connections to the provincial elite that their families had ensured they cemented during their schoolboy days. These connections mattered, clearly, and their contact in the sport continued, although Woodstock had no local cricket club of its own when they played.[36]

Lovers of cricket in Ingersoll and Woodstock thus did not let go of the sport entirely. Local newspapers covered it, especially whenever an

important match occurred elsewhere. During England's Zingari cricket tour of Canada in 1872, for example, Ingersoll and Woodstock
newspapers covered the matches, presumably because of some interest
amongst their readership. Readers followed the exploits of W.G.
Grace, viewed by some to be the best-known Englishman of his time,
as he played a match in nearby London before a crowd of some seven
thousand people.[37] Hailed as England's finest athlete of the day and
still considered by many the finest cricketer yet, Grace captivated his
live and newspaper audiences.[38] His visit, however, did little to inspire
a resurgence of the sport locally in either town. When Woodstock's
Weekly Review reflected, "perhaps the presence of the best eleven that
ever set sail from Old England may rehabilitate the noble game in some
of its afore time popular garments," its optimism was unfounded.[39]
Cricket never completely died out in the area, although it became marginal to local sporting culture. As in other places throughout the
dominion, it persisted well into the twentieth century, though several
times declared dead.[40]

Unlike the closed social enclave of the old Woodstock elite's club,
newer cricket clubs that sprang up in Ingersoll and Woodstock had a
broader social base, yet were short-lived. They competed in challenge
matches against themselves, each other, and other small towns – places
like Paris, Tillsonburg, St Thomas, Simcoe, Norwich, and Princeton –
within about a forty-mile radius connected by railway lines. They did
not play against the select teams from larger centres of cricket power
and influence, like Hamilton and Toronto. Nor did they play against
the Zingari touring teams from England and from other colonies that
visited the province. Members in Ingersoll and Woodstock's newer
clubs had none of the great social pretensions expressed by the old
Woodstock club, and were well aware that they stood outside the tightly knit social circles bound by the powerful private schools. Ingersoll's
grocer, temperance advocate, and long-time postmaster Joseph Gibson
knew this firsthand. An avid lover of the game, he became acquainted
with the sport during his childhood years in England. As described in
chapter 3, as an adult Gibson spent his summers at his Muskoka cottage, in an area well known as a playground for the province's rich and
powerful families, and there he tasted the high culture style of the game
while playing against wealthy vacationers staying at the Beaumaris
Resort Hotel.[41] Gibson apparently played impressively, with his ball
rarely being touched by those at bat.[42] As a founding member of the
Ingersoll club, Gibson likely agreed with the claim made in 1874 that
theirs was "nothing but a country club"; small beans in the grand
scheme of the sport, and a cause for strange delight among local players who did not have their own grounds or clubhouse.[43]

Many things differentiated the newer cricket clubs from the old Tory elite club. Players in the new clubs, for example, did not wear proper suits or costly uniforms to play. They still ate between the innings, but did so without the benefit of servants or a private clubhouse. If present, wives and sweethearts served players a simple picnic, not an extravagant banquet. Unlike the old club's approach, when a second inning of a match could not be finished in a day, game officials pulled the stumps and called the game. Matches did not last for days on end. Instead of ending with gala balls at private mansions, club members and their guests congregated at local hotels for post-game suppers – that is, if they had time before catching the train home.[44] Expenses, not really an issue for members of the old Woodstock club, became a concern for the newer ones. In 1874 and 1875 the ladies of Ingersoll held fund-raising concerts in the local YMCA rooms to help cover the club's travel and entertainment costs.[45] Unlike the slow, leisurely pace taken by the old Woodstock club for their journeys, newer clubs traveled in a style expressing different fiscal resources and social values. In 1879, Ingersoll cricketers kept up a frantic pace as they journeyed to Simcoe for a match, leaving "at 5:00 am to catch the 'air line' at Tillsonburg, and commencing to play cricket without a hot breakfast."[46] They returned home before the last train left town.

The newer cricket clubs, unlike the old Woodstock club, had neither clubhouses nor grounds of their own.[47] Until 1860, this had been no problem, since cricket was the only organized team sport played locally. Things changed, however, when Ingersoll's earliest organized baseball club held its practices at the "cricket field," aka the public park.[48] The cricket club's reliance upon public – rather than private – lands lessened the social distance between it and the town. One did not need an invitation to observe Ingersoll matches, and when other sports clubs – representative baseball clubs in the 1860s and lacrosse clubs in the 1870s – emerged on the local scene, cricketers shared a common playing field. Evidence shows that the cricketers obliged other team sport clubs by ending their matches early so that others could play their games.[49]

If the situation of controlled space and public access to it mattered little to Ingersoll and Woodstock cricketers, the issue of private grounds troubled patrons of the sport elsewhere throughout the province, especially urban elite clubs. They aimed to maintain exclusiveness in their sport, and controlling space achieved this, but at the same time they wanted their sport to thrive. In 1878, T.C. Patteson wrote about the precarious state of cricket in Canada in *The Canadian Monthly and National Review*. As described earlier, he knew the Woodstock scene well, spending his summers at Eastwood, the old

Vansittart estate, to be near his horses. An avid sportsman and a founder of the Ontario Jockey Club, Patteson supported Canadian cricket passionately, helping to recruit the English eleven of the Marylebone Cricket Club's tour of Canada in 1872.[50] "Without some reform from within," he argued, "the game can never really flourish here." To remedy the situation he suggested the development of a district system, much like the English county system, with strong clubs acting "as the head and fount of cricket" for each district.[51]

Patteson and his associates, however, never themselves appeared convinced of the appropriateness of making their game as widely available to the public as it was in England. Such a club "must have its absolute own grounds," Patteson proclaimed, because publicly supported commons for playing fields just wouldn't work. Taxation, he argued, was "heavy enough already, and many a horny-fisted son of toil would ask in amazement, and with complete justice, why he should still more heavily burdened to support a mere pastime, indulged in chiefly by the sons of gentlemen."[52] In doing so Patteson voiced a common notion of cricket as being naturally bound by social class: "but from our rich mercantile and professional classes throughout the Dominion we have something like a prescriptive right to look for aid."[53]

From the 1860s on, Patteson's "horny-fisted sons of toil" couldn't be found in Ingersoll and Woodstock's cricket clubs.[54] Even if they had the disposable leisure time to join a club and travel with it, club membership restrictions excluded them.[55] Nor did the new culture around cricket resemble anything like that experienced by the old local Tory elite. Instead, it came from Ingersoll and Woodstock's rising middle class of professionals and businessmen, the "rich mercantile and professional classes" to which Patteson referred. The twenty-three Ingersoll club members who played between 1866 and 1875 included no manual workers, with one-half of them Ontario-born and most belonging to Protestant denominations in local Church of England and Methodist churches.

Judging by what the local press forwarded about their game, area cricketers had good reasons for playing the sport. Most newspaper accounts claimed cricket to be a manly activity – "the very acme of sport for sport's sake" – that remedied the pervasive physical, mental, and moral ills that plagued middle-class urban men.[56] Writing to the *Chronicle,* one exponent of the manly game advocated that "if this, and other games requiring strength, activity, and endurance, were made a part of the daily business of our people ... our bills of mortality would be less formidable than they now are – we should have fewer pale faced dyspeptics meeting at the street corners, and more cases of longevity, while many of those diseases which result from sluggish inactivity would disappear from our midst."[57] Newspaper columns admonished males to play cricket to relieve the tedium of their daily toil through bodily exercise and to refresh their minds. Cricket lovers hailed their game's great complexity and praised themselves for their comprehension of its esoteric and scientific aspects. "A cricket team must work with the exactness of a piece of machinery."[58] By comparison, local propagandists depicted baseball and lacrosse as "more flashy, but less scientific than the 'old standby.'"[59]

Comparisons between cricket, baseball, and lacrosse abounded in the sporting press in the two towns and far away, yet those who brought to Canada the sporting traditions of their homeland found cricket to be a comforting and familiar activity. "This old English game will be played, and continue popular, long after the very names of many others of ephemeral renown have been forgotten," suggested Woodstock's *Weekly Review*.[60] Since the towns had sizable populations of English immigrants, cricket clubs and scrub matches found some support locally. "This noble and health giving game," one local reporter proclaimed enthusiastically in the years before the rise of organized baseball, "is bidding fair to become as universal and popular in Canada as in 'Merrie Old England.'"[61] Some people held onto cricket steadfastly as a matter of ethnic loyalty, like Ingersoll's Sons of England Association, who, after their founding in 1882, immediately set about creating a cricket club for intra club competition.[62] However, few people outside this type of circle played the game locally.

As many historians note, in both Canada and the United States cricket generally lost its pride of place to baseball.[63] In 1858, after a match between Parr's English touring eleven against selected gentlemen from Canada and the United States at Niagara, the teams played a baseball match "to lessen some of the severe losses of the promoters of the cricket match."[64] Cricket moved to the margins of local sporting culture: as chapters to follow show, baseball during the 1860s and lacrosse during the 1870s and 1880s – not cricket – highlighted civic holiday team sport competition.

Were baseball and lacrosse inherently better suited to the lifestyles of North American urban inhabitants, as some historians have argued?[65] Baseball and lacrosse games attracted sizable followings, took less time to play, and required neither expensive nor elaborate equipment and dress. Nor did they require a finely groomed playing field. The fast pace and rough physical nature of lacrosse appealed to many people, while baseball had frequent changes between offense and defense, making it a livelier, more action-packed game than cricket. Nevertheless, while these factors offer some insights into some differences between the games, they are not explanatory and do not account for the success of cricket in England, for example, one of the most urban and industrialized countries in the world during the nineteenth century, where issues of temporal pace and financial expense also presumably applied. Today cricket attracts a strong following in many places throughout the world like India, Australia, and the West Indies.

Some scholars argue that national sentiment and national character explain the fates of cricket, baseball, and lacrosse in the North American environment.[66] As Colin Howell aptly shows in his study of baseball in the Maritime provinces, while the high culture cricket of elite groups existed in large cities like Halifax and St John, cricket in small communities and outlying districts of the region held a much broader social appeal. "Throughout the coalfields of the Maritimes," he argues, "cricket was a miner's game; indeed, as coalmining output increased, so did cricket's popularity."[67] Conversely, some anti-English sentiment doubtless affected cricket's popularity, especially in the United States, as Melvin Adelman shows. Yet this reasoning does not explain why other English sports, especially equestrian sports, continued, even to this day, unimpeded by anti-English sentiment.[68] Pro-English sentiment didn't work for the sport, since cricket experienced no great upsurge in popularity during imperialism's sweep across Canada during the 1880s. Nor does this line of reasoning consider that baseball, like cricket, possessed common English roots. In fact, early baseball promoters encouraged their players to take up cricket to improve their baseball playing skills. Clearly, no universally *better suited* sport existed. The fate of any sport locally relied upon its local social construction.

What, then, accounts for the marginalization of cricket in Ingersoll and Woodstock when the sport seemingly thrived in other places? In part this happened because local AAA organizers chose not to include the sport in their sport reform agenda, even though their ranks included cricket aficionados like Ingersoll's Joseph Gibson. While Gibson got in a match whenever he could, he, like other local sport reformers, chose to put his efforts behind promoting other team sports – notably baseball and lacrosse – and moulding local teams into community representatives. The same situation occured in neighbouring Woodstock, where among AAA founders were cricket-loving men like prominent local lawyer and Dominion Telegraph manager Warren Totten, who also chose to promote other team sports.[69] Tremendously active on the local scene, Totten had spearheaded the building of the Woodstock Opera House and sat as reeve and mayor, and was involved in governing many local fraternal and sport clubs.[70] A product of the bastions of power and prestige in the province, he was one of three Woodstonians described earlier in the chapter who competed in the Gentlemen of the Province team in annual matches against Upper Canada College students in the early 1870s.[71] Beverly Ingersoll, another WAAA founder, although much younger than Totten, also learnt the game during his schooldays at Upper Canada College. When he received a hero's funeral after dying a tragic death on the WAAA toboggan slide in 1885, eulogies did not mention his cricket playing, presumably because it had little bearing on the way in which he was remembered in the sporting life of the community. Instead his work with local lacrosse and baseball received heaping praise. Like Gibson and Totten, Ingersoll did not promote cricket through his involvement in his local AAA. Writing in 1888, one proponent of the game lamented the absence of the sport in the local AAAs and tried to goad members into promoting it. No one responded to the call.[72]

Why would such men, leaders of the new middle class in Ingersoll and Woodstock, choose to ignore cricket in their social reform community agenda for sport? One might consider the need for reform in a game whose structure and cultural baggage had already been well established. Judging by what social observers said about cricket, it simply did not have the rowdiness associated with it that plagued other sports. It was not a sport in need of reform – a keen AAA agenda. No one appeared at all concerned over the social environment of a game already infused with a muscular Christian ideology long before it arrived in the colony. In many respects cricket would be the prototype for respectable organized sport. However, its most visible organized form in elite enclaves, such as Canada's private school system, made it seem inaccessible – or maybe just distasteful – to many. The promotion of this model of the sport, by extension, would be at odds with the middle-class agenda. Middle-class men wished socially and culturally to define themselves as natural leaders of a new order based upon individual respectability and personal merit. They relegated cricket to a marginal role in community sporting life, giving it – in Ingersoll and Woodstock at least – no role as a representative team sport in the mechanics of urban boosterism.[74]

FIVE

Baseball, Boosters, and the Amateur Not-for-Profit Approach to Community Sport

In August 1869, the *New York Clipper* compared the fates of cricket and baseball as it covered the Woodstonian-led baseball developments unfolding in southwestern Ontario. It remarked: "The American national game is spreading in this section of the Queen's domain, and will, ere long, completely obliterate the '*hould Henglish*' game of cricket. The masses see that it is a more exciting game than cricket; that more skill is displayed by the players, and that it is not near as tedious to witness."[1] The highly regarded sporting magazine was reporting what many others already knew: baseball was taking off as a popular organized sport while cricket's popularity was teetering.

By the mid–1860s, baseball, which had always had a strong popular tradition in Ingersoll and Woodstock, was ripe for the hands of sport reformers. Contrary to the once commonly held belief that Abner Doubleday invented baseball in 1839, a form of the game existed in Oxford County during the early decades of the nineteenth century that used a square playing field with four bases and eleven players a side.[2] Similar to types of baseball found in Massachusetts and New York, it grew from the ball-playing traditions of Loyalists and others who brought to southwestern Ontario from Britain and the United States the strongly local versions of baseball learned in their youth. The game's rules were generally simple, unwritten understandings between players, passed down by oral tradition. Players used rudimentary, locally made equipment, with bats, or clubs as they called them, drawn from blocked out cedar, although "a wagon spoke, or any nice straight stick would do." A local shoemaker made the ball from double-twisted woolen yarn and covered it with "good honest calf skin."[3]

Matches between young men highlighted community holiday events, making local baseball a much more broad-based and popular social

The Young Canadians, Woodstock's Canadian Baseball Champions, c. 1868. Formed initially to provide socially oriented competition for club members using a four-base playing field, the Young Canadians adopted today's three-base game some time in 1861. They created and dominated the Silver Ball award for the Canadian Baseball Championship in 1864, with the *New York Clipper* calling the team the "Cock of the Walk." (Courtesy of the Woodstock Museum)

affair than the cricket activities of the Woodstock elite. During a game on militia muster day in June 1838, players from Beachville played against a group from the townships of Zorra and North Oxford.[4] All were farmers, artisans, or the sons of farmers; none had access to the tight social circle of the elite. In 1886, Dr Adam E. Ford, a former Beachville resident and avid sportsman, described the event in a reminiscence published in the popular Philadelphia sporting magazine *Sporting Life*.[5] What he portrayed was in stark contrast to what that one young lad, who was his contemporary, had described at the old Woodstock cricket club at the Deedes estate. The officers of the cricket club stylized their play into a serious and solemn event. Just a mile down the road in Beachville, however, local boys and young men played a lively game of baseball, an event marked by its informality, lack of organization, and more egalitarian social nature (although both games excluded female players). Watched by a volunteer regiment from Zorra as they passed by on their way to muster, the baseball game described by Ford happened as part of the community's general celebrations for the King's birthday.[6] Like many traditional sports of the day, it involved much fun and laughter. Players had to "plug" (hit) the runners with the ball to put them out, as Ford recounts the hilarity of the spectacle: "The object ... was to get runners on the base lines, so as to have the fun of putting them out or enjoying the mistakes of the fielders when some fleet footed fellow would dodge the ball and come in home."[7]

Baseball began to take on its modern, organized form in Oxford County in the early 1860s as young men in Ingersoll and Woodstock formed the Victoria and the Young Canadian clubs to provide socially oriented competition for club members.[8] Initially playing a local version of the game, with four bases and eleven players, they soon adopted the modern three-base game that New Yorker Alexander Cartwright had codified some fifteen years earlier and which was found in Henry Chadwick's *Beadle's Dime Base-Ball Player*.[9] While, as noted, the activities of Ingersoll and Woodstock's baseball clubs were socially more broadly based than those of the Woodstock cricket club, the Victoria and Young Canadians still had no unskilled workers as members. Most were Canadian-born Protestant bachelors whose ages ranged from their early to mid-twenties.[10]

The Victoria and Young Canadian clubs sought initially to provide sporting competition and a place to socialize for the forty or so local men who belonged to them.[11] In Ingersoll and Woodstock, as in New York, where the game had first been codified, club members used baseball to promote health, recreation, and social enjoyment. They stressed and rationalized the socially oriented competition, believing that it cultivated health and provided moral training for players,[12] and their disciplined, elaborately constructed associations regulated the social environment surrounding the sport. Like their rivals, the Tecumseh Base Ball Club from nearby London, the Victorias and Young Canadians had club constitutions and bylaws governing their operation. In London, players paid one dollar a year to play, with admission depending upon a member vote.[13] During club matches two captains picked players, assigning playing positions and overseeing play. Ungentlemanly behaviour caused expulsion, suspension, reprimands, or fines ranging from twenty-five cents to five dollars. Lists of offences included using profane language, wearing another player's uniform, disputing an umpire's decision, expressing an opinion on a doubtful play, or leaving the field without the captain's permission. By signing articles of agreement, players pledged their allegiance to club rules. A two-thirds majority vote confirmed the sanctions laid against recalcitrant members.

Historians George Kirsch, Melvin Adelman, and Colin Howell have shown that early baseball clubs held a particular social appeal to men who sought rational recreation.[14] Ballplayers found local hotel owners to be gracious and supportive hosts for their organizational meetings and socializing, and Woodstock's hotel men, C.L. Wood, Patrick Farrell, J.E. Thompson, and James O'Neill promoted baseball avidly, as did the proprietors of Ingersoll's Hearn's Hotel and Jarvis Hall.[15] Club dinners and banquets held in local hotels gave baseball players and their supporters sociable occasions that bred strong bonds of loyalty and friendship. Merriment, good food, and drinking surrounded these affairs. Club officials welcomed baseball men from other places, cementing ties to a sporting brotherhood that existed well beyond local boundaries. In 1867, Woodstock's club president, Robert McWhinnie, attended the spirited banquet of Hamilton's Maple Leaf club, where the men showed manly camaraderie by raising their glasses to club members involved in repelling the Fenian menace. Hamilton club leaders and Woodstock's McWhinnie made speeches about their much-loved game that were recorded in local newspapers in a way that lost the levity of the occasion. The press described McWhinnie as having "expatiated ably on the science of baseball at some length" as he responded to a "high eulogium on the benefits of the game."[16] Ugh – could the event have been so dry and affected? Not likely; just as the *New York Clipper* had taken a jab at the *"hould Henglish"* game of cricket, the paper probably reported upon the event in a way that ridiculed the pomposity associated with high culture sport. The songs that followed the baseball banquet speeches, like the anthem *Don't Judge a Man by the Coat He Wears*, suggests a club belief in fraternal egalitarianism, telling a very different message from that encoded in the activities of the Tory elite's cricket club.

This sociability found in early baseball never died out, although it did change with the rise of urban competition and the developing intimate connection between representative sport teams and local urban boosterism. The connection between team and town began inconspicuously enough, through a search for good opponents to beat. Almost immediately after their creation, the Victorias and Young Canadians began challenging each other to friendly matches. An Ingersoll schoolteacher, Thomas Wells, caught a glimpse of an early match between the two while traveling from one town to the other in July 1860 – an unexpected treat recorded in his diary.[17] By the end of the decade, matches between the two places would be commonplace, with one Ingersoll "grumbler" complaining of that "juvenile game," which had "assumed proportions of absurd importance."[18] Whether the grumbling was a clever editorial parody is not known, but clearly baseball's magic had captivated many local people, including town mayors, councillors, the business community, and local sports lovers. This might indeed seem absurd to someone who did not believe that baseball expressed *anything* important, but local people saw in baseball teams a place for their communal aspirations. Team victories became, in the minds of many townspeople, another way of expressing their community's worth and success.

The nice fit between baseball and urban boosterism stemmed from the rise of competitive inter urban baseball, something led by Ingersoll and Woodstock in the province. After winning many matches against their Ingersoll opponents, Woodstock's Young Canadians forged a plan to show off their talent and test their mettle against all other clubs from towns and cities in the province. In August 1864, C.L. Wood, a former New Yorker who owned Woodstock's Royal Hotel, sent word out that his town was ready to "*play ball.*" He and local club organizers invited other clubs to a meeting aimed at promoting inter urban competition.[19] Clubs from towns connected by the Great Western and Grand Trunk Railway lines attended – from Ingersoll, Guelph, Barton, Hamilton, Dundas, and Flamborough. The meeting produced the earliest-known baseball association in the country, the Canadian Association of Base Ball Players (CABBP), modeled on the seven-year-old American National Association of Base Ball Players (NABBP).[20] The new Canadian association promoted its game at the provincial exhibition in Hamilton the next month, treating exhibition-goers to something new – representative urban baseball competition – through a well-publicized match. Nine picked from eastern clubs (Hamilton, Flamborough, and Dundas) played against a team from west (Ingersoll, Woodstock, and Guelph).[21] By the time they replayed the event two years later, most people had grown accustomed to watching representative inter urban baseball competition.[22]

The Silver Ball trophy, the token of the CABBP's championship, created by Woodstonians "wild over the game," helped stimulate intense rivalries between hometown teams. They invented the trophy after collecting cash subscriptions, melting down American silver dollars, and crafting them into a regulation-sized ball, an "elegant specimen of silver work."[23] The Young Canadians set down the rules governing the Silver Ball competition, known in eastern Canada and the United States as the Woodstock rules for baseball.[24] According to them, the quest for the Canadian championship ran between mid-June and October. Teams challenged the reigning champions, who responded by setting a match date within at least ten days. NABBP rules as published by

Chadwick's *Beadle's Dime Base-Ball Player* governed match games.[25] Teams winning the Silver Ball posted a $40 surety, being able to keep the ball if they defended it successfully for three years running, with Woodstock donating a new ball for another championship trophy.[26]

After initially getting their wires crossed over who was supposed to be challenging whom, the Silver Ball competition got underway soon after the Woodstonians advertised their rules. Hamilton's Maple Leafs took on the Young Canadians in the first Silver Ball match in August 1864, only to be trounced by the home team by a score of 30–2, an auspicious beginning for Woodstock.[27] The Young Canadians held the championship title for seven years, with Ingersoll's Victorias only marring this record slightly when they won it from them (although just for a week) in 1868.[28] Baseball historian William Humber has stated that in the 1860s, the best baseball in Ontario was to be found in Woodstock.[29] This is true. In defense of their title, the Woodstonians always had the home field advantage, beating teams from Hamilton, Newcastle, Dundas, Guelph, and London, to the joy of local crowds. So many victories with so little effort prompted the *New York Clipper* to dryly describe the Young Canadians as the "Cock of the Walk." Compared with the baseball goings-on in the New York area, Woodstock's baseball may have been small beans, but Woodstonians did not seem at all fazed by this fact. Of the Young Canadian team's connection to its small but ambitious town, the *New York Clipper* noted, "the Woodstock people and the press blew pretty strongly for them."[30]

Baseball promoters and civic leaders in Woodstock may have been the earliest sports reformers in the province to realize the potential for urban boosters through baseball. This popular sport in its organizational infancy could provide a venue to promote their town through respectable representatives, while helping shape a sense of community pride and identity. Civic officials and community leaders in both Woodstock and Ingersoll used the Queen's Birthday and Dominion Day holidays to celebrate their hometowns and highlight their town's teams. Baseball matches on civic holidays drew local businesspeople, sports promoters, and community supporters like a magnet. In 1868, some five hundred excursionists from Guelph accompanied their team to Woodstock to watch a fiercely contested Dominion day match between the Young Canadians and Guelph's Maple Leafs.[31] At a Dominion Day tournament held by the Woodstonians the next year, some five thousand people – a thousand people more than the town's population – attended the affair, sitting on hastily erected spectator stands.[32] Seven teams from six towns played in the event, causing the *New York Clipper* to praise the Woodstonians for undertaking "any scheme that had for its object the encouraging and fostering of the game."[33] In the 1860s, baseball aficionados "in the know" viewed Woodstock as Canada's premier baseball town; no other community put as much heart and soul into fortifying the connection between team and town. Hosting tournaments for teams throughout the region, the Woodstonians enhanced baseball's image as a skillful, manly game through awarding prizes for outstanding catching, pitching, and baseline play. Even sartorial splendour fortified the team-town connection, with the Woodstonians giving out prizes for the neatest uniforms that a club sported, like the London Tecumseh's smart outfits of cricketing flannels and scarlet hose. Not since the days of the old cricket club had local athletes in Woodstock worn distinctive uniforms for play, yet this time team uniforms meant something altogether different – they were emblems of the community at large, not of a small, tightly knit enclave within it.

The local citizenry's responses to team victories and losses at times could be overwhelming. When the Victorias, the underdog in the contest, managed to wrest the Silver Ball from the Young Canadians in 1868, town officials and the local citizenry reacted to the victory with a huge party, rivaled only by the celebration thrown when the first train of the GWR arrived in town so many years ago. Meeting their triumphant ball team at its station, joyous citizens paraded the Victorias' team captain William Hearn atop their shoulders through the streets. No doubt the local iron finisher and sometime assistant fire chief relished this moment forever. At the town hall, councillors and leading citizens feted Hearn and the Victorias. Later, at a banquet in the Royal Hotel, the new marvel of photography recorded the occasion for posterity. Outside in the streets, citizens lit bonfires to celebrate their victory, frolicking well into the night. During the week following, curious onlookers stopped by at the corner of Thames and King Streets to catch a glimpse of the Silver Ball on display in the window of the Victorias' president Ralph Woodcock's bookstore, superbly advertising the team, the town, and the enterprising Woodcock himself.[34] With the Silver Ball in its possession Ingersoll appeared to have had it made. Newspapers all over – in New York City, Toronto, and London – reported on the town's good fortune. Yet, as with most sporting victories, this was a short-lived day in the sun. Within one week, the Victorias lost a re-match to the Young Canadians, giving up their coveted Canadian championship title, the Silver Ball, and the joy that the victory brought.

In Ingersoll, Woodstock, and elsewhere throughout the province, sport reformers entrenched deep ties between the home team and the honour of the town. Yet at times in the heady days of early competition the behaviours of players and their sporting public surrounding hotly contested matches threatened middle-class notions of appropriate behaviour. Some fifteen hundred spectators, nearly one-half of Woodstock's entire population, watched the Young Canadians beat the Dundas Mechanics at a match in 1866.[35] Two years later three thousand people, nearly three-quarters of the town, attended a Silver Ball Match between the Young Canadians and the Victorias.[36] Within months, the town of Guelph gave its citizens a holiday so that they could accompany their home team to Woodstock[37] to watch the fiercely contested match between the Young Canadians and Guelph's Maple Leafs.[38] Nearly five hundred excursionists took the trip, while stragglers, unable to make the costly one dollar trip but rich enough to stake money on the game, congregated at Guelph's telegraph office to keep abreast of match developments.[39] At the Woodstock fair grounds excursionists received their money's worth in breathtaking entertainment. In the first inning, Woodstonian McKay's homerun ball crashed through the window of the nearby agricultural hall. The crowd loved it. In the sixth inning Guelph's spectacular triple play, although "lustily cheered" by Guelph supporters, could not prevent Woodstock's decisive 36–28 victory.

Despite reports that "the best of good feeling prevailed between the players throughout the contest," spectator violence and rowdyism marred the day for event organizers. Fistfights broke out, likely egged on by some good whiskey, as "toughs" threatened people in the stands while "no one dared to interfere with them in their nefarious work."[40] The excursionists returned home to Guelph to continue the unrest into the evening and throughout the next day. In the weeks that followed, newspaper editors in Woodstock and Guelph continued the rivalry and name-calling in their papers. Guelph's *Evening Mercury* likened Woodstock to "a huge snake after getting a knock on the head, [which] writhes about in a fearful mental agony."[41] As sport sociologists Richard Gruneau and David Whitson have commented, in instances such as these, violent spectators need "to make a point about their own competence and worth as men, as members of a particular social group, or as residents of a proud community. The momentary sense of superiority or inferiority expressed when a 'representative' player or team won or lost became especially significant to people who didn't have much power over other areas of their life."[42] Vast contradictions thus existed between the notion of respectability presumed by promoters of representative sport and the deeper messages that at times accompanied crowd unruliness.[43] Mudslinging by the press – an institution integral to the local shaping of respectability – is just another contradictory part of the association between baseball and urban boosterism.

Baseball's popularity among all segments of the local population added to the tensions associated with the sport. Intense competition between towns fueled organized baseball's evolution, changing it from a game played for its own sake and for the social benefits believed to accrue from it to a sport in which winning really mattered the most. Baseball victories became a symbol of the relative merits of the team and town, "a focus of heated celebration of local identity."[44] The earliest Silver Ball competition came from clubs that began as local voluntary organizations with a strong social agenda rather than fierce economic motivation. Initially not predominantly profit-seeking ventures, they lacked a framework for early competition. Yet these things would come – first locally and then between towns – as the popular game spread and teams sought out better competition. At an early match game in 1864, the Young Canadians lent a player to their challengers from Ingersoll, prompting the *New York Clipper* to muse that the event "savored much more of a social than a match game."[45]

Within five years, however, such a thing would be unthinkable. Competitive teams like Guelph's Maple Leafs padded their players' roster with ringers, including players from other towns, to gain a competitive edge – something Timothy Bonney-James points out "itself was a symbol of urban competition."[46] When the Young Canadians faced the Brooklyn Atlantics in 1868 at a tournament in Niagara, some four thousand fans watched them compete with players borrowed from the Guelph and London clubs. No one made much ado about it.[47] Even with their fortified numbers, the Young Canadians were way out of their league. The Atlantics, former American champions, trounced them 30–17. Nearly every team with competitive aspirations got into the act of doing whatever they could to win. London's Tecumsehs struck players off their first and second nines if they could get better players by other means, such as offering inducements like traveling expenses to attract out-of-towners to help them win.[48] Rumours also implicated Ingersoll and Woodstock clubs in under-the-table dealings: the Victoria and Young Canadian clubs considered amalgamating, opponents charged, "for the simple reason that they could not muster a nine equal to any of the first class clubs in the province."[49]

Intense competition also made visible unseemly parts of the game, like the rowdyism and betting of the Guelph-Woodstock fracas. The ever-present spectre of betting made a player's poor showing during a match a cause for suspicion. After a match between the Young Canadians and the London Tecumsehs in 1869, newspaper reports pointed to bets freely offered and taken.[50] Amid rumours that the game against the Young Canadians "was sold before it had begun," London player James Brown faced his Tecumseh club executive over the serious matter of game fixing. He protested his innocence, claiming that he "had not sold the match at Woodstock, nor had he bet against the club, nor had he made, nor did he expect to make any money by the club."[51] Had the Woodstonians or another interested party fixed it? After some deliberations, the Tecumseh executive found no wrongdoing and concurred with Brown's plea of innocence.

The growing emphasis upon winning, which became obvious by the early 1870s, marked the beginnings of a new era in local involvement in organized inter urban baseball. Both Woodstock and Ingersoll led Ontario clubs as promoters and competitors in socially oriented club competition before that watershed. They had alone possessed the Silver Ball, the token of the Canadian championship. In 1869, however, Woodstock's team could not beat Guelph's Maple Leafs, and they passed the emblem onto this team, an emerging Canadian baseball powerhouse.[52] The new champions coveted the title and recruited ringers to play for their team. They defeated all comers for three successive years and, according to Silver Ball rules, became the owners of the trophy.[53] As Bryce's 1876 *Canadian Baseball Guide* observed, the passing of the Silver Ball from local hands hurt clubs in Ingersoll and Woodstock.[54] It certainly affected local pride and the local sport scene. Championship games, played on the incumbent's home field, now occurred only in Guelph. Because both Ingersoll and Woodstock organizations had begun as social clubs, they had not cultivated second nines to advance when the clubs' premier players retired, leaving local fields for "younger and less skillful men." Without an available pool of skilled talent, they had little chance of defeating teams that stressed competitive achievement rather than social enjoyment. This burst their bubble.

Baseball mania, first experienced in Ingersoll and Woodstock, continued to sweep urban Ontario as highly competitive clubs from large industrial cities such as Toronto, Hamilton, Guelph, and London created a new regulatory agency to develop and oversee a new, provincial competitive league. In 1876, their Canadian Association of Base Ball Players (CABBP), formed at Toronto's Walker House hotel, replaced the earlier association and changed the face of inter urban baseball competition in the province. Ingersoll and Woodstock clubs, formerly at baseball's vanguard, played no role in the new association's formation as smaller places in the province were left by the wayside.[55] Discarding the Woodstock rules for challenge competition, the CABBP turned its baseball competition into a strict business, no longer subject to the voluntary and piecemeal funding given by participants, fans, and hometown businesspeople. Firmly tied to the cash nexus, visiting clubs received 40 per cent of the gate receipts to pay for regular team travel between cities in the league.[56] While claiming to be an amateur agency, the CABBP's rules avoided the issue of player payment, although it prohibited the movement of players between teams within a thirty-day period.[57] The highest bidder could thus recruit the best players. After a disputed championship in 1878, the association's president, Guelph's George Sleeman, charged bitterly that the league was "managed by a few wire pullers, each trying to outwit the others in the interests of a particular club."[58] The new CABBP was in turn replaced, in 1880, by the Canadian Association of Amateur Base Ball Players (CAABBP), which attempted to redress many of the organizational problems that plagued its precursor, but this happened in vain.[59] Many debates undermined this and other baseball ventures, as historian Alan Metcalfe points out, including the merits of professionalism, the financial instability and short life span of member clubs, and generalized dissent over how to best develop inter urban competition.[60]

Amid the chaos, and with teams like Guelph's Maple Leafs and Harriston's Browns buying imported players, critics exhorted: "Stop the farce and boldly acknowledge the professionalism."[61] Yet even the most notorious offenders didn't know whether Canada could finance successful professional baseball. George Sleeman, historian William Humber observes, "was notably guided by his pocketbook, alternately cursing imports one year and hiring them the next."[62] At one point Sleeman argued that "Canada is not a rich enough country for men who are after money and nothing else, the sooner such men get out into the States the better for the game here."[63] Yearning for baseball as it had begun in Ingersoll and Woodstock during the early 1860s, he uttered words that would be prophetic for the playing of the sport in the two towns: "Until baseball is played in Canada as it used to be, *for the love of the game and the honour of the town or city represented*, it never will be a success" (my emphasis). Local identification with home team players, he argued, was essential for baseball, boosterism, and the ultimate success of organized competition. To Sleeman, "there was more enjoyment and certainly far more interest in the game when every member of the team was a [local] native."[64]

Baseball promoters in Ingersoll and Woodstock had already come to this conclusion themselves, something that influenced their desire to create a respectable sport culture in the two communities. If they did not have enough athletic talent and money to create and sustain winning professional teams, baseball promoters and town boosters could find other solutions. Both towns strove for teams that could win while keeping the connection between team and town tightly knit. Amateur sport provided both a moral imperative and practical approach to

Boys' baseball team, Woodstock area, n.d. Baseball leagues, focused upon shaping boys into manly men and keeping them off local street corners, drew support from middle- and working-class homes alike. In the 1870s and 1880s junior teams far outnumbered senior representative teams in both Ingersoll and Woodstock. (Courtesy of the Woodstock Museum)

sporting success by creating teams that played "for the love of the game" (the amateur ethos) and the "honour of the town or city repre- sented" (urban boosterism). This gave Ingersoll and Woodstock sports leaders opportunities to etch a league of their own, so to speak. Sport sociologists Richard Gruneau and David Whitson suggest that many small communities took the same tack, ensuring that cheering for the home team "meant cheering for teams that were likely composed of family, friends, or at least acquaintances. It could be credibly argued that the quality of the team's performance actually said something about the community that produced it – not only about the skill level of its players, but also about the character of its people."[65] In 1884, the Woodstocks, a newly formed amateur club, presented a strongly word- ed view of the matter: "we have no sympathy whatever with 'profes- sional sport,' as it is now carried on in the interests of speculators and gamblers ... the result of a professional baseball match has no more interest for us than the result of a fight between two ownerless street curs."[66] That year the team, with the local lacrosse and bicycle clubs, formed the WAAA to provide socially oriented amateur competition for locally based sport. When the town of Ingersoll created its own AAA in 1889, baseball figured prominently in its formation.

The AAAs promoted amateur baseball among other sports they believed to be wholesome and respectable and which fed town pride while stimulating town health. To do this they combined shrewd business sense and the authority granted to them from local government to govern local sport, especially on the civic holidays. Local newspapermen, ardent supporters of the amateur movement, shook their finger at those who failed to do their civic duty by supporting their home team. After all, the AAA aimed to project the town's greatness through fostering amateur sport competition. Indeed, the popular connection between team and town led the press sometimes to place blame for defeat upon the shoulders of an errant citizenry, not poor playing. Local clubs needed community support to "eke out a respectable existence."[67] The AAAs helped matters along. When the Woodstocks suffered from poor gate revenues, for example, the WAAA got rigs to take spectators to the games for free.[68] People who questioned the amateur, not-for-profit approach met with counterclaims that they had little faith in the town. In 1889, "a well known Woodstock baseball man" apparently questioned publicly the fiscal viability of an amateur league composed of teams from Galt, Guelph, Stratford, Woodstock, and Ingersoll, making his case "for the simple reason that it would not pay." The editor of the *Sentinel* repudiated the charge forcefully, citing the popular wisdom that "a winning team is always financially successful."[69] The community just needed to get behind their home team and limit the competition to a manageable and presumably winnable level – a fair playing field, so to speak.

Strangely enough, AAA focus upon local sporting talent led the organizations to promote, in a roundabout way, professional baseball, despite whatever rhetoric about the evils of professionalism that came from their mouths. After beginning his baseball career on Woodstock's amateur ball fields, Canadian baseball legend and eventual Canadian Baseball Hall of Fame member Edward 'Tip' O'Neill left town to play with the St Louis Browns, where he led his team to four pennant titles in the late 1880s and held league batting and homerun personal records.[70] Although he gained his fame on professional playing fields, the WAAA and the local press voiced no concern about his moral welfare, choosing instead to see his successes as vindication of the town's amateur approach to sport. His talent, after all, had been cultivated through local amateur teams. O'Neill provided just one of many local success stories. Through the years the town celebrated the professional exploits of other homegrown talents, covering the careers of 'Billy'

Bain Factory Club first nine, Woodstock, 1898. First nine teams from local
factory clubs competed in a semi-professional league against teams from
Toronto, Chatham, Stratford, Detroit, and Hamilton, something that garnered WAAA support, despite the association's rhetoric about the moral
natures of amateur and professional sport. Notice Hamilton-born Bill
"Hippo" Galloway of Afro-Canadian descent in the back row, whose story is
told in William Humber's *Diamonds of the North*. (Courtesy of the Woodstock Museum)

Farrell, Alex Ross, Alf and George Weeks, George Brazer, and Charley
O'Neill. All hailed as "sons" of Ingersoll and Woodstock, they represented their hometowns in faraway places.[71] Town officials and amateur agents conveniently overlooked their playing "inlegitimate sport."
Winning apparently spoke volumes to townspeople in search of community identity.

   In their support of local factory workers' baseball, Ingersoll and
Woodstock's AAAs developed creative ways of tying together community social welfare, booster, and corporate capitalist interests. The connections between these elements were always tenuous and subject to
resistance, but in principle, at least, all parties involved – workers,
AAA promoters, and the owners of local factories – gained something
through baseball. Always a stalwart pastime of workers, local baseball
competition happened along occupational lines just for fun, small bets,

and beer.[72] For workers, writes Bryan Palmer, baseball diamonds created a special world where "the tensions of life dissipated with the excitement of a close match, the clowning of a particular player, or the refreshment of a glass of beer, a keg of which was usually within reach."[73] In Ingersoll, men from Noxon's Agricultural Works challenged teams from Brown's Carriage Works, Hault's and Ellis's furniture companies, and other local factories.[74] In Woodstock, men from Scarff's Carriage Shops, Richards Soap Factory, the Thomas and Karn Organ factories, Thompson's Mills, and other work sites played on Saturday afternoons.[75] By the mid–1880s, the WAAA provided playing fields for these games and for the forty or so members of the Bain Wagon Works and Hay's Furniture Factory clubs, giving local workers rare access to the WAAA facilities denied them through membership restrictions.[76] First nine teams from both clubs competed in a semi-professional league against teams from Toronto, Chatham, Stratford, Detroit, and Hamilton, something that garnered WAAA support, despite the association's rhetoric about the moral natures of amateur and professional sport.

A conjunction of local interests informed this support, creating a tenuous consensus about the importance of baseball to community cultures. Accommodating the workers on its playing fields no doubt carried association rewards. Grounds fees, for example, went into AAA coffers to fund amateur sport, something that also happened in Hamilton, where the Tigers rugby football team played on the local AAA grounds. More importantly, that workers had to rely upon AAA facilities for their games reinforced the WAAA's position as gatekeeper for local sport. By extension, it naturalized the power of the amateur agency. Reliance upon WAAA facilities and ostensible acceptance of the behavioural restrictions imposed upon users of the WAAA grounds appeared to some as evidence of the association's local authority.

The WAAA's alliance with the town's industrial capitalists influenced the situation. As every urban booster knew, town prosperity depended upon industrial prosperity. The tides of fortune for prominent factory owners like J.G. Hay and J.A. Bain had repercussions for the entire local economy, and consequently for the quality of everybody's life. These owners themselves had good, practical reasons for promoting workers' ball clubs. Management considered promoting a loyal, respectful workforce through paternalism to be effective; through baseball, the town's workers could feel a sense of community of their own making.[77] Providing healthy exercise and recreation was supposed to keep them from drink and dissipation. This, in turn, might translate into well-running workplaces, something that some local factories struggled to achieve. In 1896, for example, Woodstock's D.W. Karn

Bain Factory Club members, 1896. By the mid-1880s, the WAAA provided playing fields for the forty or so members of the Bain Wagon Works club, giving local workers rare access to the facilities of an association that had a restricted membership. Except for Sundays and Saturday half-holidays in the summer, working men had few opportunities to get in a good game of base-ball. Notice the little boy in the front row on the far right, presumably a mascot for the club. (Courtesy of the Woodstock Museum)

reported to the Royal Commission on the Liquor Traffic that worker drunkenness robbed his organ factory of at least two months' worth of productivity a year because when men like piano tuners could not make it in to work, their absence affected the entire production line.[78] Perhaps baseball could solve the problem. Company uniforms and team mascots accentuated the ties between workers and their factories, giving them a sense of larger community within the town. Doing so on the community's public facilities – the AAA grounds – reinforced their community roots. Workers' clubs posed attractive possibilities to factory owners and AAA ideologues, entertaining and potentially pacifying workers and promoting self-interest though advertising.[79] By the 1890s, factory leagues provided a solid venue for boosting the town and its interests through baseball.

Nevertheless, it would be naive to assume that workers had no social agenda of their own making. Their ball playing, based upon their own cultural needs, did not aim to fulfill the social agenda of amateur ideologues and industrial capitalists. A clash of cultures, or fundamental

differences between the world-views of amateur ideologues and factory men were readily apparent. Sometimes it revealed itself through
overt and subtle acts of worker resistance to the AAA agenda. Soon
after gaining access to the WAAA facilities, for example, townspeople
could see workers playing Sunday afternoons, which went against Sabbatarian law and AAA practice.[80] Shocked by Sunday activity, the WAAA
hired a constable to keep recalcitrants off its grounds and to arrest Sabbath offenders.[81] Yet, while they battled on this front, the AAA did little about the close connection between workers' sport and alcohol:
despite warnings posted all around the grounds prohibiting alcohol
consumption, kegs of beer remained a part of the workers' game. Neither did they actively monitor wagers between workers' teams,
although in AAA eyes this contravened the essence of respectable sport.

SIX

Lacrosse:
Idealized Middle-Class Sport
for Youth

In June 1871, the neophyte players of Ingersoll's Shamrock lacrosse club devoted themselves to learning their new fast-paced sport. As if out of nowhere, lacrosse arrived in town as the first wave of local baseball mania floundered. The Shamrocks practised assiduously, learning the difficult throwing, catching, and dodging skills needed to play lacrosse. Pleased with their progress, but realizing that they didn't have anyone to play against, they challenged the baseball players from the then-retired Victoria baseball club, taunting them "to awake from their lethargy and take up the lacrosse stick" for a Dominion Day match.[1] Accustomed to having good holiday sport, townspeople relished the chance to get a glimpse of their old heroes and the new sport of lacrosse at the same time. Some three thousand townspeople thronged to the unusual event to witness their town's newest representative team, a good-looking group of young athletes dressed in smart blue and white uniforms donated by local merchants Holmes and Gillespie.

What townspeople saw on the playing field, however, looked more like a bloodbath than respectable sport. Being totally unfamiliar with lacrosse, the more competitively experienced Victorias resorted to violent physical force to vanquish the younger though more highly skilled opponents. This brutish *modus operandi*, labeled "a gross libel upon lacrosse, and an outrage upon common sense," drew criticism from community members and the press for being "cowardly and unmanly."[2] Directing harsh words at the offenders, a writer in the *Chronicle* commented sarcastically, "We would suggest that lacrosse is a game entirely distinct from either football or shinny, and that it has certain rules, the strict observance of which are the very essence of the game."[3] The bewildered Victorias learned this essence at the expense of their competitive pride. They found organized lacrosse quite unlike their more familiar game of baseball, a game for which they had – briefly –

won the Silver Ball and Canadian championship. Many people – males and females alike – knew the popular childhood game of baseball well, having experienced it as players or spectators. Lacrosse, however, seemed to appear out of the blue, carried along on the momentum of baseball mania stirred up by sports reformers and urban boosters. Picking up where baseball left off, lacrosse captivated the hearts of local sporting enthusiasts in both towns eager to be entertained through sport: as the *Sentinel* observed, "with the loss of the late lamented Silver Ball lacrosse seems to be favoured game this season."[4] That lacrosse had none of the stigma associated with cricket helped its appeal to urban boosters and sport reformers alike.

Despite its lengthy tradition in North American Indian religion, tradition, and society, lacrosse's organized form appeared in Ingersoll and Woodstock as a sport without a past.[5] Montreal sportsman Dr W. George Beers virtually reinvented and codified the traditional Indian game, popularizing it through his treatise *Lacrosse the National Game of Canada* (1869). His sport carried a specific social agenda: to cultivate Canadian nationalism, manliness, and respectability in male youth, and to keep the leisure activities of males in check, so to speak.[6] With such idealistic trappings, lacrosse quickly found popularity in Ingersoll, Woodstock, and other Canadian towns and cities. Due to its newness, sport reformers considered it a socially clean and morally pure sport, having none of the "debasing accompaniments, the bar room association" that other sports with roots in popular social traditions possessed.[7] In 1871, just as local sport reformers introduced it to the townspeople of Ingersoll and Woodstock, lacrosse had its own governing body, the National Lacrosse Association (NLA), to provide rules and codes of behaviour governing the structural, strategic, and moral aspects of the game.[8] The NLA worked to ensure that *its* way of playing the game would become *the* way.

People in Ingersoll and Woodstock adopted the sport in ways that built upon the growing local connection between team and town. Town boosters who sought locally feasible ways in which to play sport considered lacrosse a respectable sport that enhanced the physical and moral health of local male youth; honourable pursuits like lacrosse ultimately turned boys into men. The repeated themes of boyish sport and young manhood, echoed in early writings on lacrosse, became central to its promotion locally and nationally.[9] Locally, social and sport reformers held great concerns over the problem of how male youth should spend their leisure time. With high school enrolments increasing, and with a decline in the apprenticeship system, middle-class boys and youth depended upon their families for longer periods than before.[10] By the turn of the century, 80 to 90 per cent of five- to six-teen-year-olds in Ingersoll and Woodstock attended school 200 days a year.[11] They increasingly came under female scrutiny – both in schools and in the home – prompting some social observers to fear for the loss of male role models. Under female influences, would local male youth become more feminine?[12]

Historians David Howell, Peter Lindsay, and David MacLeod point out the intricacies of the 'young boy problem' of the day. Social critics of the times argued that, unchecked, this situation would cause males to become physically weak and therefore powerless and unmanly.[13] Keenly concerned about this, parents and social reformers sought appropriate spare-time activities to occupy male youth, ones that, as Steven Riess observes, defined manliness and created ways to achieve it.[14] Organized lacrosse aimed to expose young males to respectable versions of masculinity while teaching them the importance of physical activity for their physical and spiritual health in an increasingly seden-tary world. George Beers offered a list of those who would do well to pick up a lacrosse stick – socialites, sissies, and unmanly men: "Fellows who 'spree,' who make syphons [sic] of their esophagi, and who can-not make better use of their leisure than to suck mint juleps through straws, those model specimens of propriety who think a man on the road to perdition unless he is always reading good books, and making himself a bore to his friends by stale, hypocritical conversation. Those nice young men in black broadcloth who never can take a joke, [and] those whining schoolboys who creep unwillingly to school."[15] All of them would do well to take up lacrosse.

Keeping local crime rates down and keeping youth off the streets motivated Ingersoll and Woodstock community boosters to promote organized lacrosse for local boys. Truancy and street crime in the towns paled by comparison with the province's large cities, yet many townspeople knew well that these problems affected local males; as one Ingersoll social observer cried, "the wheels of our social mecha-nism are out of order!"[16] Local newspapers reported sensational tales from the cities, where the young boy problem became a fixture.[17] But they didn't just happen far away in big cities: local people saw loafers hanging around, haunting street corners on evenings and, worse, on Sundays. These "dirty wretches" insulted passersby, spitting out tobac-co juice and obscenities.[18] Where did people like this come from? The local press fingered the toughs as those living near the railway tracks on the north side of town, where, not coincidentally, many workers and their families lived. Asked by the Commission Appointed to Enquire into the Prison and Reformatory System about potential cures for such idleness, Woodstock's gaoler offered a simple solution: "I would keep children employed at something or other," he proclaimed, and give them "good honest play, a game of lacrosse or similar amusement."[19] Woodstock's chief constable, T.W. McKee, held the nickname "Tzar of the Beavers Club" for his efforts to keep boys suitably occupied and on the right path.[20]

Lynne Marks argues cogently in her book *Revivals and Roller Rinks* that late nineteenth-century Protestant ministers in small-town Ontario did what they could to promote rational recreation, using the mostly male worlds of leisure and associational life to accomplish this aim; however, their social agenda found resistance on several fronts.[21] Sermons given in Ingersoll and Woodstock repeatedly stressed the relationship between manliness and male leisure. Their titles reveal local preoccupations: "How Does Physical Welfare Affect Moral Conduct?," "Young Man's Leisure," "Where Do You Spend Your Time?," "True Manhood," and "A Manly Man."[22] Marks shows that oftentimes most young men weren't in church to hear them.[23] Providing reprints of sermons that could be clipped out of local newspapers gave clergymen, social reformers, teachers, and parents another opportunity to impress important messages upon youth. Aiming squarely at the community's young men in 1872, Ingersoll's Reverend P. Wright claimed that local boys lacked a conception of true manhood, a "fruitful source of failures in young men."[24] Yet, with a grasp of this idea, he assured all who heeded his words, "evil has no chances for young men." Strength and courage needed to be suitably controlled for a lad to be considered manly. Public places like lacrosse playing fields and the streets, as well as more private spheres such as the home, provided opportunities to display this control. Sermons reminded Ingersoll boys of their social responsibility to females: "Don't make a great bluster and be rough and hard, thinking to be manly. Be a little quiet in the house, gentle with your little sisters, and not tiring mother with a great deal of noise ... When your work is over and it is the right time for sport kick up your heels and have lots of fun outdoors."[25]

Even the most private matters regarding male sexuality needed suitable control, according to sermons from local clergymen. In a sermon given to the Brantford YMCA, Woodstock's Reverend Dr Nichol warned boys against the evils lurking in the hearts and bodies of young males. He spoke "very strongly against practices that were destroying the manhood of thousands and supplying our insane asylums with occupants."[26] This thinly veiled reference to masturbation, popularly known as the "curse of Onan" or "the secret vice," doubtless shocked many. By the turn of the century, however, the notion that healthy physical activity expended vital energy in morally appropriate ways became a standard claim for advocates of sexual science as well as

promoters of youth sport, who worked to create an "athlete of conti-
nence, not coitus, continuously testing his manliness in the fires of self-
denial."[27]

Local sport promoters knew well that at its outset lacrosse superbly
embodied the idea that games build character, a key ingredient in muscular Christianity.[28] Through lacrosse they aimed to instill the valued
character traits such as teamwork, self-sacrifice, courage, manliness,
and achievement that they believed could be transferred from playing
fields to other, real-life situations. These high motives for the sport distinguished it from rowdy, idle diversions, making it seem a morally
uplifting activity, an able contender against the social upheavals that
plagued small towns changing because of their urban and industrial
growth.[29]

The National Lacrosse Association's premier award for amateur
competition, the Claxton Flags, was donated by a charter member and
sometime president of North America's first Young Men's Christian
Association.[30] Montreal millionaire, philanthropist, and social
reformer James T. Claxton's intent for the flags, valued at $250, aimed
to foster "clean, amateur athletics amongst the youth of Canada."[31]
This occurred long before the YMCA became known chiefly as a sports
institution.[32] The flags, like Woodstock's Silver Ball baseball trophy,
awarded winners in challenge competition. Nevertheless, while Woodstock's Silver Ball rules laid out only the technical rules for baseball
matches, the Claxton Flags lacrosse competition had a deep moral
imperative written into its codified rules. Soon after Woodstonian amateur sport promoters created a lacrosse club locally, the town's Ladies
Benevolent Society graced the Beavers with their own lacrosse pennant,
an impressive piece painstakingly made by local women, "worked in
gold, surmounted by a Beaver, with *BLC* embroidered underneath."[33]
Like the Claxton Flags, it reminded people of the Beaver club's social
and moral aspirations.

Lacrosse playing rules kept sharply focused on the moral intent
behind the sport's organization. They demanded that players develop a
rational, educated strength, with the idea of 'right action' restricting
physical and social play.[34] The key to this approach rested in the stren-
uous physical exertion bordering on combat required by the sport,
coupled with its potential for violence. Twenty players on the field,
sticks in hand, needed to be careful when charging after a single ball.
The Ingersoll Victorias' approach and the reaction it provoked at that
Dominion Day match in 1871 showed that players had to downplay
brute force to avoid the kind of physicality that scraped bodies and
broke bones. On the game's scientific approach, George Beers wrote,
"that there is a science in the game is proved by the fact that many

throws, dodges, checks, etc., are explained by fixed principles, from which no one can deter and be successful."[35] Still, physics alone did not make for good lacrosse; the science also stressed the concomitant development of social and sports skills on the playing field. According to such beliefs, a sense of fair play needed to rule the day. Only unmanly men turned to brute force to vanquish their opponents.

Ingersoll and Woodstock's organized clubs reinforced the social and moral learning experiences believed to be inherent in the game. To accomplish this they built what Beers called a sporting freemasonry, a term aptly intended to appeal to his middle-class male audience.[36] Both masculine enclaves, lacrosse and nineteenth-century freemasonry alike emphasized camaraderie, an esoteric body of knowledge, and rituals of play and costume. Both boasted sub-communities within national and provincial networks. To cultivate this freemasonry Beers admonished lacrosse players everywhere to "learn by heart and practice in conscience that beautiful verse of Thackeray's": "Who misses or who wins the prize, / Go, lose or conquer as you can, / But if you fail, or if you rise / Be each, pray God, a gentleman."[37]

The spirit of gentlemanliness encouraged club members to express their sense of honourable camaraderie.[38] Woodstock's Beavers did this in 1879 when they honoured their club secretary, local merchant Edward W. Nesbitt, on the eve of his wedding. They presented him with an exquisite silver tea service along with a beautiful parchment scroll at a testimonial dinner. Elaborately detailed in gold, the scroll's inscription speaks volumes about the club's social and moral goals for training young males for success in sport and life:

We feel it is no empty boast when we say that it is an honour to belong to the *Beaver Lacrosse Club* of Woodstock. The Young men who organized this Club nine years ago have retired and now occupy positions of trust and honour in our community leaving their places in the Club to be filled by other and younger men who bid fair to follow in the footsteps of their predecessors. At home and abroad the name of the *Beaver Lacrosse Club* has been and is now a synonym of honesty, uprightness, and fair dealing. Taking defeat in the same good natured and gentlemanly manner that they have scored victories, and on all occasions, recognizing the golden rule, *To do to others as they wished to be done by.*[39]

Through lacrosse clubs, middle-class men like Nesbitt and other community members in positions of trust and honour carried out a specific social agenda. They believed that they could lead local male youth to develop respectable values that would help them along life's journey and that the success of local lacrosse teams would be the town's success as well. Nesbitt would carry on his crusade for years to come, eventually taking the helm of the Canadian Lacrosse Association, a high accomplishment for someone from small-town Ontario.

Men of similar social and economic backgrounds masterminded this agenda for lacrosse in Ingersoll and Woodstock. Of the seventy-two men governing local amateur clubs in the towns between 1871 and 1890, sixty-nine had Protestant religious affiliations, even though Roman Catholics comprised as much as one-third of the local populations. As with others involved in sport reform, these men's occupational backgrounds united them and differentiated them from other local males. All but five of the lacrosse club organizers held non-manual occupations, working in local banks, law offices, stores, publishing offices, and the like, where roughly only one-quarter of the jobs in town could be found. Only five working men – skilled ones at that – governed local lacrosse clubs, even though they came from the largest occupational sector, one-half of all local occupations, recorded on local manuscript censuses. Although unskilled workers accounted for another one-quarter of the local workforce, none could be found amongst lacrosse organizers. The local voluntary association and political involvement of lacrosse club organizers also provide highly suggestive glimpses into the world-views shared by these socially prominent local men. Clearly men on the go, one in every three lacrosse organizers at some time sat on town council, while one in six belonged to the board of trade.

While club organizers possessed remarkably similar social backgrounds, club members held diverse ones. This suggests cooperation, presumably based in consent, from community members from other social groups. Junior lacrosse clubs far outnumbered senior, representative ones, as in baseball.[40] Between 1880 and 1889, three-quarters of 147 club lacrosse members in Ingersoll and Woodstock fell between the ages of fifteen and twenty-one years, where just 15 per cent of the local populations came from. As with baseball, lacrosse players came from a broader social base than did Woodstock's old cricket club did. Sons of skilled manual workers played beside those of non-manual workers, a strategy that Gillian Poulter points out helped transmit desired values through a more socially diverse population.[41] Lacrosse promoters, focused upon shaping these boys into manly men, drew male youth from middle- and working-class homes alike.

Baseball could not be beat as an activity rooted in popular culture, yet, as an activity geared toward youth as earnestly designed by sport reformers, nothing beat lacrosse, in its heyday *the* game of boys and young men locally. Club leadership positions brought public approval and recognition to young males: "The boys who are envied are the

Dufferin lacrosse club, Ingersoll, n.d. Local senior lacrosse clubs, like Ingersoll's Dufferins, a charter member of the IAAA, lasted for decades. Its members competed in regional divisions of senior and intermediate play in the
National Lacrosse Association and, after 1887, in the newly formed Canadian Lacrosse Association. (Courtesy of the Ingersoll Cheese Factory Museum)

captains of the lacrosse teams," praised a writer in the *Sentinel*.[42] Field
captains, chosen on their own merit, held an office that was "no
sinecure."[43] Junior clubs played matches against other teams in town.
With its own national association, lacrosse began locally within an
already established non-local organized sport framework, with rules
already codified and a national governing body already in place. A
writer in the *Chronicle* once opined of this quintessentially organized
sport, "no one who ever heard of lacrosse would suppose for a
moment that it could exist without a head to govern it, to form rules,
etc. There is not in Canada one club that could really be called a
lacrosse club that does not belong to some one of the associations."[44]
NLA rules stipulated that member clubs could not compete against non-
members, closing the ranks of competition by design and working to
control the sport's development, presumably to keep a tight reign on its
moral imperative and behavioural restrictions laid out in club constitutions and bylaws. While baseball held a resilient tradition in the

informal culture of shop and factory, not to mention the culture of children, the game of lacrosse created by sport reformers seemed to be a sport without a past, holding no such roots for the first generation of local boys who played the game in the 1870s.

If one looks at the well-publicized intermediate and senior divisions of play where teams represented the town, however, one can see reform ideals falling quite short of their mark. Local senior lacrosse clubs, like Ingersoll's Dufferins and Woodstock's Beavers, both charter members of their local AAAS, lasted for decades. The two competed in regional divisions of senior and intermediate play in the NLA and, after 1887, in the newly formed Canadian Lacrosse Association (CLA).[45] As in baseball, representative inter urban lacrosse competition provided a way in which the two communities could puff themselves up and bring glory to the hometown – a serious business indeed. To perfect their game, Woodstock's players trained carefully, restricting their diet and practising three times a week at the ungodly hour of 6 am. Neighbours from the village of Norwich poked fun at their earnestness and the intensity of their regimen: "they are already feeding on dried beef and drinking milk and raw eggs for their 'wind.' We hardly think that they need any extra supply of that commodity."[46]

As in baseball, community members ardently supported winning teams. In 1888 Ingersoll's citizenry petitioned the mayor to declare a half-holiday to watch the Dufferins' match for the Southern District championship.[47] In 1901, for Woodstock's birth as a city, the *Sentinel-Review's* Inaugural Edition reflected upon that town's sporting past, proclaiming that the town's Beavers club had given Woodstock "an enviable reputation in the realm of sport."[48] The characteristic Woodstonian drive and determination that had made the team such a success, it argued, also led to Woodstock's rise to city status. There, as in other small communities throughout Canada, team uniforms, symbols of order and respectability, and team names reinforced hometown ties, providing myth-makers with opportunities to tell stories about themselves and their reality.[49] To them, lacrosse fields provided symbolic battlegrounds.

Community organizations, mayors, local professional men and merchants, families, and friends all found ways to support their town's team. Hoping to mould a winning team, they offered rewards for players' social and sport skills. Of course, rewards would be needless if players always behaved in desired ways. In 1871, following the tradition established by local baseball teams, Ingersoll citizens banded together to offer a $10 prize for the best team in the local Dominion Day match; however, symbolic prizes and rewards – some opulent, some simply sentimental in nature – displaced cash prizes soon thereafter.[50] The prominent local jeweller, H. Richardson, for example, offered a gold pencil prize for the Dufferin benefit garden party, while a local firm, Mason and Company, handed out a gold-lined silver cup for a throwing competition.[51] In 1888, James Vance, the local barrister and town councillor who became president of both the IAAA and Dufferin lacrosse club as well as the CLA, commissioned a gold medal to award a running competition.[52] Woodstonians also did their share of rewarding the efforts of local lacrosse players. In 1874, Dr Turquand, a well-known civic leader, temperance man, and sometime mayor, donated a silver cup for the best all-round local player.[53] A few years later, local jeweller Samuel Woodroofe, an active sport promoter of the local bicycle and football clubs and executive member of the WAAA, handed out a silver medal for a running competition between club members. A shrewd businessman, he placed the medal in his store window for a week, calling attention to the team while bringing curious customers into his store.[54] Local grocer E.W. Nesbitt, whose impending wedding had prompted the Beavers to throw him a testimonial dinner, also got into the act of rewarding local youth for their effort and expertise on local lacrosse fields. A sometime president of both the WAAA and the CLA, he gave a diamond pin for the best all-round player who attended practices punctually.[55]

The town and its lacrosse team had a well-cultivated connection. From the early 1870s on, club and holiday organizers in both towns featured lacrosse matches for their Dominion Day celebrations some nineteen times between them over a span of twenty years. Thousands of holiday-goers flocked to view these sport spectacles and the other holiday events – noontime parades, speeches from local dignitaries, track and field events, and community picnics. The profits made from ten-cent admission fees to holiday matches alone funded a club's entire season. At a time when Wild West shows were all the rage elsewhere, Woodstock's clubs, like clubs from Montreal and Toronto, arranged holiday exhibition matches against Native Indian teams from nearby reserves.[56] The matches sparked the interest of George Gray, an Ingersoll schoolteacher, who saw two of them in Woodstock and recorded them in his diary.[57] Unfortunately, Gray didn't describe the spectacles that followed the matches in any detail, something that newspaper reports of the time suggest consisted of the Indians dancing a "war dance" to the beat of ceremonial drums. Face-painted, wearing headdresses and other ethnic garb, they played a tightly choreographed role, but whatever they themselves thought of that role, or even who had gotten the spectacle up, remains to be discovered. While Native Indian teams never visited Ingersoll, local people still went along with the theme, dressing up as Indians for their

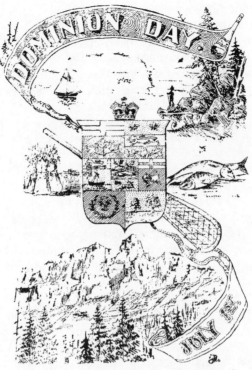

Dominion Day lacrosse sketch, 1893. The *Sentinel-Review's* Dominion Day tribute shows a crest with symbols for each province surrounded by scenes of the Canadian wilderness (including a Native Indian on a rocky shore) and a well-placed lacrosse stick lying across it, suggesting that lacrosse, geography, and climate together united the nation. (*Sentinel-Review* 1 July 1893)

Dominion Day nighttime torchlight procession in 1879.[58] Lacrosse propagandists and local civic leaders used the extravaganzas and their images to juxtapose symbolically and celebrate what they viewed Canada *had been* against what it *had become*. The productions fortified their pride in their locality and in the Canadian nation in a way that evoked images of the sport's distant origins in Native culture, a theme also highlighted in the 1876 and 1883 Canadian lacrosse tours to Britain.[59] In 1893 a sketch published in the *Sentinel-Review's* Dominion Day tribute showed a crest with symbols for each province surrounded by scenes of the Canadian wilderness (including a Native Indian standing on a rocky shore) and a well-placed lacrosse stick lying across it, suggesting that lacrosse, geography, and climate together united the nation.[60]

While local sanctioning came from middle-class community leaders, lacrosse clubs received substantial grassroots support from local fans. Intent upon making team victories their own, fans were often just way too boisterous, something that town leaders and lacrosse organizers abhorred. This residual element of rowdiness could be found within the connection between team and town that capitalist boosterism fostered. With its tremendous popularity in the late 1870s and 1880s, and with the increasing associations between lacrosse teams and the corporate urban community, the gap between what sport reformers hoped to achieve through lacrosse and what actually happened widened significantly.[61] Pressures for victory, coupled with intense fan and player identifications with the home team, undermined reformers' efforts.[62] So, too, did greater player commitment to winning for the glory of the team and the honour of the town. An earnestness to win at times displaced earnest people's desire for self- and social improvement.

Despite prohibitions, newspapers frequently reported money won and lost on the games, showing that fans loved to bet on the representative matches of their hometown team.[63] In 1879, Simcoe's team and their backers arrived for a match in Woodstock "supplied with heaps of wealth" that Beaver supporters "readily took up."[64] As had happened in local baseball, only short steps separated betting from game fixing and under-the-table payments to amateur players. In July 1887 the Brantford Brants courted Beaver players Kennedy, Kelly, and Laird with offers of jobs, guaranteeing a sizable $20 per week playing season salary.[65] Certain Brantford fans also reportedly offered Beaver player and Patterson Factory worker Ed Kennedy $20 to throw a game.[66] A writer for the *Sentinel* decried the action, praising Kennedy's apparent refusal to take part in it and claiming, "this is the sort of thing that is ruining lacrosse, it is the betting spirit that leads to such attempts at fraud. Unless betting and the influence of betting men is stamped out, amateur lacrosse is dead – in fact it don't deserve to live."[67]

Sport reformers' efforts to clean up betting and other bad behaviours at local lacrosse playing fields just didn't seem to work. Obviously, many resisted them. Some flatly refused to abide by the behavioural regulations of amateur clubs at the town's athletic grounds. Others refused to participate in the community event, finding other spots, like the cemetery hill overlooking the WAAA grounds, where they could watch the performances free.[68]

Ingersoll and Woodstock lacrosse organizers also had a hard time constraining other forms of resistance, like the violence that accompanied senior level matches, something that was nothing new, as historians Alan Metcalfe and Barbara Pinto show about Shamrock team competition around the same time in Montreal.[69] Like hockey today, the sport bred player violence during emotion-packed competition. Ironically, this enhanced the sport's appeal to those inclined that way. During one visit to Ingersoll in 1888, for example, heavily charged competition put Woodstock players under attack.[70] During the match – refereed by what the Woodstock press called "daisy umpires" – one Woodstock player body-checked his opponent and sent him flying. Hundreds of outraged Ingersoll fans charged the field, mobbing him and his teammates. The mêlée lasted fifteen minutes. After the field cleared and play recommenced, one obscenity-screaming spectator chased down a rough Woodstock player and, catching him by the throat, thrashed him. Strangely enough, the rowdy spectator needing to be restrained happened to be the town's police chief.

Lovers of the sport throughout southwestern Ontario knew how playing field antics led to antipathies between the two towns. Commenting on this state of affairs, the Embro *Courier* pointed a harsh finger at overzealous fans who took the game personally, with the connection between team and town going too far: "if the spectators of these two towns would keep quiet and not interfere so, much of the bad feeling between the boys would die out."[71] The Tillsonburg *Liberal* similarly blamed local spectators, who, it instructed, should "keep their mouths shut and not interfere with the players disputes which occur on the field."[72] A reporter from Ingersoll's *Chronicle* responded to the indictment, acknowledging the displaced rowdiness inherent in intense inter urban competition: "if you expect the spectators in rival towns to keep quiet you make a great big mistake."[73] With fans "howling like maniacs," lacrosse competition, encouraged by boosterism, undercut images of respectability in the sport.[74] While rowdiness occurred often in the stands, rather than at the centre of public display, sport reformers nevertheless had a hard time with its high visibility.

Local newspapers often stepped into the battle, admonishing locals to act in a gentlemanly, respectable way. Yet members of the press, too, exhibited elements of displaced rowdyism. After a riotous Woodstock match, a writer in the *Chronicle* suggested, "had the spectators stepped in and hammered some of them and maimed them for life the punishment would be no less than they deserve."[75] This situation, although testifying to lacrosse's immense popularity as a form of action-packed competition and entertainment, undercut the reforming of local sport. With its rising popularity and its intricate ties to urban boosterism, lacrosse emerged by the turn of the century as an antithesis to the vision of Canadian youth and sport first expounded by middle-class sport reformers. As the gap between ideation and behaviour widened, it clearly did not live up to expectations as a truly national, respectable game that could unite social groups under the leadership of a small, select group of local men.

SEVEN

A Respectable Man's World:
Amateurism and Local Culture

In 1901, the editor of the *Toronto Telegram* devoted a column to lambasting Woodstock for its hypocrisy over importing formerly professional hockey players to represent the town on its amateur team. This happened after a Stratford team, full of grievance after losing to the heavily stacked Woodstonian team, complained to the Ontario Hockey Association. In its coverage of the incident, the paper pointed to the town's history of letting its amateur ideals lapse in the face of fierce sporting competition. It called for Woodstonian pride in its tradition of amateur sport to keep it on its straight and narrow path. Woodstock, it noted, "is pledged by all of its sporting traditions to the theory that a representative team should have its roots in the enthusiasm of the local boys who play the game. It was this theory that made Woodstock a giant in baseball. It was the other theory that made Woodstock a joke in lacrosse ... Woodstock people should sit calmly down and ask themselves whether the hockey game is worth the candle if Cornwall importations are to crowd the home-grown players off the ice."[1]

While the *Telegram* showed the practice of importing ringers to be inherently unfair to other communities in the league, the crux of its case lay upon the effect that the practice had upon Woodstonian youth, while undermining the idea of representativeness espoused by its local amateur sports promoters: "Woodstock's greatest injustice was to the boys of its own town. These boys should be encouraged to play hockey by the certainty that the rest of them will get a chance to show in the colours of their home team. They can have no such chance if the Woodstock team is to be made up of winter boarders from Cornwall."[2] These sentiments expressed dissatisfaction with developments found in amateur representative teams everywhere. Many small cities, towns, and villages throughout the country experienced the same dilemma as they strove to cultivate their own niche in the developing inter urban amateur competitive leagues from which representative hometown teams grew. Some three decades earlier, a disgruntled George Sleeman had lamented over the fate of his Guelph Maple Leafs, stating, "Until baseball is played in Canada as it used to be, *for the love of the game and the honour of the town or city represented*, it never will be a success."[3]

But what precisely did these appeals to "honour" and "representation" mean? From the 1860s until the closing years of the century, local representative sport was circumscribed by the amateur tenet that players who played for the love of the game rather than for pecuniary profit somehow more legitimately represented their urban community. A player's moral standing, as implied in the muscular Christian principles of amateurism, indicated the relative social and moral health of the town overall. Town officials and citizens alike found symbolic victories through representative sport team victories. If the team did not win, players and townspeople could take consolation in the spirit and manner that it took its defeat. You could lose a game and still be a winner. Or could you? Judging by some of the behaviours surrounding amateur competition in Ingersoll and Woodstock, this may have been too tall a task for ardent organizers, players, fans, and urban boosters.

The claims of representativeness quite simply thus beg the questions 'whose representative?' and 'what is being represented?' There can be no doubt regarding the first. In instance after instance, middle-class men and their sons in both towns dominated their civic holiday committees and organized amateur sports governance. They also dominated the playing fields of local representative teams, using their sport to buttress their vision of reality and express themselves as a distinct local social group. They also wanted to clean up what they viewed as problematic leisure practices associated with working-class culture. Yet unskilled workers really did not exist in their amateur sporting world, save, perhaps, as spectators. Working men's leisure had already been checked primarily through structural constraints, not middle-class control. The case is less clear about the exclusion of Roman Catholics.

Their exclusion of women, however, is more straightforward. Whereas informal communal activities like those found on early civic holidays typically included gender-specific activities for both males and females, organized amateur urban sport clubs were created by and for males.[4] This emulated the distinction between the public and private spheres of life that culturally bound male and female activities. Organized sport reinforced and emphasized cultural notions of masculinity by inculcating and publicly displaying "manly" qualities – physical courage, strength, stamina, will power, and self-control.[5] Since these qualities stood as being antithetical to femininity, organized sports erected an effective philosophical barrier against female participation, which reinforced their subordination to males.[6] Biological arguments posed by medical men predicated upon women's supposed physical frailty, like fears that playing sport would make women sterile or masculine, supported this barrier, giving scientific support to the notion of their proper sphere. Only after the First World War did females begin to gain a public role in sport outside the confines of schools.[7] Before then they participated sporadically, depending upon circumstances surrounding the activities. Involvement in tennis and cycling, for example, challenged existing conventions and helped somewhat to emancipate local females. But as has been seen, even if they managed to make their way onto the public forum of civic holiday parades riding bicycles, females in Ingersoll and Woodstock treaded carefully when they stepped onto male cultural terrain.

The answer to the question 'what is being represented?' lay at the crux of this situation. Organized amateur sport represented many things, for example, gender territory and culturally appropriate spheres of action for males and females, as well as respectable cultural roles for men and women. It also represented the class-based and highly discriminatory values of an emerging dominant system. Despite the amateur code's meritocratic illusion (i.e., the suggestion that sporting grounds offered a special space for equality of opportunity and equality of the outcome to occur), and contrary to how the IAAA and WAAA presented themselves as community representatives, the AAAs were undeniably 'pets of a class.' The notion that teams and their players could somehow represent the urban community was just another such 'pet.' As the English aristocracy in an earlier era had used their anti-utilitarian approach to sport to assert and perpetuate their own class identity, so did the middle class use representative amateur sport in the late nineteenth century. Both groups used certain sports – and particular approaches to playing the game – to express their own value system. Amateurism helped create and propel a middle-class culture as it evolved through time, emphasizing things that expressed its self-consciousness as a distinct social formation. Representative amateur sport repeated the themes found in other types of middle-class fraternal and voluntary organizations – themes of respectability, self-improvement, temperance, and piety.

Why so much effort for something as 'simple' as sport? Like any other aspect of culture, sport had within it serious stuff – something that Marshall McLuhan observed about professional baseball in the early 1950s.[8] But, much more than that, it was and is, in the words of historian Bruce Kidd, a contested social territory.[9] This fact is readily apparent in the half-century worth of dramatic changes that occurred to the sporting culture of Ingersoll and Woodstock. After industrialism created for large segments of the population the structured time necessary to the organization of regularized sporting competition, and from the moment that mid-century transportation improvements broke down the boundaries of locality and inland isolation, sport in both Ingersoll and Woodstock, like many other places in the province, reared its head as a social issue of pressing local concern. Questions of idle diversion or rational recreation, the rowdy or the respectable, were key as those who desired social power shaped a world of sport that reflected their particular world-view. Negotiations for this social power happened locally.

Apparently certain differences in local social practices resulting from Ingersoll and Woodstock's different early settlement histories lingered and affected the local social construction of sport for some time. As late as the 1870s parts of Woodstock's old aristocratic enclave still lingered, even though the retired officer elite was long gone. No recognizable group of Ingersoll inhabitants, by contrast, asserted such illusions of grandeur. Did the rising class of middle-class men in Woodstock have to push harder to establish themselves? Or were they given a 'hand up' in a process of accommodation, being introduced to wider circles of power? Both views might help explain Woodstock's decided lead in adopting sporting innovation throughout the latter part of the century. The evidence provided by the communities suggests this. In league formation, for example, Woodstock led other places in the region. In 1864, local baseball men inspired and hosted the organization of the Canadian Association of Baseball Players. They created the Silver Ball award and the Woodstock rules that governed inter urban competition throughout the province for a dozen years. After the town was displaced by Guelph in senior level competition, it turned toward cultivating junior level competition, creating in 1877 a junior baseball league for southwestern Ontario at the Royal Hotel – the place where over a dozen years earlier Ontario's organized inter urban competition had been born. By the early 1880s, John Forbes' Commercial Hotel hosted the founding of a provincial level trotting and turf association; the hotel also, when under the proprietorship of Charley Pyne, became a local headquarters for the Canadian Wheelmen's Association.

Beyond this, Woodstonians tended to be much more heavily involved in provincial- and national-level sport governing bodies than Ingersoll sportsmen. Whether, in truth, the WAAA had been the second amateur athletic association created in Canada as it claimed cannot be ascertained. Certainly it stood as one of the earliest in the province. The IAAA's creation, in 1889, followed non-local developments, and only Michael Walsh, 1886 vice-president of the Western Ontario Lawn Tennis Association, and C.L. Vance, 1891 president of the Canadian Lacrosse Association, appear to have stood at the helm of national or regional associations. Both of these men began their term in office as second in command to a Woodstonian. By contrast, the names of Woodstonians frequently graced the executives of non-local sport agencies. In 1864, C.L. Wood was the first president of the Canadian Association of Base Ball Players. In 1886, Judge Finkle sat as the first president of the Western Ontario Lawn Tennis Association, while the next year his WAAA colleague, W.A. Karn, held the presidency of the Canadian Wheelmen's Association. Samuel Woodroofe and Andrew Pattullo held the same office years later. E.W. Nesbitt presided over the Canadian Lacrosse Association in 1889, while Frank Hyde led the Ontario Hockey Association in 1901 – the very time that Woodstock was being lambasted for importing former professional players to play for its hometown team. Woodstock's hosting of what they considered to be national-level championships in baseball (the Silver Ball), horseracing (the Queen's Plate), and cycling (the CWA championship), while Ingersoll hosted none shows how much more connected the Woodstonians were to other men in non-local agencies.

Woodstock thus set its sights on high goals in sport; this, however, did not catapult the town outside the orbit of its not-so-terribly-high status in the urban hierarchy. Despite its visions of itself as "the Industrial City" and its being the seat of county government, Woodstock held much more in common with its rival Ingersoll than it did with large cities like Toronto or Montreal – something revealed when the WAAA's prominent role occupied in local civic holidays is considered. While some social distance between WAAA members and other local people was nevertheless ever-present, it was smaller by comparison than the social distance between MAAA members and the people excluded from its prestigious businessmen's club. The self-identification of local AAAs in Ingersoll and Woodstock with their communities speaks to their strong grassroots involvement in community life.

Contrary to the commonly held perception that national-level sport regulatory agencies, which grew out of the prestigious and powerful sporting clubs in Toronto and Montreal, carried considerable power at the expense of other, smaller areas, the Ingersoll and Woodstock cases suggest that local self-interest played a strong role in shaping the activities of the lesser AAAs. Woodstock, for example, chose to affiliate with the Amateur Athletic Association of Canada only when one of the town's representative athletes needed reinstatement. The large cities may have wielded considerable power nationally, but local men negotiated their power locally; it took merely the word of prominent local

AAA men for Woodstock's Billy Farrell to be reinstated as an amateur athlete.

The ascendancy of amateurism in Ingersoll and Woodstock came from its ties with urban boosterism and its place in local civic celebrations. Both local cases produced essentially the same result: a new social order strove to equate the town's interests with that of their own. Middle-class amateur promoters pursued ways to create a class culture while making themselves appear natural social leaders locally. In the final analysis, however, their efforts created neither simple nor straightforward results. Although the AAAs managed to order and structure civic holiday sports (encoded with their carefully crafted messages of respectability), they failed to obliterate totally the rowdiness found in local sport and society, or to control all meanings associated with sport competition. Nor could they. Those who used cemetery hillsides as spectator stands, or who played in the streets, of course, were expressing only one type of opposition. Other forms abounded, apparent for example in local workers' August holiday sports, where local men and their families enjoyed dog-racing, catch-as-catch-can wrestling, and traditional games of inversion. Opposition is also seen in the resilient legacy of spectator gambling and betting on inter urban matches, and in the frequency with which cockfights and other blood sports garnered the attention of the local press – despite its own protestations of the very illegality of the contests. Some local people quite simply ignored AAA rules governing playing fields that told people when and how they could play. The repeated exhortations of reformers about organized amateur sport being a cure-all for the ills of a society simply point out that the rosy-coloured world of respectability did not exist as they would have liked to have had it. Even so, as the case of factory baseball players using AAA grounds for professional competition shows, the AAA's control of local athletic facilities reinforced an illusion that they controlled local sport. Workers, like others, at times deferred to this authority to achieve their own ends, while town sanctioning of AAA-run holidays reinforced the illusion.

If the mechanisms involved in the amateur ascendancy happened similarly in both towns, so came similar results. Their very reliance upon the ideology of amateurism, an ideology whose basic premise denied the ultimate importance of victory (that is, sport was a means to a character-building end and not an end in itself, and the social and moral lessons of sport were somehow more important than winning itself), created a tremendous paradox for local sport. If the social construction of local sport emphasized the notion that sports teams represented the town and that playing field victories became, in effect, the town's victory, then the moral underpinnings of the amateur code would be constantly at issue as towns and their teams pursued increasingly greater competition and victories. On the one hand, the endorsement of amateurism (and opposition to rowdyism, gaming, drinking, and professionalism) expressed a desire for social order and reform under middle-class leadership. On the other hand, middle-class capitalistic competitiveness, for themselves, their corporate class, and also for their town, caused civic leaders to ally representative sport with urban boosterism. This would be the most serious threat to middle-class amateurism: the enemy from within, based upon boosterism. In Ingersoll and Woodstock, the notions of "love of the game" and "the honour of the town or city represented" inherent in the rise of representative amateur team sports in themselves represented the views of only a handful of men whose logic was at times ill-founded. In neither Ingersoll nor Woodstock could these two notions comfortably fit together; the cultivation of one undermined the other.

This tension between ideation and behaviour – between what sport promoters professed to believe and what their actions produced, along with those of players, fans, and others – was readily apparent in two small towns in the sports-conscious decades of the last century and remains central to the riddle of representative sport. It is found everywhere that representative sport exists today: fueling the contradictions between Olympic ideals and the shady athletic practices that are covertly and overtly sanctioned; between the promoters of sports clubs for moral good and the actions of hooligan fans, including parents acting out their rage at hockey games; and within big-time college athletics. So long as athletes and their playing field victories are used as surrogates for communal aspirations and glory-seeking, sport will continue to be rife with struggles in a contested cultural terrain. Even so, the extent to which local culture still shapes the meanings of sport at the start of our new millennium – as we venture into Marshall McLuhan's global village – remains to be seen.

Notes on Methodology and Primary Sources

In this work I address the paucity of social and sport history written on small communities in Ontario. Although no single community is representative of the province or nation, a community study broadens the perspectives drawn from studies done on the national and provincial levels. My focus on small towns has clear advantages for elaborating Canada's sporting history, some of which are related to methodology.[1] Although broad, national overviews help us understand Canada's social and sporting past, they miss the local variation that local studies neatly capture and suggest that change in sport flows from the metropolis to the hinterland.[2] While developments elsewhere influenced what went on in Ingersoll and Woodstock, local inhabitants created their own meanings for the sports they experienced in their daily lives. Studying small places allows for the use of individual level data, which helps to achieve some precision in getting at issues such as class relationships in sport, and in providing penetrating views into the social background of local amateur sport promoters. National-level studies often rely on aggregate level data. Or, when they use local level data, often it is derived from metropolitan places like Toronto or Montreal. Studying small towns and villages provides manageable units for analysis, enabling historians to examine and document the immediate environment in which urbanites lived out their lives. Local manuscript censuses, directories, parish registers, tax rolls, and membership lists of voluntary associations contain valuable demographic, occupational, and family information about people involved in sport. This information cannot be captured at the national level, and metropolitan places are just too big to study in this way. The issue of size, however, is at times a double-edged sword. For a variety of reasons, sport club minute books and records are much more easily available for large cities with city and university archives than for small towns and villages.

Creating a data set from primary source materials on sport in Ingersoll and Woodstock involved a number of steps. Since few sport club records remain from local clubs for the period studied, this book relies heavily upon the sport reporting in a variety of different types of newspapers: local weeklies and dailies; newspapers from large cities such as Toronto and Montreal as well as smaller ones like Hamilton and Stratford; sporting newspapers from Canada and the U.S.; and popular magazines.

I examined available issues of local newspapers (most of which were available on microfilm) to obtain information on sport in the two towns between 1842 and 1895. In instances when either community boasted more than one paper, I examined and then compared the reporting in both papers. Competing local newspapers tended to cover sport well and overlap in their coverage, confirming the importance of sports – particularly inter urban competitions – to the community culture. It is, however, impossible to ascertain everything that happened in the towns. The collection of nineteenth-century newspapers remaining from Ingersoll is excellent. Woodstock newspaper holdings, however, are scant during the 1850s and early 1860s. To redress this problem, I examined papers from selected corresponding communities – Hamilton, Guelph, London, Stratford, St Mary's, and Toronto – to supplement information on the town's sporting activities. In many cases the Ingersoll press reported on Woodstock happenings, regardless of whether the two towns had competed against each other.

The collecting, collating, classifying, and presenting of the Ingersoll and Woodstock sport database derived from the newspapers and other primary sources of information listed in the bibliography was a painstaking process in the early 1980s, before personal computers and data management software became popularly available. To create the database, I extracted the names of sport players and organizers from all available sources, including newspapers; memorabilia such as team photographs and trophies; local history sources such as maps, gazetteers, directories, and genealogies of local families, housed in various libraries and museums in Oxford County; and sport-related collections housed in national, provincial, regional, and local archives. Often these materials listed the player/organizer by last name only, or sometimes by last name and first initial. I considered this information to be insufficient unless it could be corroborated by other sources of data, and thus I omitted many names from the database for analysis.

I linked the verified names in the data set to corresponding manuscript census returns for the urban populations of Ingersoll and Woodstock for each of the five censuses taken between 1851 and 1901. Some of the machine-readable forms of the Ingersoll censuses were kindly supplied to me by George Emery. The censuses were alphabetically sorted while keeping households consisting of people with the same surname intact. Record linkage was done forward as well as backwards (i.e., a name derived from a newspaper account in 1866 was linked to both the 1871 and 1861 censuses). I eliminated certain people from the list if I found more than one individual with the same name and other records could not discriminate between the two people. I recorded the following information from the record linkages for each sporting person: surname, first name, occupation, age, place of birth, race/ethnicity, religion, marital status, household head, and their relationship to the head of the household. I corroborated the occupational information and supplemented and/or verified it using town, village, and provincial directories; tax assessment rolls; local history name indexes; insurance and other maps; local cemetery and parish rolls; and membership lists of Ingersoll and Woodstock fraternal orders kindly supplied to me by Oxford County historian Christopher Anstead.

I must cite several caveats must about my sport database. No single primary source of information stands alone. Occupational designations, for example, taken from primary sources sometimes give conflicting information about occupation, partly because individuals sometimes changed jobs or advanced in their employment. Since occupational data is classified according the broad categories described below, however, I found that these shifts generally did not change the classification of the data substantially. The gazetteers and directories published periodically that I consulted focused mainly, although not exclusively, on household heads. They helped little in identifying young and unestablished people in the community. The censuses, on the other hand, recorded these people and provided sources of information regarding the occupations of household heads. Yet they occurred only at ten-year intervals. A more serious problem is way in which gazetteers, directories, and censuses under-recorded unskilled workers, as well as people who came and left town in the years between the publishing of directories or the taking of the censuses. That being said, when used cautiously and when applied in combination with other sources of primary information, the information derived from the above materials can be invaluable. The relatively small size of Ingersoll and Woodstock's populations facilitated the process by limiting the size of the pool of potential linkages.

This study uses the occupational taxonomy devised for the Saguenay Project by Gerard Bouchard and Christian Pouyez to categorize the occupations of sports players and organizers as well as the local workforce.[3] It is based upon two fundamental criteria: the manual/

non-manual nature of the occupational task and the complexity of the task, including technical difficulty and level of responsibility, or how much control over one's own and others' tasks an individual possesses. For greater sensitivity to occupational variation, three auxiliary criteria further subdivide the occupations: the geographical area of management units (regional, municipal, and other); the task's legal jurisdictional status (private, public, and other); and the economic sector of the task (manufacturing and sales, professional services, primary production, secondary production, and other).

Notes

ABBREVIATIONS

NA   National Archives of Canada
UWO   J.J. Talman Regional Collection, D.B. Weldon Library, University of
      Western Ontario

INTRODUCTION

1 McLuhan, "Baseball is Culture," 214.
2 Kidd, *The Struggle for Canadian Sport*, 267.
3 Metcalfe, "The Anatomy of Power," 41.
4 Mott, "Flawed Games, Splendid Ceremonies."
5 Redmond, "Some Aspects of Organized Sport," 98.
6 Ladd and Mathison, *Muscular Christianity*, 16.
7 Haley, "Sport and the Victorian World."
8 Lorenz, "Local Teams in a 'World of Sport.'"
9 Artibise, "In Pursuit of Growth."
10 Pope, "Amateurism and American Sports Culture."
11 For good discussions of the importance of locality and sport development, see Tomlinson, "Shifting Patterns of Working Class Leisure,"
   193–5; Bonney-James, "More Than a Game," 3–4; Melville, "From
   Ethnic Tradition to Community Institution."
12 Huggins, "Second-Class Citizens?" Andy Holman's *A Sense of their Duty*
   provides a penetrating analysis of middle-class formation but only touch-
   es briefly on organized sport. Other works, like Blumin's *The Emergence
   of the Middle Class* and Gilkeson's *Middle Class Providence, 1820–1940*,
   are also suggestive but cursory on the topic of sport. A good overview of
   the respectable theme in Canadian sport is found in Howell, *Blood,*

Sweat, and Cheers, 28–50; for class-related sporting developments in America, see Riess, *Sport in Industrial America, 1850–1920,* and Riess, "From Pitch to Putt."

13 On this tendency, see Howell, *Blood, Sweat, and Cheers,* 40–1, 144–5.

CHAPTER ONE

1 Mills, *The Idea of Loyalty in Upper Canada, 1784–1850;* Wise, "Upper Canada and the Conservative Tradition"; Johnson, *Becoming Prominent: Regional Leadership in Upper Canada, 1791–1841;* Armstrong, "The Oligarchy of the Western District."

2 Holman, *A Sense of their Duty.*

3 For a good overview of the creation of the farming economy in the province before the railway, see Wood, *Making Ontario.*

4 Chapman and Putnam, *The Physiography of Southern Ontario,* 231–3.

5 His daughter by the first of his three marriages, Laura Secord, would overshadow her father's fame after her involvement in the War of 1812. See essays by Ruth McKenzie, George C. Ingram, and Cecilia Morgan reprinted in "Invented Tradition: Laura Secord and the War of 1812," in C.M. Wallace and R.M. Bray, *Reappraisals in Canadian History: Pre-Confederation* (Scarborough: Prentice Hall Allyn and Bacon Canada, 1999), 226–60.

6 G.C. Patterson, *Land Settlement in Upper Canada, 1783–1840* (Toronto: Printer to the King, 1921), 189; Shier, "Some Aspects"; Dawe, *Old Oxford is Wide Awake!*

7 Cropp, "Beachville the Birthplace of Oxford."

8 Ingersoll apparently believed the rescission of his grant to be the work of "some evil-minded person [who] reported to the home government that Governor Simcoe was likely to injure the country by encouraging Americans to settle here." Cited in Dawe, *Old Oxford is Wide Awake!,* 11–12.

9 Shier, "Some Aspects," 7–12; see also Byron Jenvy Scrapbooks, Ingersoll Public Library.

10 Shier, "Some Aspects."

11 Wilson, "Reciprocal Work Bees," 439.

12 Samuel Strickland, *Seven Years in Canada West; or the Experience of One Early Settler* (London: Richard Bently, 1854), 35; on masculine culture and sport, see Wamsley and Kossuth, "Fighting it Out."

13 Alex Matheson Sutherland Notebook, Woodstock Museum; see also Conway, "Memoirs of the 1880s," Oxford County Library.

14 Alex Matheson Sutherland Notebook, Woodstock Museum.
15 *Woodstock Weekly Review* 14 July 1871; Wilson, "Reciprocal Work Bees," 451.
16 J.T. Fitzgerald, "Indians were Camped Along River in 1828," *London Free Press* 11 January 1933.
17 Jameson, *Winter Studies and Summer Rambles*, 127–9; 119.
18 Bouchier and Barney, "A Critical Examination of a Source on Early Ontario Baseball."
19 *Sporting Life* 5 May 1886.
20 Wamsley and Kossuth, "Fighting it Out"; DeLottinville, "Joe Beef of Montreal"; Christie, "The Function of the Tavern in Toronto."
21 Byron Jenvy Scrapbooks, "1830–1850 a Development Era," (undated clipping), Ingersoll Public Library.
22 *Chronicle* 26 April 1865.
23 Dawe, *Old Oxford is Wide Awake!*
24 These issues, the basis of much discussion in local taverns, are well documented in Dawe, *Old Oxford is Wide Awake!*; see also Read, *The Rising in Western Upper Canada.*
25 Ireland, "Andrew Drew and the Founding of Woodstock," 231–3.
26 Craig, *Upper Canada*, 226ff.
27 *Concise Dictionary of National Biography* (London: Oxford University Press, 1965), 133; Canfield, *Vice Admiral Henry Vansittart.*
28 Ireland, "Andrew Drew and the Founding of Woodstock," 229–32.
29 On the officers, see W. Bettridge Papers, Ontario Archives; "Andrew Drew," *Dictionary of Canadian Biography* 10, 259–60; Ireland, "Andrew Drew, the Man Who Burned the Caroline"; Ireland, "Andrew Drew and the Founding of Woodstock."
30 Gates, *Land Policies in Upper Canada.*
31 Blunderbus, *A History of Brighton*, 14.
32 For a glimpse of the social network that existed, see Dommett, *Canadian Journal.*
33 Anstead and Bouchier, "The 'Tombstone Affair,'1845"; see also Armstrong, "The Oligarchy of the Western District."
34 As cited in Dawe, *Old Oxford is Wide Awake!*, 47.
35 Shenston, *The Oxford Gazetteer*, 86–8.
36 Shenston, *The Oxford Gazetteer*, 115–18; Dawe, *Old Oxford is Wide Awake!*, 40–1. James Hamilton Ingersoll, the son of Charles Ingersoll (and brother-in-law of William Hamilton Merritt), remained in the village, taking over the family's local enterprises.
37 Dawe, *Old Oxford is Wide Awake!*, 64.
38 Morgan, "'In Search of the Phantom misnamed Honour,'" 549; *Globe* 29 January 1852.

39 I have drawn this point from my reading of Gruneau's theoretical analysis of the Canadian case in *Class, Sports and Social Development*, 95ff. On the Tory tendency toward conservatism see Wise, "Upper Canada and the Conservative Tradition."

40 McCleneghan and Riggs, *Aristocratic Woodstock 1834–1850*.

41 "That Aristocratic Neighborhood of Woodstock." *Globe* 24 May 1878, reprinted in the *Globe and Mail* 24 July 1967.

42 Veblen, *The Theory of the Leisure Class*.

43 Dawe, *Old Oxford is Wide Awake!*, 82.

44 Sawtell Scrapbook #2, "Regal and Vice Regal Visits to Oxford County," Woodstock Public Library.

45 *Globe* 24 May 1848, reprinted from the *Long Point Advocate*.

46 Blunderbus, *A History of Brighton*, 14.

47 An advertisement for what must have been one of the last steeplechases, with a list of stewards, is found in "Horse Racing," 7 July 1853, Vertical File F-C, Woodstock Public Library.

48 Smith, *Smith's Canadian Gazetteer*, 223; Shenston, *The Oxford Gazetteer*, 115–24.

49 Dawe, *Old Oxford is Wide Awake!*, 46.

50 Read, *The Rising in Western Upper Canada*; Dunham, *Political Unrest in Upper Canada*.

51 *Upper Canada Sundries*, "Loyal Address from Woodstock," 14 May 1836 v.167, 91098.

52 Read, *The Rising in Western Upper Canada*; Crawford, "Captain Andrew Drew"; Ireland, "Andrew Drew, the Man who Burned the Caroline."

53 Canfield, "Canon Bettridge." On St Paul's Church itself see Arthur Sweatman, *A Sketch of the History of the Parish of Woodstock* (Woodstock: Times Job Dept., 1902[?]); Maurice S. Baldwin, *Old St Paul's Church Ninetieth Anniversary, 1834–1924* (Woodstock: B.J. Rae Printer, 1924); *100th Anniversary 1834–1934, Old St Paul's Church* (Woodstock, 1934); Elliott, "The Parish of Woodstock."

54 "Statement of Pewholders and Pew Rentals Due St Paul's Church, Woodstock 1848, Woodstock Public Library."

55 Anstead and Bouchier, "The 'Tombstone Affair,' 1845."

56 Anstead and Bouchier, "The 'Tombstone Affair,' 1845"; see also Dawe, *Old Oxford is Wide Awake!*, 57–8.

57 Dawe, *Old Oxford is Wide Awake!*, 78.

58 Shenston, *The Oxford Gazetteer*, 124. Shenston acted as the returning officer for this election.

59 *Globe* 24 May 1878; Elliott, "The Parish of Woodstock," 94–5.

60 Dawe, *Old Oxford is Wide Awake!*, 89–90; Neutel, "From 'Southern' Concept," 30–47.
61 As returning officer for the County of Oxford in 1847 Vansittart had overruled Hincks's decided victory in the provincial election on a technicality. Vansittart eventually received a reprimand for the incident. Shenston, *The Oxford Gazetteer*, 95–6.
62 Gruneau's *Class, Sports and Social Development* makes this case at the provincial level; see also Careless, "Some Aspects of Urbanization," 65–79.
63 *Globe* 24 May 1878, reprinted in the *Globe and Mail* 24 July 1967.
64 Artibise, "In Pursuit of Growth."
65

Table 1.1
Summary of urban growth and local services for Ingersoll and Woodstock, 1830–1901

	Ingersoll	Woodstock
village incorporation	1852	1851
town incorporation	1861	1857
city incorporation	–	1901
1st railway	1853	1853
2nd railway	1879	1876
3rd railway	–	1879
weekly newspaper	1853	1840
daily newspaper	1879	1870
board of trade	1874	1877
electrification	–	1881
municipal electr. takeover	–	1901
street rail	1901	1900
private waterworks	1891	1880
municipal waterworks	–	1890
sewage	–	1895
library service	1872	1832
hospital	–	1895

Source: Bloomfield et al., *Urban Growth and Local Services.*

66 This point is made in Spelt, *Urban Development in South-Central Ontario.*
67 On the impact of railways on the cost of shipping local goods, Shenston, *The Oxford Gazetteer*, 83; *Fisher and Taylor's Gazetteer and General Directory for the County of Oxford, 1874–1875;* see also Talman, "The Development of the Railway Network," 83.
68 Emery, *Noxons of Ingersoll, 1856–1918;* Cartwright, "Cheese Production

in Southwestern Ontario"; Mennil, "A Regional Study of the Economy of Ingersoll."

69

Table 1.2
Industrial employees and number of manufacturing establishments
in Ingersoll and Woodstock, 1871–1891

	1871		1881		1891	
	Ingersoll	Woodstock	Ingersoll	Woodstock	Ingersoll	Woodstock
establishments	69	72	86	81	103	105
employees	627	435	668	858	668	1593
ratio employees/ establishment	9	6	8	11	6	15

Sources: Bloomfield, et al. *Urban Growth and Local Services*; Ontario, *Bureau of Industries Reports* 1886, 1888, 1890.

70 Bloomfield, "Industry in Ontario Urban Centres."
71 Cartwright, "Cheese Production in Southwestern Ontario"; *Chronicle* 25 May 1872.
72 This happened with a $50,000 grant given to the railway. Woodstock also gave $68,000 to acquire access to the Credit Valley line. *Consolidated Bylaws of the Town of Woodstock*. See also Lavell, *100 Years Young: Woodstock Board of Trade and Chamber of Commerce, 1877–1977*.

73

Table 1.3
Ingersoll and Woodstock census populations and the number of Ontario urban municipalities by population size, 1851–1901

Population size	1851	1861	1871	1881	1891	1901
1,000	2	21	28	61	72	82
1,000–2,499	21	34	45	78	96	103
2,500–4,999	7	15	24	35	38	40
5,000–9,999	2	4	7	14	15	18
10,000–24,999	2	4	3	2	5	6
25,000+	1	1	2	3	4	4
total	35	79	109	193	230	253
Ingersoll	1,190	2,577	4,022	4,318	4,191	4,571
Woodstock	2,112	3,353	3,982	5,373	8,612	8,833

Note: The shaded areas indicate which population size category Ingersoll and Woodstock fit into; Woodstock had moved ahead of Ingersoll by the time of the 1881 census.
Sources: Canada, *Census Reports*, 1851–1891; Bloomfield et al., *Urban Growth and Local Services*.

74

Table 1.4
Place of birth in percentage of total populations, Ingersoll and Woodstock inhabitants, 1851–1901

	Places of Birth									
	Canada		British Isles		U.S.		Other		Total	
	Ing.	Wdsk.	Ing.	Wdsk.	Ing.	Wdsk.	Ing.	Wdsk.	Ing.	Wdsk.
1851	44	40	47	56	8	3	1	1	1,194	2,097
1861	54	52	35	42	10	5	1	1	2,576	3,316
1871	64	63	30	33	5	3	1	1	4,009	3,956
1881	71	64	25	32	3	3	1	1	4,308	5,364
1891	75	76	20	21	4	2	1	1	4,193	8,541

Source: Ingersoll and Woodstock manuscript censuses, 1851–1891.
Note: Figures are in rounded numbers. There are slight discrepancies between calculations from the manuscript censuses and the published aggregate data.

75 According to the Ingersoll and Woodstock Fraternal Order Membership Collection created and held by Christopher Anstead, Ingersoll had the St George's Society (1858), St Andrew's Society (1870), Sons of Canada (1889), the Emerald Benefit Association #13 Sacred Heart (1891), Sons of Scotland Heart of Midlothian #64 (1891), and the Sons of England Lodge Imperial #176 (1893). Woodstock was home to the Princess Alice #5 (1891), Order of Scottish Clans Clan Sutherland #37 (1887), Sons of Scotland Edinburgh #95 (1892), International Order of the King's Daughters Court St Mary's #350 (1893), and the Daughters of the King (1894).

76

Table 1.5
Per cent distribution of occupational breakdown,
Ingersoll and Woodstock, 1851–1891

	1851		1871		1891	
	Ingersoll	Woodstock	Ingersoll	Woodstock	Ingersoll	Woodstock
non-manual	17	12	20	29	26	26
manual skilled	46	49	51	50	50	51
manual unskilled	37	39	29	21	24	23
total n.	371	643	1,204	1,046	1,365	3,075

Source: Ingersoll and Woodstock Manuscript censuses, 1851–1891; calculated for the male workforces aged 15 years and older.

77 See Spelt, *Urban Development in South-Central Ontario*, 150–86.
The demise of Ingersoll's cigar manufacturing firm was attributed to its

inability to compete against a firm from London. *Sun* Industrial Ingersoll Illustrated, 25th Anniversary Souvenir Edition, February 1907; on local boards of trade, see Bloomfield, "Boards of Trade and Canadian Urban Development"; Statutes 37 Victoria Ch. 54 (26 May 1874).

78 See *Ingersoll Bylaws* #144 (November 1880); #235 (April 1887); #238–9, 252 (July 1887); #246 (August 1887).

79 *Sentinel Review* 26 October 1886.

80 *Chronicle* 14 August 1884.

81 Ontario, *Report of the Inspectors of Factories for the Province of Ontario, 1888.*

82 Emery, *Noxons of Ingersoll, 1856–1918*, 38.

83 One photograph of a Woodstock factory baseball team held in the Woodstock museum shows a man in the first row of players noticeably without a thumb.

84 *Sentinel* June 1893; Woodstock manuscript census, 1891.

85 Ontario, *Sessional Paper No. 74, Annual Report of the Bureau of Industries for the Province of Ontario, 1888, Part IV Wages and Cost of Living*, 82–3.

86 Marks, *Revivals and Roller Rinks; Sun* Industrial Ingersoll Illustrated, February 1907.

87 Emery, *Noxons of Ingersoll, 1856–1918*, 38–9.

88 *Sentinel-Review* Express Industrial Number, February 1906.

89 *Sentinel* 17 November 1886.

90 Marks, *Revivals and Roller Rinks*; Anstead, "Fraternalism in Victorian Ontario."

91 Anstead, "Fraternalism in Victorian Ontario," 74.

92 Careless, *Frontier and Metropolis*, 62.

93 Holman, *A Sense of their Duty.*

94 Anstead, "Fraternalism in Victorian Ontario," 347–84.

95 Emery and Emery, *A Young Man's Benefit*; Anstead, "Fraternalism in Victorian Ontario."

96 Noel, *Canada Dry.*

97 Dumenil, *Freemasonry and American Culture, 1880–1939*; Blumin, *The Emergence of the Middle Class.*

98 Anstead, "Fraternalism in Victorian Ontario," iii-iv.

99 Artibise, "In Pursuit of Growth"; Betke, "Sports Promotion in the Western Canadian City"; Huskins, "'A Tale of Two Cities.'"

100 See, for example: *Sun* Industrial Ingersoll Illustrated, 25th Anniversary Souvenir Edition, February 1907; *Sentinel-Review* (Woodstock) *Inaugural Edition*, 1901; *Sentinel-Review* The Garden of Ontario Special Edition, May 1897; *Sentinel-Review* Express Industrial Number, February 1906; *Sentinel-Review* 50th Anniversary Edition, 11 September 1936; *Sentinel-Review* Diamond Jubilee Edition, 25 October 1947.

101 *Chronicle* 31 October 1878; *Sentinel* 14 November 1884; 30 October 1885; and 8 October 1886.

102 "That Aristocratic Neighborhood of Woodstock," *Globe* 24 May 1878; *Sentinel-Review* The Garden of Ontario Special Edition, May 1897; *Sentinel-Review* Inaugural Edition, *1901*.

103 On McIntyre's notoriously bad poetry, see Deacon, *The Four Jameses*.

104 On 5 June 1873 the *Chronicle* reported that cattle grazed on the town park for a fee, to be turned out when the space was needed for recreational purposes.

105 *Sentinel* 3 June 1879.

106 On the need for Ingersoll parks, town council debates over the parks, and parks developments refer to *Chronicle* 10 June 1869; 7 July 1870; 6 July 1871; 10, 17, 24 April 1873; 8 May 1873; 5, 10 June 1873; 16 November 1883; 7 June 1883; 21 May 1885; 8, 10 June 1886; 7 June 1888; 1 April 1890; 17 July 1890. See also *Ingersoll Bylaws* #16 (1 March 1869), #69 (7 April 1873), #153 (12 September 1881), #173 (7 May 1883), and #58 (7 May 1885). On Woodstock parks development and town council activities, see *Sentinel* 26 May 1871; 21 July 1871; 25 August 1871; 1 September 1871; 17 May and 31 May 1872; 31 Jan, 9 May, 31 June and 30 May 1873; 12 June 1874; 9, 25 April, 29 May, 18 July, 25 October, 7 November 1879; 19 May 1882; 20 April 1883; 12 June 1885; 9, 17 May 1887. Apparently the local habit of referring to the town park as the "old cow pasture" was not easily shaken: the expression was still used in 1883 (*Sentinel* 27 April 1883).

107 On public health related issues and specific suggestions for local parks development see *Chronicle* 17 July 1879; Emery, "Adam Oliver, Ingersoll and Thunder Bay District."

108 *Chronicle* 10 June 1875.

109 *Chronicle* 7 June 1888.

CHAPTER TWO

1 On civic celebrations and parades, see Farber, "High, Healthy and Happy"; Turner, *The Ritual Process*; Huskins, "Public Celebrations"; Heron and Penfold, "The Craftsmen's Spectacle"; Goheen, "Symbols in the Streets"; Goheen, "The Ritual of the Streets"; Goheen, "Negotiating Access"; Davis, *Parades and Power*; Glassberg, "Public Ritual and Cultural Hierarchy"; Ryan, "The American Parade"; Rosenzweig, *Eight Hours for What We Will*.

2 On urban and inter urban sport see Hardy, "Sport in Urbanizing America"; Hardy, *How Boston Played*; Bale, *Sport, Space and the City*; Riess, *City Games*; Somers, *The Rise of Sports in New Orleans, 1850–1900*.

3 Geertz, "Notes on the Balinese Cockfight" in *The Interpretation of Cultures*, 417.

4 *Statutes* 8 Victoria Ch. 4 (1845). When the popular monarch died in 1901, the 24th became a permanent national holiday; *Statutes* I Edward VII Ch. 12 (1901); see also Goheen, "Negotiating Access."

5 *Ingersoll Chronicle* 22 May 1857. No Woodstock papers remain from this period, however oftentimes Ingersoll papers reported on Woodstock happenings. The information for this description is gleaned from the *Chronicle* 25 May, 1 June 1855; 22, 29 May 1857; 11, 25 May 1860; 31 May 1861; 16, 23 May 1862; 22 May 1863; 13, 20, 27 May 1865; 25 May 1866; 9, 16, 30 May 1867.

6 *Chronicle* 16 June 1881. See also *Chronicle* 18 June and 2 July 1874; 23 May, 3 July 1879; 16 June 1881; 26 May 1892; 25 May 1893.

7 Canada, Debates of the House of Commons, 14 March 1902, 1437. One member of Parliament chanted this little ditty during the debate in the House over designating the day a permanent national holiday – a piece that my parents sang during their schooldays in Toronto in the 1930s and I chanted with my neighbourhood pals during my childhood in Ottawa in the 1960s.

8 The following analysis draws heavily from Davis, *Parades and Power*.

9 Davis, *Parades and Power*, 49–112.

10 According to Mathews, the term callathumpian possibly stems from "Gallithumpians," those who disturb order in Parliament. Mathews, *A Dictionary of Americanisms*, 248.

11 On the "antiuniformity" of the callathumpian parade gnre, see Huskins, "Public Celebrations," 218–25.

12 Such "outlandish, carnivalesque mockery," argue Heron and Penfold, provided subordinate classes with rare access to the pageantry of the streets. Heron and Penfold, "The Craftsmen's Spectacle," 364–5.

13 *Sentinel* 3 July 1874.

14 Heron and Penfold, "The Craftsmen's Spectacle."

15 Huskins, "The Ceremonial Space of Women."

16 Huskins, "Public Celebrations."

17 Palmer, "Discordant Music." For the revolutionary potential of the chivaree, see Greer, "From Folklore to Revolution."

18 *Chronicle* 10 July 1879.

19 *Chronicle* 23 May 1862, 25 May 1882; *Consolidated Bylaws of the Town of Ingersoll* lists numerous bylaws concerning morality and public order. On the policing of municipalities see John Weaver, *Crimes, Constables and Courts: Order and Transgression in a Canadian City* (Montreal and Kingston: McGill-Queen's University Press, 1995).

20 James Sinclair, 1907, as cited in Brian Dawe, "Ingersoll's 'Monster.'"

Hundreds see Pond Drained." Undated newspaper clipping, Vertical Files, Ingersoll, Oxford County Library.

21 Heron and Penfold, "The Craftsmen's Spectacle," 365.

22 *Sentinel* 27 May 1880.

23 *Sentinel* 27 May 1880.

24 Sawtell *Scrapbook*, Woodstock Public Library Collection.

25 *Sentinel* 25 May 1888.

26 *Sentinel* 27 May 1892. Some years earlier, after a fight a vigilante mob of some 200 angry white men combed the streets and ransacked the homes of terrorized black residents. *Chronicle* 4 July 1878.

27 Davis, *Parades and Power*; Ryan, "The American Parade"; Glassberg, "Public Ritual and Cultural Hierarchy."

28 *Chronicle* 31 May 1861.

29 *Chronicle* 25 May 1889.

30 McIntyre, "Victoria Park and the Caledonian Games."

31 Marks, *Revivals and Roller Rinks*; Anstead, "Patriotism and Camaraderie."

32 Anstead, "Patriotism and Camaraderie."

33 Ibid., 247.

34 For example, *Chronicle* 25 May 1860.

35 Marks, *Revivals and Roller Rinks*, 117.

36 *Sentinel* 9 August 1878.

37 Poet James McIntyre found his own way of thanking these local heroes for their ongoing service to the community in the poem "Our Firemen": "The firemen, now, their only strife, / It seems to be a race for life, / Which engine first shall reach the fire / And cause the wild flames to expire." In his "The Great Fire of Ingersoll," McIntyre writes optimistically of the town: "Our once fair town is now in woe, / And we have had our Chicago; / But soon a nobler town will rise, / For Ingersoll's all enterprise." McIntyre, *Musings on the Banks*. For more on the fire, see James Sinclair, *A History of the Town of Ingersoll* (Ingersoll: n.p., c. 1924), 38–40.

38 Canada, *Report of the Royal Commission of the Relations of Labour and Capital in Canada, 1889*; Kealey, "Introduction," ix–xxvii.

39 Emery, *Noxons of Ingersoll, 1856–1918*, 31–2.

40 *Chronicle* 26 May 1887.

41 *Chronicle* 26 May 1887.

42 *Chronicle* 5 July 1888.

43 *Chronicle* 7 July 1887; on the Knights' organizing activities in 1886–87, see Kealey, *Toronto Workers Respond*, 296.

44 *Chronicle* 7 July 1887.

45 McIntyre, "Victoria Park and the Caledonian Games."

46 *Chronicle* 3 August 1866.

47 *Chronicle* 21 May 1868.

48 *Sentinel* 30 May 1884; 29 May, 5 July 1885.
49 *Gormully and Jeffery Manufacturing Co, Catalogue 1891* (Chicago). The company's "American Light Champion" penny-farthing ran between $115 and $143. Cycle uniforms came in all sizes and included trouser guard, club cap, flannel Norfolk blouse, leggings, bicycle hose, a cyclist belt, knee breeches, and cycling shoes. Costly accessories included lamps, bicycle stands, tool bags, belt pouches, bells, special seats, and peddles.
50 According to Bureau of Industries reports on wages and cost of living statistics, the fifteen organ tuners in Woodstock worked a 57-hour work week and would have made $622.50 in yearly wages. Accounting for the cost of living, their surplus income came to $105. The fifty-five case makers at the factory were also relatively well off, having $110 in annual surplus income. The twenty-five finishers at the factory had roughly one-half that amount left over. Ontario, *Annual Report of the Bureau of Industries for the Province of Ontario, 1888* Table 10: Yearly Wages and Cost of Living; Woodstock 1891 manuscript census.
51 Such concerns, especially about dissipation amongst organ tuners, led him to testify about the influence of drink upon his workforce at local hearings of the Royal Commission on the Liquor Traffic. See Spence, *The Facts of the Case*, 59.
52 Cited in Humber, *Freewheeling*, 9.
53 *Sentinel* 19 June 1874.
54 *Sentinel* 30 April 1887.
55 *Sentinel* 23 May 1884.
56 Adelman, *A Sporting Time*; Guttmann, *From Ritual to Record*.
57 For a good description of the passing down of local communal games traditions by such men as 'Old' Ned Dolson, see the reminiscence of Adam Ford in Bouchier and Barney, "A Critical Examination of a Source on Early Ontario Baseball."
58 Sutton-Smith, "Games of Order and Disorder"; Sutton-Smith, "The Study of Games." See also Huskins, "Public Celebrations," 280–309.
59 The sack and wheelbarrow races would be typically associated with the Caledonian Games. See Redmond, *The Caledonian Games in Nineteenth Century America*; Redmond, *The Sporting Scots of Nineteenth Century Canada*.
60 *Chronicle* 26 May 1865.
61 On muscular Christian and rational approaches to sport, see McIntosh, *Sport in Society*; Mangan, *Athleticism in the Victorian and Edwardian Public School*; Mangan, *The Games Ethic and Imperialism*; Brown, "Athleticism in Selected Canadian Private Schools." On social tensions surrounding traditional games forms, see Gruneau, *Class, Sports and Social Development*, 100–1.
62 Bailey, *Leisure and Class in Victorian England*.

63 Strutt, *Sports and Pastimes of the People of England*. See Book I, especially "Rural Exercises Practiced by Persons of Rank."

64 Every year the retired officers held a socially exclusive steeplechase. On military sport traditions generally, see Day, "The British Army and Sport in Canada."

65 Wamsley and Kossuth, "Fighting it Out."

66 Guillet, *Pioneer Days in Upper Canada*, 188.

67 Woodstock *Herald* 26 September 1845.

68 For example, *Consolidated Bylaws of the Town of Woodstock* Bylaw #168: "To regulate slaughter houses and prevent charivaris and immoderate driving." 22 February 1864.

69 Metcalfe, *Canada Learns to Play*, 147.

70 Dodds, *Canadian Turf Recollections*; Jones, *History of Agriculture in Ontario*. For a discussion regarding "better breeding" in a sport context see Sumner, "The State Fair and the Development of Modern Sports," 139–41.

71 Metcalfe, *Canada Learns to Play*, 148.

72 *Chronicle* 26 May 1865; 30 May 1867; 19 January 1888.

73 *London Free Press* 1 October 1938.

74 *Chronicle* 26 April 1865. For other Innkeepers Purse events see Christie, "The Function of the Tavern in Toronto," 55; Roxborough, *One Hundred Not Out*, 21.

75 Bull, *From Rattlesnake Hunt to Hockey*, 124.

76 Huggins, "Culture, Class and Respectability."

77 Joyce, "Sport and the Cash Nexus in Nineteenth Century Toronto," 157–8; see also Bonney-James, "More Than a Game," 53–8.

78 Metcalfe, *Canada Learns to Play*, 146–7; Dodds, *Canadian Turf Recollections*.

79 *Sentinel* 31 June 1873.

80 Because no Woodstock newspapers remain from this period the exact date of the formation of the Woodstock Association is not known. On the Association's origins see *Sentinel* 5, 26 May 1871; *Weekly Review* 21 July, 25 August, 1 September 1871.

81 Dodds, *Canadian Turf Recollections*, 41; *Sentinel* 30 April and 1, 3 May 1919; see also Leonard W. Taylor, *The Sourdough and the Queen: The Many Lives of Klondike Joe Boyle* (Toronto: Methuen, 1983).

82 *Sentinel* 28, 29 September, 1 October 1886.

83 Dodds, *Canadian Turf Recollections*, 56.

84 For Thomas Charles Patteson's obituary see *Globe* 21 September 1907. A tribute to his sporting involvement is found in the *Globe* 23 September 1907; on Patteson, see W. Stewart Wallace, *The Macmillan Dictionary of Canadian Biography* (Toronto: Macmillan, 1978 ed.), 653; Joyce, "Sport and the Cash Nexus in Nineteenth Century Toronto," 158–9; Gillespie, "Wickets in the West," 53ff.

85 *Sentinel* 1 July 1901; *Globe* 24 May 1878.

86 *Canadian Gentleman's Journal and Sporting Times* 2 June 1876.

87 Ibid.

88 *Sentinel* 9 May 1873.

89 *Sentinel* 30 May 1873.

90 Woodstock *Weekly Review* 28 May 1875; Trent Frayne, *The Queen's Plate* (Toronto: McClelland & Stewart, 1971 ed.); Louis Cauz, *The Plate: A Royal Tradition* (Toronto: Deneau Publishing, 1984).

91 *Sentinel-Review* Inaugural Edition, 1 July 1901.

92 *Chronicle* 21 May 1874.

93 *Canadian Gentleman's Journal and Sporting Times* 6 August 1875.

94 Bull, *From Rattlesnake Hunt to Hockey*, 148.

95 Brown, "Thoroughbred Horse-Racing Receives an Imperialist Nod"; Waters, "Operating on the Border."

96 *Royal Commission in Racing Inquiry*, 10 George V no. 67 (1920); Canada, Debates of the House of Commons, 6 April 1910, 6398–504 and 7 April, 6509–98. See Metcalfe, *Canada Learns to Play*, 145–59, for an excellent overview of the horseracing debate surrounding the "Act to Amend the Criminal Code Bill" to prohibit betting at race tracks; see also Catriona Beaton Parratt, "Sport and Hegemony: Windsor c.1895 to c.1929," (M.A. thesis: University of Windsor, 1985), 32–36.

97 The ongoing coverage of horseracing in the St Mary's *Journal-Argus* on 22 and 29 September and 6 October 1871 reveals some of the feelings of people on both sides of the debate.

98 Start, *Fair Play*.

99 *Chronicle* 17 August 1882.

100 Ibid.

101 Mott, *Sports in Canada*, 7.

102 See Greg Gillespie, "Roderick McLennan, Professionalism, and the Emergence of the Athlete in Caledonian Games."

103 Ibid.

104 *Chronicle* 19 June 1876.

105 A poetic tribute to Hodge, "A Civic Holiday Trip," penned by James McIntyre in August 1882, is found in the poet's *Musings on the Banks of the Canadian Thames*, 35.

106 *Chronicle* 4 May 1882; Woodstock hired Hodge to run their Dominion Day event that same year. *Sentinel* 30 June 1882.

107 *Chronicle* 24 May 1882.

108 *Chronicle* 7 May 1884.

109 *Chronicle* 26 May 1881.

110 Gillespie, "Roderick McLennan, Professionalism, and the Emergence of the Athlete in Caledonian Games."

111 Robinson, "Professional Sport a Half Century Ago."

112 Ibid.

113 Ibid.
114 St Mary's *Journal-Argus* 26 May 1886.
115 *Chronicle* 28 May 1884.
116 *Chronicle* 3 June 1886.
117 *Chronicle* 18 October 1883.
118 Metcalfe, *Canada Learns to Play*, 99–132; Kidd, *The Struggle for Canadian Sport*, 44–93.
119 *Chronicle* 28 May 1884.
120 *Chronicle* 3, 10 June 1886.
121 *Chronicle* 3 June 1886.

CHAPTER THREE

1 Howell, *Northern Sandlots*, 60.
2 *Sentinel* 4, 11, 18 April 1884; *Woodstock Amateur Athletic Association Constitution and Bylaws* (Woodstock, 1908).
3 *Sentinel* 4 April 1884.
4 The connection between local government and the local AAA ran deep. Between 1884 and 1896, men who were – or were to become – current town councillors held one-quarter of the governing positions on WAAA executive boards. *Chronicle* 21 March 1889, 30 May 1890; *Sentinel-Review Inaugural Edition*, 1 July 1901, 10.
5 Kidd, *The Struggle for Canadian Sport*, especially chapter 2, "The Making of Men," 44–94.
6 Like the MAAA, and in contrast to the New York Athletic Club, the WAAA (and later the IAAA) did not generate income from food and liquor sales. The WAAA received fees from its socially restricted membership, with profits from civic holiday celebrations funding its yearly activities. The association's lifeblood thus rested on the town council-holiday connection; holiday success determined WAAA overall financial success. This, in turn, influenced the association's day-to-day operations. On other AAAs see Morrow, *A Sporting Evolution*; Morrow, "The Powerhouse of Canadian Sport"; Metcalfe, *Canada Learns to Play*; Redmond, "Some Aspects of Organized Sport and Leisure in Nineteenth Century Canada"; Wise, "Sport and Class Values in Old Ontario and Quebec"; Heine and Wamsley, "'Kickfest at Dawson City.'"
7 See, for example, Morrow, *A Sporting Evolution*; *Gazette* 23 May 1884, 22 May 1885; Ballem, *Abegweit Dynasty, 1899–1954*.
8 Morrow, *A Sporting Evolution*; Morrow et al., *A Concise History of Sport*, 19–20.
9 Abbott, "Cold Cash and Ice Palaces."
10 Ibid.
11 *Sentinel* 7 August 1885.
12 Dodds, *Canadian Turf Recollections*.

13 Stratford *Herald*, n.d., as reported in the *Sentinel* 25 April 1884
14 *Sentinel* 21 March 1881; 23 November 1883.
15 *Sentinel* 23 November 1883.
16 *Sentinel* 15 July 1881. Earlier that year Forbes had held $2,000 in bets for a race between James Quirk of Brantford and Charles Biggar of Fergus for a $1,000 stake. The race was held in the dead of winter on the ice of Miller's pond. *Sentinel* 18 February 1881.
17 *Sentinel* 11 September 1936.
18 Ibid.
19 *Sentinel* 25 April 1884.
20 Woodstock, too, had hired Hodge in 1882, having him run their Dominion Day games that year. *Sentinel* 30 June 1882.
21 *Chronicle* 23 May 1884.
22 In the eyes of earnest civic boosters athletes whose professional careers had ended had no real occupation or trade to fall back on, making them less than desirable citizens. This sentiment lingered in the town a long time: in the 1920s Frank Hyde, a prominent WAAA member and sometime president of the powerful Ontario Hockey Association, repeated this message in public lectures and through his writings in the local press. All too frequently, he complained, "do we find boys entering the arena of professional sport losing sight of the obligation they owe themselves in the rounding out of a career that ultimately assures them a meritorious place in the duties of citizenship." "Rumour that Woodstock Man Might Become Head of New Pro. Loop Causes Well-Known OHA Officer to Chuckle." Newspaper clipping, Frank Hyde Papers, Woodstock Museum.
23 Cited in Morrow, "A Case Study in Amateur Conflict," 175. The AAA of C governed track and field, gymnastics, handball, fencing, boxing, and wrestling. See Kidd, *The Struggle for Canadian Sport*, 22; Metcalfe, "The Meaning of Amateurism."
24 Morrow, "A Case Study in Amateur Conflict," 175.
25 *Sentinel* 23 May 1884; the development of good character traits through sport, of course, would be the most highly coveted prize in any amateur competition. Yet as Alan Metcalfe observes, the conditions under which bad behaviours increasingly found their way onto playing fields – despite the AAAs – came from the overarching structures of society, not professionalism itself. "The true and lasting meaning of amateur," Metcalfe argues, "has been encapsulated in the idea of playing within 'the spirit and letter of the law.'" Amateurs did not have a monopoly on good behaviour; nor did professionals have a monopoly on bad behaviour. Metcalfe, "The Meaning of Amateurism," 46.
26 Adelman, *A Sporting Time.*
27 Robinson, "Professional Sport a Half Century Ago.".
28 *Toronto Mail* 2 April 1887.

29 Ibid.

30 *Sentinel* 1 February 1888.

31 This followed the resolution of difficulties over obtaining acceptable playing field space. *Sentinel* 4, 11, 18 April 1884; *Chronicle* 3, 10 June 1886; 29 March 1889; 1 April, 30 May 1890; *Ingersoll Amateur Athletic Association Constitution and Bylaws*; *Chronicle* 21 March 1889. On 1 April 1890 the *Chronicle* reported on the creation of a committee to confer with the town council and agricultural society regarding preparing Victoria Park.

32 Ingersoll had initially proposed this move in 1887 before the founding of its AAA. *Sentinel* 29 April 1887.

33 *Chronicle* 16 May 1895.

34 *Sentinel* 30 May 1884.

35 Ibid.

36 *Sentinel* 22 May 1891.

37 Ibid.

38 The Oxford Museum in Woodstock recently has obtained some wonderful photographs of females lining up for and running holiday races on the WAAA track around the time of WWI. I don't know when this practice began and have not seen evidence for it in the period under study. They are all wearing long skirts, however, and judging by the emblems on their sweaters, some belonged to some sort of club or association. Their running styles, manner, and deportment are a stark contrast to the photographed male athletes competing in athletic events on the same day.

39 *Sentinel* 25 May 1888.

40 On female physical and social constraints see Vertinsky, *The Eternally Wounded Woman*; Mitchison, *The Nature of their Bodies*; Lenskyj, *Out of Bounds*; Smith, "Graceful Athleticism or Robust Womanhood."

41

Table 3.1
Per cent distribution of occupational breakdown,
Ingersoll and Woodstock AAA executives and the local populations, 1884–1896

	% Total AAA	% Populations	
	Executives	Ingersoll	Woodstock
non-manual	95	26	26
manual skilled	5	50	51
manual unskilled	0	24	23
total n.	103	1,365	3,075

Sources: Ingersoll and Woodstock manuscript census returns, 1881, 1891, and the sport data base. Ingersoll and Woodstock male workforce > 15 years. In rounded figures.

42 Very good treatments of this are found in Anstead, "Fraternalism in Victorian Ontario;" Clawson, *Constructing Brotherhood*.

43 My idea of life cycle involvement in sport and recreational activity is informed by John R. Kelly, *Leisure Identities and Interactions* (Boston: George Allen & Unwin, 1983), 69*ff*.

44 Art Williams and Edward Baker, *Bits and Pieces – A Montage of Woodstock, Ontario in Text and Pictures* (Woodstock: Commercial Print Craft Ltd., 1967), 24–7; 48.

45 Woodstock North Women's Institute. Tweedsmuir History. Oxford Book 1, 49. Oxford County Library.

46 *From Forest to City; Woodstock Old Boys and Girls Home Coming [sic] Reunion and Diamond Jubilee Celebration.*

47 *Pioneer* article as reprinted in the *Sentinel-Review* 13 December 1920.

48 Woodstock's hotel proprietors, C.L. Wood, Patrick Farrell, J.E. Thompson, and James O'Neil, like those of Ingersoll's Hearn's Hotel and Jarvis Hall, all promoted baseball, as discussed in chapter 5.

49 *Pioneer* as reprinted in the *Sentinel-Review* 13 December 1920.

50 Gilkeson, *Middle Class Providence*. On clubs, sport, and Toronto's interlocking social elite, see Simpson, "The Elite and Sport Club Membership." See also Alan Metcalfe, "The Evolution of Organized Physical Recreation in Montreal, 1840–1895." *Histoire Sociale/Social History* 11 (21)(May 1978):144–66; Wise, "Sport and Class Values."

51 WAAA, *Constitution and Consolidated Bylaws,* Article II; IAAA *Constitution and Bylaws*, Article II. On gentlemanliness and its social origins in the English social class system, see Metcalfe, *Canada Learns to Play*, 120–1.

52 AAA of C *Annual Meetings and Reports*; AAA of C Correspondence, Letter from D.S. Kendall to W.S. Weldon, 20 March 1890, V 11 file 11–1, both MAAA Papers, NA.

53 *Second Annual Report of the AAA of C 1885*, 3–4, MAAA Papers, NA. See, Morrow, "The Powerhouse of Canadian Sport;" Metcalfe, "Organized Sport and Social Stratification," 82; S.F. Wise, "Sport and Class Values."

54 Ballot dated 21 March 1890. AAA of C Papers, MG 28 I 351 V 2 file 11–1, MAAA Papers, NA.

55 For example, letters between WAAA officials and AAA of C dated 20 March, 21 March, and 7 April 1890. AAA of C Correspondence.

56 AAA of C Correspondence, letter dated 2 April 1890, MAAA Papers, NA. The seventh annual report of the AAA of C, 18, reports Farrell's reinstatement of 28 April 1890. The actual complaint against Farrell does not remain. Local newspaper reports suggest that Farrell had a lengthy history of receiving money for races. In 1881, for example, he ran a running match for $25, and 1883 he ran against A.N. Elder for $50, and against Mayberry in Paris for an unspecified amount. These, of course, occurred

before the creation of the WAAA and presumably in 1884 all local athletes began from scratch. In June 1885, however, Farrell is reported as having signed on with Sleeman's Guelph Maple Leafs to play baseball, and as signing on as a pitcher for a team in the Michigan State League in May 1887.

57 *Eleventh Annual Report of the AAA of C 1894,* 6, MAAA Papers, NA. St Catharines' membership had also lapsed.

58 Gilkeson, *Middle Class Providence,* 136–74.

59 *Chronicle* 13 December 1894.

60 IAAA *Constitution and Bylaws,* 14–15; WAAA *Constitution and Bylaws,* 14–15.

61 Adelman, *A Sporting Time.*

62 IAAA *Constitution and Bylaws,* 15–16; WAAA *Constitution and Bylaws,* 17–18.

63 WAAA *Constitution and Bylaws,* 15–17.

64 *Chronicle* 13 December 1894.

65 *Chronicle* 13 February 1890.

66 Ibid.

67 *Chronicle* 13 December 1894.

68 The WAAA's first building would later be occupied by the store of J.J. Lanigan, while its second building would later house the firm of Bean and Westlake. *Sentinel* 30 December 1886; *Sentinel-Review* Express Industrial Edition.

69 *Sentinel* 27 December 1886.

70 *Chronicle* 13 February 1890.

71 IAAA *Visitor's Register, 1890–1939,* UWO.

72 *Sentinel* 27 December 1886. Presumably his business acumen, coupled with having cultivated connections with the "right" visitors from Montreal, resulted in Pyne being considered a strong candidate for the position of manager of the Montreal AAA in 1889. *Sentinel* 12 April 1889.

73 *Chronicle* 13 February 1890.

74 *Chronicle* 26 April 1894.

75 *Chronicle* 19 April 1894.

76 *Chronicle* 14 March 1889.

77 *Chronicle* 13 February 1890.

78 *Sentinel* 30 May 1884; *Chronicle* 14 March 1889.

79 On the relationship between the church and sport see Howell and Lindsay, "Social Gospel and the Young Boy Problem 1895–1925."

80 *Chronicle* 28 March 1895.

81 *Sentinel* 3 January 1890.

82 Ibid.

83 "Melancholy and Fatal Accident," transcript of *Times* newspaper article in Canfield Collection, Notebook No. 19, 27–9. Woodstock Public

Library; *Sentinel* 27 February 1885; Beverly's father, Colonel James
Ingersoll – a son of Thomas Ingersoll, the founding father of the town
bearing his name – had relocated from Oxford Village (Ingersoll) to
Woodstock in 1847, when the registry office was moved from the one village to the other.

84 "Melancholy and Fatal Accident," transcript of *Times* newspaper article
in Canfield Collection, Notebook No. 19, 27–9, Woodstock Public
Library.

85 Ibid.

86 *Sentinel* 16 May 1884.

87 Joyce, "Canadian Sport and State Control," 24–6; Schrodt, "Sabbatarianism and Sport in Canadian Society."

88 On corporate paternalism and the lack of provisions for sabbatarian
recreation for workers, see Zahavi, *Workers, Managers, and Welfare
Capitalism*, 26–8, 50–3. Thanks to George Emery for bringing my attention to this interesting source.

89 *Sentinel* 14 November 1884.

90 *Sentinel* 13 November 1886.

91 Ibid.

92 *Sentinel* 13 October 1886.

93 *Sentinel* 1 February 1888.

94 *Sentinel* 24 July 1885.

95 *Chronicle* 12 February 1874.

96 *Chronicle* 24 March 1884.

97 *Chronicle* 25 April, 2 May 1879.

98 Donnelly, "Sport as a Site for 'Popular' Resistance." More generally, see
Scott, *Domination and the Arts of Resistance*.

99 *Chronicle* 28 June 1888.

100 *Sentinel* 1 August 1884.

101 *Sentinel* 11 March 1892.

102 *Chronicle* 16 May 1879; 9 March 1882; 27 August 1885; 15 April
1886; 24 April 1886. In May 1886 the Ingersoll town council refused
to sanction the use of the town hall for "sparring," returning hotel
keeper William McMurray's rental deposit. After an intense debate
between town councilors over whether "scientific" fighting was indeed
harmful to athlete or spectator, McMurray's appeal squeaked through
by a narrow margin of 6 to 5. The following week the paper reported
that "a large and respectable audience" had attended the sparring contest (6, 13 May 1886). In Woodstock a similar debate had occurred
some years earlier but with a different outcome: on dogfighting, see
Sentinel 8 June 1883; 4 April 1887; on cockfighting, Woodstock
appears to have been at the centre of a highly organized cockfighting
circuit. *Chronicle* 5 April 1888 and 18 May 1890; *Sentinel* 16 April
1887. See also *Sentinel* 4 July 1889 and 8 April 1891.

103 Joyce, "Canadian Sport and State Control," 30.
104 Canada, *Statutes*. Victoria 44 Ch. 30 (1881).
105 *Sentinel* 27 May 1879.
106 Bonney-James, "More Than a Game," 58.
107 Joyce, "Canadian Sport and State Control," 29.
108 *Sentinel* 16 April 1887. On Bittle and his fisticuffs style, see Joyce, "Canadian Sport and State Control," 30.
109 Bouchier and Cruikshank, "The War on the Squatters."
110 *Spirit of the Times* 13 June 1888.
111 The cockfight occurred on Good Friday. Transcript of the article, Woodstock Museum, x983.1, 430.
112 *Sentinel* 27 December 1886; the names of the others arrested who have been record-linked to the 1891 census, the 1897 Woodstock directory, and "Petition to Messrs. Hay & Co., from Employees." *Sentinel* 28 December 1887.
113 Interview #1, interview by author, August 1989, Woodstock, Ontario.
114 *Sentinel* 3 July 1885.
115 Robinson, "Professional Sport a Half Century Ago." See also *Weekly Review* 11 August 1871 and *Sentinel* 31 October 1884; 12 June 1885; 26 June 1885; 2 April 1887; 26 September 1887; 1, 13, 20 February 1888; 31 July 1888; 18 June 1889.
116 Robinson, "Professional Sport a Half Century Ago."
117 Ibid.
118 *Chronicle* 29 June 1880; 4 August 1881; *Sentinel* 7 August 1885; 29 August 1894.
119 *Sentinel* 29 August 1894.
120 Joyce, "Canadian Sport and State Control," 34–5.

CHAPTER FOUR

1 The author of this reminiscence remains unknown. His reminiscence includes a full description of the building of the Woodstock pitch: "A Cricket Sheaf" (uncatalogued newspaper clipping, n.d., Oxford County Library); "The Thames Valley" (Scrapbook #2, Sawtell Scrapbook Collection, Woodstock Public Library) provides a description of the pitch and Sawtell's recollections of playing in 1845. Joshua Brink apparently sold the land to Deedes.
2 Mangan, *The Games Ethic and Imperialism*; Mangan, ed., *Pleasure, Profit, Proselytism*; Mangan, ed., *Making Imperial Mentalities*.
3 Lillywhite, *The English Cricketers Trip to Canada*, 63–4.
4 Sandiford, "Cricket and Victorian Society," 303. See also Bowen, *Cricket*, 252.

5 Ibid.

6 Lindsay, "The Impact of Military Garrisons on the Development of Sport in British North America," 33. On cricket generally see Robert Moss, "Cricket in Nova Scotia During the nineteenth Century," *Canadian Journal of the History of Sport and Physical Education* 9 (2)(December 1978):58–75; Lindsay, "A History of Sport in Canada"; Wise and Fisher, *Canada's Sporting Heroes*, 8; Day, "The British Garrison at Halifax."

7 Gruneau, *Class, Sports and Social Development*, particularly chapter 5, "Outline of the Canadian Case."

8 "That Aristocratic Neighborhood of Woodstock," *Globe* 24 May 1878; reprinted 24 July 1967.

9 Jameson, *Winter Studies and Summer Rambles in Canada*; Smith, *Smith's Canadian Gazetteer*, 123–9.

10 Manuscript census of Woodstock, 1851; Shenston, *The Oxford Gazetteer*, 115–24. On the officers, see Bettridge Papers, Ontario Archives; "Henry Vansittart," *Concise Dictionary of National Biography* (London: Oxford University Press, 1965), 133; "Andrew Drew," *Dictionary of Canadian Biography* 10:259–60; Dommett, *Canadian Journal*; Ireland, "Andrew Drew, the Man Who Burned the Caroline"; Ireland, "Andrew Drew and the Founding of Woodstock;" and Canfield, *Vice Admiral Henry Vansittart*.

11 Sawtell, "The Thames Valley," Sawtell Scrapbook Collection, Woodstock Public Library. Colonel Deedes' house and the board fence is captured on one of the earliest known photographs taken by local photographic amateur Robert Stark in 1865. Keith Douglas DeLellis Collection, PA 207182, NA.

12 "A Cricket Sheaf," uncatalogued newspaper clipping, n.d., Oxford County Library.

13 On the social atmosphere of pre-Confederation cricket see Lindsay, "A History of Sport in Canada," 98*ff*; Booth and Batts, "The Political Significance of Organized Sport in Upper Canada, 1825–1867."

14 *Woodstock Herald and Brock District Advertiser* 26 September 1845. The Cricketer's Hotel, located near Beachville, is listed in Sutherland, *Oxford Gazetteer and General Business Director for 1862–1863*, 107. Its location is identified on the map found in M. Cropp, *Beachville, The Birthplace of Oxford 1784–1969* (reprint, Beachville Centennial Committee, 1967), 24.

15 *Woodstock Herald and Brock District Advertiser* 15 September 1849.

16 *British American* 29 September 1849.

17 These points are taken from George Kirsch, review of Adelman, *A Sporting Time: New York City and the Rise of Modern Athletics. Journal of Sport History* 13 (2) (Summer 1986):155. See also Kirsch, *The Creation of American Team Sports*.

18 On the high costs of transportation before 1840, see Pred, *Urban Growth and the Circulation of Information.*

19 The *Woodstock Herald and Brock District Advertiser, British American,* and Hall and McCullough, *Sixty Years of Canadian Cricket* all reported on Woodstock cricket club matches. On travel in the area at the time, see W.B. Hobson, "Old Stage Coach Days in Oxford County," *Ontario Historical Society Papers and Records* 17 (1919):33-6. On the province's bad roads generally, see Edwin C. Guillet, *Pioneer Travel in Upper Canada* (Toronto: University of Toronto Press, 1976).

20 Jameson, *Winter Studies and Summer Rambles in Canada,* 119.

21 On Oxford County newspapers in the period, see Brian Dawe, *Old Oxford is Wide Awake!,* 96-7. The *Woodstock Herald and Brock District Advertiser* (1840-48), the first paper in Oxford County, voiced a moderately Tory political view while the *Monarch* (1842-48) held an extreme Tory view. The *British American* (1848-53), was a conservative journal, with J.G. Vansittart, son of the vice admiral, as its principal proprietor. The *Oxford Star* (1848-49) expressed reform views.

22 *British American* 29 September 1849.

23 Bowen, *Cricket.*

24 Sawtell, "The Thames Valley," Sawtell Scrapbook Collection, Woodstock Public Library.

25 Phillips, *Canadian Cricketer's Guide and Review,* 14; Along the same vein, R.A. Fitzgerald claims in his *Wickets in the West* that "to our mind there is ... no bad taste displayed in an invitation handsomely couched and generously accepted. Cricket admits of no distinctions, it is a sport of all sports which affords an open platform to all classes" (325).

26 C.L.R. James's *Beyond a Boundary* (London, 1963) offers a poignant social and cultural analysis of this aspect of cricket in the West Indies. See also Alan Metcalfe, "C.L.R. James and his Contributions to Sport History," *Canadian Journal of History of Sport* (December 1987):52-7.

27 The club did not employ a professional. On the distinction between "gentlemen" and "players" in this practice see Sandiford, "Cricket and Victorian Society"; Kirsch, *The Creation of American Team Sports*; Lincoln Allison, "Batsman and Bowler: The Key Relation of Victorian England," *Journal of Sport History* 7 (2) (Summer 1980):5-20.

28 *Canadian Cricket Field* 26 July 1882.

29 St Catherine's Cricket Club, *Canadian Cricketer's Guide and Review,* 71.

30 Roxborough, *One Hundred Not Out*; Wise,"Sport and Class Values"; Joyce, "At Close of Play"; Mott, "Manly Sport and Manitobans."

31 This happened across Canada, including in British Columbia. See Barman, "Sports and the Development of Character."

32 Gruneau argues that muscular Christian precepts and the rational approach to sport popularized by the public schools "educated the young

bourgeoisie in a sense of gentlemanly propriety which would subvert their individualistic tendencies and integrate them into a broader, more organic commitment to the collectivity" (*Class, Sports and Social Development*, 103). On the use of sport in the public schools, see Mangan, *Athleticism in the Victorian and Edwardian Public School*; Brown, "Sport, Darwinism, and Canadian Private Schooling to 1918."

33 Mangan, *Athleticism in the Victorian and Edwardian Public School*; Brown, "Sport Darwinism, and Canadian Private Schooling to 1918."

34 Brown, "Athleticism in Selected Canadian Private Schools," 65.

35 *Patriot* 15 July 1836.

36 Woodstock *Weekly Review* 30 June 1871; 13 September 1872; *Roll of Pupils of Upper Canada College from 1829 to 1898* (Toronto, 1898); George Dickson and G. Mercer Adam, *A History of Upper Canada College, 1829–1892* (Toronto: Rowsell & Hutchison, 1893).

37 Fitzgerald, *Wickets in the West*, 131–60; Gillespie, "Wickets in the West." More generally, see Brown, "Canadian Imperialism and Sporting Exchanges."

38 Holt, "Cricket and Englishness"; Mandle, "W.G. Grace as Victorian Hero."

39 Woodstock *Weekly Review* 24 May 1872.

40 Phillips, *Canadian Cricketer's Guide and Review*, 47; *Chronicle* 21 August 1873, 4 September 1879; Woodstock *Weekly Review* 24 May 1872, 16 July 1880; on the death of cricket, see: Cooper, "Canadians Declare 'It Isn't Cricket'" [1996]; Gillespie, "Wickets in the West." On cricket exceptionalism see Melville, "From Ethnic Tradition to Community Institution."

41 On the variety of ways in which Canadians played cricket, see Metcalfe, *Canada Learns to Play*, 80–95; Howell, *Northern Sandlots*, 13–36.

42 *Pioneer* article reprinted in the *Sentinel-Review* 13 December 1920.

43 *Chronicle* 17 September 1874.

44 *Chronicle* 21 August 1873; 27 May 1875; 29 July 1875.

45 *Chronicle* 17 September 1874; 4 March 1875.

46 *Chronicle* 21 August 1879.

47 Formed sporadically, these clubs typically played between one and three matches a season. Ingersoll clubs competed in 1857, 1859, 1860, 1862–65, 1874, 1875, and 1879. In Woodstock clubs competed in 1859–60, 1863–64, 1871, 1879 and 1882.

48 *Chronicle* 27 July 1860.

49 For example, *Chronicle* 27 July 1869, 11 August 1871, and August 1874; *Sentinel* 11 August 1874.

50 Gillespie, "Wickets in the West."

51 [Patteson], "The Recent Cricket Match," 611.

52 Ibid.

53 Ibid. Patteson appears to not have tried to revive the game in Woodstock, where the elite tradition had so clearly died.

54 Club membership lists have been record-linked to local directories, gazetteers, and manuscript census of the Canadas. Ingersoll, 1860, 1875.

55 *Chronicle* 17 April 1873.

56 *Sentinel-Review* 14 July 1927.

57 *Chronicle* 17 August 1860.

58 *Chronicle* 4 September 1874. On the scientific approach to the game, see *Felix on the Bat.*

59 Woodstock *Weekly Review* 24 May 1872.

60 Woodstock *Weekly Review* 28 March 1871.

61 *Chronicle* 3 August 1860.

62 On ethnic associations in the towns see Anstead, "Fraternalism in Victorian Ontario."

63 Metcalfe, *Canada Learns to Play*; Howell, *Northern Sandlots*; Cox, "A History of Sport in Canada, 1868–1900"; Lindsay, "A History of Sport in Canada, 1807–1868." For American developments, see Kirsch, *The Creation of American Team Sports.*

64 Lillywhite, *The English Cricketers Trip to Canada*, 53.

65 Metcalfe makes this point in *Canada Learns to Play*, 82. See also Cox, "A History of Sport in Canada, 1868–1900," 70–1, and Lindsay, "A History of Sport in Canada, 1807–1868," 104–5.

66 Kirsch, *The Creation of American Team Sports*; Adelman, *A Sporting Time*; and Tyrrell, "The Emergence of Modern American Baseball c. 1850–1880."

67 Howell, *Northern Sandlots*, 33.

68 Adelman, *A Sporting Time.*

69 *Sentinel* 20 December 1899.

70 Anstead, "Fraternalism in Victorian Ontario," 264–6.

71 Woodstock *Weekly Review* 30 June 1871; 13 September 1872; *Roll of Pupils of Upper Canada College from 1829 to 1898.*

72 *Sentinel* 20 April 1888.

CHAPTER FIVE

1 *New York Clipper* 14 August 1869.

2 Bouchier and Barney, "A Critical Examination of a Source on Early Ontario Baseball"; Henderson, *Ball, Bat and Bishop.*

3 *Sporting Life* 5 May 1886.

4 Cropp, "Beachville the Birthplace of Oxford," 18.

5 *Sporting Life* 5 May 1886. Ford's obituary can be found in the *Denver Post* 18 May 1906 and in the *Annual of the Ontario Curling Association for 1906–1907* (32), 29–30. See also Bernie McLay, *The Cruttendon*

Family (Unpublished manuscript, St Mary's Museum, St. Mary's Ontario), 21–42. On Ford's involvement in organized sport see Bouchier and Barney, "A Critical Examination of a Source on Early Ontario Baseball."

6 Ford supposed the date to be George IV's birthday, since that was the monarch who reigned just before Ford's birth. In fact, the date was George III's birthday, as designated by *Statutes of Upper Canada*, 33 George III ch.1, 1793 (passed 9 July 1793). *An Act for the Better Regulation of the Militia in this Province.*

7 *Sporting Life* 5 May 1886. The practice of "plugging," "soaking," or "burning" a runner was commonplace until the Cartwright game replaced the manoeuvre with the practice of tagging base runners. See William Clarke, *The Boy's Own Book* (London and Boston, 1829); Robin Carver, *The Book of Sports* (Boston, 1834).

8 *New York Clipper* 18 August 1860. The Victorias at first were named the Rough and Ready club. On early baseball club formation generally, see Adelman, *A Sporting Time*; Kirsch, *The Creation of American Team Sports*; Seymour, *Baseball: the Early Years.*

9 *New York Clipper* 18 August 1860. On 22 June 1861 the *New York Clipper* reported on a match between Young Canadian Players and nine picked from the town of Woodstock, which was "the first match that has ever been played there on the New York system"; Humber, *Diamonds of the North*, 23–8; see also Chadwick, ed., *Beadle's Dime Base-Ball Player.* Apparently Chadwick sold some 50,000 of this volume annually. See Hardy, "Entrepreneurs, Organizations and the Sport Marketplace," 17.

10 Of thirty-three Victoria players, roughly 87 per cent were Ontario-born, with the remaining players American and then British-born. 63 per cent of the group were under the age of twenty-one, whilst the ages of the remaining players ranged from twenty-two to thirty-three years. All were Protestant (one-half Methodist and the remaining distributed through the Church of England, Presbyterian, and Baptist Churches). Of twenty-five Young Canadian players, roughly 75 per cent were Ontario-born, with the remainder being distributed equally among American and British-born. Roughly equal numbers of the players were under twenty-one years of age and between twenty-two and thirty-three years old. All but one of these players was Protestant (one-half of which were Methodist, with slightly more Presbyterians than members of the Church of England and Baptist Church).

11 Voigt, *American Baseball*; Seymour, *Baseball: The Early Years.*

12 Adelman, *A Sporting Time*, 141–2; Howell, *Northern Sandlots*; Howell, "Baseball, Class and Community in the Maritime Provinces, 1870–1910."

13 Tecumseh Baseball Club of London Minute Book, UWO.

14 Kirsch, *The Creation of American Team Sports*; Adelman, *A Sporting Time*; Howell, *Northern Sandlots*.
15 *Chronicle* 9 June 1865; 27 April 1866; 26 March 1868; 1 April 1869.
16 *Hamilton Times* 23 February 1867. See also *Chronicle* 3 August 1863.
17 Thomas Wells Diary, v. 2, 296, Public Archives of Ontario; George A. Gray Diaries, 2, 3 July 1869, Woodstock Museum.
18 *Chronicle* 18 August 1869.
19 *New York Clipper* 22 June 1864; 14 September 1864; *Hamilton Times* 24 August 1864; *Chronicle* 26 August 1864; undated clipping from Toronto *Star Weekly*, Louise Hill Collection, UWO; on C.L. Wood, see Humber, *Diamonds of the North*, 25.
20 Adelman, *A Sporting Time*.
21 *Hamilton Spectator* 29 September 1864.
22 *Hamilton Times* 29 September 1866.
23 *Hamilton Spectator* 11 August 1864. Whatever became of the Silver Ball trophies, two of which are pictured in the *Star Weekly* 19 July 1924, is not known.
24 *Hamilton Spectator* 11 August 1864; *New York Clipper* 28 May 1871; *Sentinel* 28 May 1880.
25 Chadwick, ed., *Beadle's Dime Base-Ball Player*.
26 *New York Clipper* 26 June 1869; 28 May 1871.
27 *New York Clipper* 14 September 1864.
28 *Chronicle* 3, 13 August 1868.
29 Humber, *Diamonds of the North*, 5.
30 *New York Clipper* 14 September 1864.
31 Guelph *Evening Mercury* 5 August 1868; Bonney-James, "More Than a Game"; Bernard, "The Guelph Maple Leafs."
32 *New York Clipper* 19 June 1869.
33 *New York Clipper* 17 July 1869.
34 *Chronicle* 13 August 1868.
35 *Chronicle* 3 August 1866.
36 *Chronicle* 21 May 1868.
37 Bonney-James, "More Than a Game," 78–80.
38 Guelph *Evening Mercury* 5 August 1868.
39 Ibid. Also see Guelph *Evening Telegram* 27 September 1923. On this match see Humber, *Cheering for the Home Team*, 29.
40 Guelph *Evening Mercury* 5 August 1868.
41 Guelph *Evening Mercury* 15 August 1868. See also *Evening Mercury* 6, 8 August 1868.
42 Gruneau and Whitson, *Hockey Night In Canada*, 69.
43 Howell, "Baseball, Class and Community in the Maritime Provinces, 1870–1910."
44 Humber, *Diamonds of the North*, 26.

45 *New York Clipper* 14 September 1864.

46 Bonney-James, "More Than a Game," 87.

47 *Chronicle* 16 June 1868; "Astronomical Baseball Scores," *London Free Press* 15 July 1968.

48 Les Bronson, Address on Baseball, UWO; Tecumseh Baseball Club Minute Book, 19 April 1869; 14 June 1869, UWO.

49 *New York Clipper* 31 July 1869.

50 *New York Clipper* 17 July 1869.

51 Tecumseh Baseball Club Minute Book, 21 August 1869, UWO.

52 Bernard, "The Guelph Maple Leafs"; Humber, *Diamonds of the North*; Bonney-James, "More Than a Game."

53 Guelph *Evening Mercury* article, undated 1917, George Sleeman Collection, File 4065, UWO; *Star Weekly* 19 July 1924.

54 *Bryce's 1876 Canadian Baseball Guide*, 8; see also *Hamilton Times* 16 June 1871.

55 *New York Clipper* 22 April, 6 May 1876; *Bryce's 1876 Canadian Baseball Guide*; *Canadian Gentleman's Journal of Sporting Times* 28 April 1876.

56 See Bonney-James, "More Than a Game," 89*ff.*

57 *Bryce's 1876 Canadian Baseball Guide.*

58 *Canadian Gentleman's Journal of Sporting Times* 28 April 1876.

59 *Globe* 22 May 1880.

60 Metcalfe, *Canada Learns to Play*, 86.

61 *Sentinel* 30 July 1880, reprinted from the London *Advertiser*; *Mail and Empire* 24 May 1880; *Globe* 22 May 1880.

62 Humber, *Diamonds of the North*, 5.

63 Guelph *Evening Mercury* undated article, 1917, in George Sleeman Collection, UWO; *Globe* 17 May 1884.

64 Guelph *Evening Mercury* undated article, 1917, in George Sleeman Collection, UWO. Humber and Bonney-James both point out that Sleeman never really held to this position.

65 Gruneau and Whitson, *Hockey Night in Canada*, 67.

66 *Sentinel* 18 April 1884.

67 *Sentinel* 21 July 1889.

68 *Sentinel* 22 July 1889.

69 *Sentinel* 27 April 1889.

70 Stephen J. Gamester, "You Can't Tell the Canadian Big-League Heroes Without a Program. Here it is." *Maclean's Magazine* 22 August 1964. O'Neill has been inducted into Canada's Sports Hall of Fame and the Canadian Baseball Hall of Fame.

71 *Sentinel* 19 June 1885; 10 May, 5 March, 29, 30 June, 5 August 1887; 12, 28 April, 18 May, 22 June 1888; *Ingersoll Sun* Industrial Ingersoll Illustrated, 25th Anniversary Souvenir Edition, February 1907.

72 For example, *Chronicle* 6 July 1866; 20 June 1878; 8 May 1890; *Sentinel* 13 August 1880; 25 August, 8 September 1882; 28 August 1885, 30 May, 15 July, 15, 23 August 1887; 14 August 1888.

73 Palmer, *A Culture in Conflict*, 52.

74 *Chronicle* 8 June 1878; 30 July 1885; 7 July 1888; 8 September 1888; 25 April 1889; Emery, *Noxons of Ingersoll, 1856–1918*, 39–40.

75 *Sentinel* 27 August 1875; 9 September 1878; 13 August 1879; 25 August 1882; 29 August 1884; 15 August 1887. Ontario, *Report of the Inspectors of Factories for the Province of Ontario, 1888*.

76 *Sentinel-Review Illustrated Supplement* 4 February 1899; "Recall When Bain Wagons Brought Fame to Woodstock," newspaper clipping, 21 February 1957, Tunaley Collection, Woodstock Public Library.

77 Sangster, "The Softball Solution"; see also Zahavi, *Workers, Managers, and Welfare Capitalism.*

78 Spence, *The Facts of the Case*, 59.

79 Gelber, "Their Hands are all out Playing," 27.

80 Although not the case in Ingersoll and Woodstock for the period studied, some factory owners strengthened alliances with their workers by standing up against Sabbatarian legislation on their behalf. See Zahavi, *Workers, Managers, and Welfare Capitalism.*

81 *Sentinel* 16 April 1888.

CHAPTER SIX

1 *Chronicle* 6 July 1871.

2 Ibid.

3 *Chronicle* 13 July 1871.

4 *Sentinel* 16 June 1871.

5 I use the terminology used by lacrosse writers of the era. For a view of the game from the Native Indian oral tradition, see *Tewaarathon (Lacrosse): Akwesasne's Story of Our National Game*. On European interpretations of lacrosse in Indian cultures: Culin, "Games of the North American Indians"; George Catlin, *Letters and Notes on the Manners, Customs and condition of the North American Indians* vol. 2 (London: The Egyptian Hall, 1871); Salter, "The Effect of Acculturation." See also Poulter, "Playing the Game."

6 Beers, *Lacrosse;* Metcalfe, *Canada Learns to Play*, 181–218; Morrow et al., *A Concise History of Sport*, 45–68; Burr, "The Process of Evolution of Competitive Sport"; Weyand and Roberts, *The Lacrosse Story.*

7 Beers, *Lacrosse*, 35.

8 Morrow, "The Institutionalization of Sport."

9 Beers, "Canadian Sports"; Goal Keeper, *The Game of Lacrosse;* "The Ocean Travels of Lacrosse," *Athletic Leaves* (September 1888):42;

"A Rival to Cricket," *Chambers Journal* 18 (December 1862):366–8; McNaught, *Lacrosse and how to play it.*

10 Houston, "Politics, Schools, and Social Change in Upper Canada"; Houston, "Victorian Origins of Juvenile Delinquency"; Houston and Prentice, *Schools and Scholars in Nineteenth Century Ontario;* Prentice, *The School Promoters;* Gidney and Millar, *Inventing Secondary Education.*

11 I have gleaned this information from the *Annual Report of the Normal, Model, Grammar and Common Schools in Ontario* found in the Ontario Sessional Papers Report of the Minister of Education (No. 3) 1893.

12 Riess, "Sport and the Redefinition of Middle Class Masculinity"; Mangan and Walvin, eds., *Manliness and Morality;* Rotundo, "Body and Soul"; Maguire, "Images of Manliness and Competing Ways of Living."

13 Howell and Lindsay, "Social Gospel and the Young Boy Problem, 1895–1925"; MacLeod, "A Live Vaccine."

14 Riess, "Sport and the Redefinition of Middle Class Masculinity," 5.

15 Beers, *Lacrosse,* 42–3.

16 *Chronicle* 10 April 1873.

17 For example, *Chronicle* 23 March, 24 September 1868; 10 April 1873; 16 May 1878; 27 November, 4 December 1884. To keep its readers abreast of criminal happenings, the *Chronicle* instituted a new regular column, "Crimes of the Week."

18 *Chronicle* 27 November 1884.

19 Ontario, *Report of the Commissioners Appointed to enquire into the Prison and Reformatory System,* 1891, 529. Thanks to Susan Houston for bringing this item to my attention.

20 *Sentinel* 19 April 1880.

21 Marks, *Revivals and Roller Rinks.*

22 Reprints of sermons, in whole or part, found in *Sentinel* 20 November 1887; *Herald* 14 March 1845; *Chronicle* 25 October 1888; 30 January 1868.

23 Marks, *Revivals and Roller Rinks,* 122.

24 *Chronicle* 7 November 1872.

25 *Chronicle* 20 June 1867.

26 *Sentinel* 29 January 1889.

27 As cited in Riess, "Sport and the Redefinition of Middle Class Masculinity," 11; Mrozek, *Sport and American Mentality, 1880–1910;* B.G. Jefferis, *Light on Dark Corners. A Complete Sexual Science* (Toronto: J.L. Nichols and Co., 1895).

28 McIntosh, *Sport and Society,* 69–79; Redmond, "The First Tom Brown's Schooldays and Others"; Lewis, "The Muscular Christianity Movement."

29 Beers, *Lacrosse.*

30 On the development of lacrosse generally, see Metcalfe, *Canada Learns*

to Play, 181–218; Lindsay, "A History of Sport in Canada, 1807–1867," 114–32.

31 Claxton's obituary from *Sunday World*, 1908, as cited in Cross, *One Hundred Years of Service with Youth*, 144.

32 See Cross, *One Hundred Years of Service with Youth*. Local connections between lacrosse and the YMCA in Woodstock also predated the association's full-scale involvement in sport. At its outset in 1871 the Woodstock YMCA's aim, "the improvement of the religious, mental, and social conditions of young men in Woodstock," overlooked sport, but within two years the Beavers and the YMCA were contemplating combining their energies to form a gymnasium. By 1874 the Beavers used YMCA clubrooms for lacrosse meetings. *Sentinel* 24 October 1873, 29 May 1874; W. Stewart Lavell, *All This Was Yesterday: The Story of the YMCA in Woodstock, Ontario, 1868–1972* (Woodstock: Talbot Communications, 1972).

33 *Sentinel* 7 July, 28 November 1871. Today the pennant is kept in the Woodstock Museum.

34 Weiler, "The Idea of Sport in Late Victorian Canada."

35 Beers, *Lacrosse*, 52; Burr, "The Process of Evolution of Competitive Sport."

36 Beers, *Lacrosse*, 50; Anstead, "Fraternalism in Victorian Ontario"; Dumenil, *Freemasonry and American Culture, 1880–1930*; Gilkeson, *Middle Class Providence, 1820–1940*.

37 Beers, *Lacrosse*, 42.

38 *Chronicle* 7 July 1887; *Sentinel* 30 June 1887.

39 "Testimonial to Edward W. Nesbitt. Woodstock 26 November, 1879" [my emphasis]. Woodstock Museum.

40

Table 6.1
The number of senior and junior baseball and lacrosse clubs in
Ingersoll and Woodstock, 1860–1889

	Jr baseball		Jr lacrosse		Sr baseball		Sr lacrosse	
	Ing.	Wdsk.	Ing.	Wdsk.	Ing.	Wdsk.	Ing.	Wdsk.
1860–64	0	0	–	–	1	1	–	–
1865–69	2	2	–	–	1	1	–	–
1870–74	5	5	1	6	2	2	3	4
1875–79	8	11	2	4	2	2	0	3
1880–84	7	2	7	12	1	2	4	7
1885–89	5	16	13	15	2	2	5	5
total	27	36	23	37	9	10	12	19

Source: Ingersoll and Woodstock sport database in author's posession.

41 Poulter, "Playing the Game."
42 *Sentinel* 20 June 1887.
43 McNaught, *Lacrosse and how to play it*, 19.
44 *Chronicle* 13 September 1888.
45 On the founding of the CLA see Toronto *Mail* 8, 9, 13, 15, 18, 20, 23, 26 April 1887. More generally, see Metcalfe, *Canada Learns to Play*, 206–8.
46 *Norwich Gazette* 15 July 1886.
47 *Chronicle* 14 September 1888.
48 *Sentinel-Review* Birth of the Industrial City Edition 9 July 1901.
49 On the relationship between team and town, see Mott, "One Town's Team"; Betke, "Sports Promotion in the Western Canadian City."
50 *Chronicle* 13 July 1871.
51 *Chronicle* 30 June 1885; 19 May 1887.
52 *Chronicle* 10 May 1888.
53 *Sentinel* 1 April 1874.
54 *Sentinel* 21 May 1880; 21 November 1884.
55 *Sentinel* 16 May 1888.
56 In 1871 the Beavers paid the Grand River Indians $60 to compete against them in the May 24th match. Ten-cent admissions covered this outlay and brought a $159 profit to the club (*Sentinel* 7 July 1871). Other Native Indian teams were the Tuscaroras, Onondagas, Muncitown, Sioux, and Six Nations. *Sentinel* 7 July 1871; 31 May, 23 August 1872; 26 June 1874; 23 May, 4 July 1879; 30 April 1880; 23 June 1882; 25 May 1887; *Chronicle* 9 May 1877. See Daniel Francis, "Marketing the Imaginary Indian," in *The Imaginary Indian: The Image of the Indian in Canadian Culture* (Vancouver: Arsenal Pulp Press, 1992), 173–90; Poulter, "Playing the Game."
57 George A. Gray Diaries, 3 July 1871; 24 May 1872, Woodstock Museum.
58 *Chronicle* 3 July 1879.
59 Wamsley, "Nineteenth Century Sport Tours"; Poulter, "Playing the Game"; Morrow, "The Canadian Image Abroad"; Brown, "Canadian Imperialism and Sporting Exchanges."
60 *Sentinel-Review* 1 July 1893.
61 On escalating violence and rowdyism in lacrosse see Metcalfe, *Canada Learns to Play*, 192–203; Metcalfe, "Sport and Athletics"; Burr, "The Process of the Evolution of Competitive Sport."
62 Pinto, "Ain't Misbehavin.'"
63 *Sentinel* 22, 29 August 1879; 25 August 1882; 15 September 1886; 28, 30 June 1887; *Chronicle* 23 June 1887.
64 *Sentinel* 22 August 1879.
65 *Sentinel* 20 July 1887.

66 *Chronicle* 23 June 1887.
67 The editorial went on to say, "Betting, slugging, and professionalism follow in natural order. Suppress the first and the other evils are easily dealt
with." *Sentinel* 30 July 1887.
68 *Sentinel* 3 July 1885.
69 Pinto, "Ain't Misbehavin' "; Metcalfe, "Sport and Athletics."
70 *Sentinel* 6 September 1888.
71 Reported in *Sentinel* 7 August 1885. Related to the incident, see *Sentinel*
7, 14 August 1885; *Chronicle* 6 August 1885.
72 Tillsonburg *Liberal* editorial reprinted in the *Sentinel* 30 July 1887.
73 Tillsonburg *Liberal* editorial reprinted with comments, *Chronicle* 28 June
1888.
74 *Chronicle* 28 June 1888.
75 *Chronicle* 30 July 1885.

CHAPTER SEVEN

1 *Toronto Telegram* as reprinted in the *Sentinel-Review* 5 March 1901.
2 Ibid.
3 Guelph *Evening Mercury* article (my emphasis), undated 1917, File 4065,
George Sleeman Collection, UWO.
4 For feminist analyses of sport, see Hall, *Feminism and Sporting Bodies;*
Hargreaves, *Sporting Females.*
5 Mott, "The British Protestant Pioneers and the Establishment of Manly
Sports in Manitoba"; Mott, "One Solution to the Urban Crisis"; Rotundo, "Body and Soul"; Haley, "Sports and the Victorian World"; Stearns,
Be a Man!, 101–2; Hall, "Rarely Have We Asked Why"; Lenskyj, *Out of
Bounds;* Reet Howell, ed., *Her Story in Sport* (New York: Leisure Press,
1982).
6 Hall, *The Girl and the Game*; Vertinsky, The Eternally Wounded Woman;
Costa and Guthrie, eds., *Women and Sport*; Mangan and Park, eds.,
From Fair Sex to Feminism; McCrone, *Sport and the Physical Emancipation*; Hall and Richardson, *Fair Ball*; Smith, "Graceful Athleticism or
Robust Womanhood."
7 Kidd, *The Struggle for Canadian Sport,* 94–145; Hall, *The Girl and the
Game*; Smith, "Graceful Athleticism and Robust Womanhood"; Marion
Pitters-Casswell, "Women's Participation in Sporting Activities as an Indicator of a Feminist Movement in Canada, 1867–1914," *Proceedings of
the Third Canadian Symposium on the History of Sport* (Halifax: Dalhousie University, 1974).
8 McLuhan, "Baseball is Culture."
9 Kidd, *The Struggle for Canadian Sport.*

APPENDIX

1 For good overviews of the issue of locality and sport see Tomlinson, "Shifting Patterns of Working Class Leisure," 193–5; Bonney-James, "More Than a Game," 3–4; Melville, "From Ethnic Tradition to Community Institution."
2 On this tendency, see Howell, *Blood, Sweat, and Cheers*, 40–1, 144–5.
3 Bouchard and Pouyez, "Les Categories Socio-Professionelles: Une Nouveau Grille de Classment."

Bibliography

ARCHIVAL SOURCES

J.J. Talman Regional Collection, D.B. Weldon Library,
University of Western Ontario (UWO)

Dr Charles Augustus Sippi Diaries
Ethel Canfield Papers
George Sleeman Collection
Ingersoll Amateur Athletic Association. Visitor's Register
Louise Hill Collection
Stanley J. Smith Papers
Tecumseh Baseball Club of London. Minute Book 1868–1872
Victor Lauriston Oxford County Collection
Les Bronson, Address on Baseball. Unpublished paper given to the Middlesex
  Historical Society, 1972

Local History Room, Woodstock Public Library

Art Williams Scrapbooks
Colonel Alexander Walley Light Diary, 1833
Edwin Bennett Collection
Ethel Canfield Collection, Notebooks
Pearl W. Hunter Scrapbook Collection
R.W. Sawtell Scrapbook Collection. "The Thames Valley," Scrapbook #2
Statement of Pewholders and Pew Rentals Due St. Paul's Church, Woodstock
Tunaley Scrapbook collection
Woodstock Public Library Name Index
Woodstock Scrapbooks
Young People's Christian Association. *Constitution, Bylaws, and Order of*
  Exercises. Woodstock, 1862

National Archives of Canada *(NA)*

Canadian Cycling Association Papers
Montreal Amateur Athletic Association Papers
  Bicycle Correspondence Letterbook 1890–1897
  AAA of C Minute Books 1883–1887; Annual Reports 1884–1896, 1898;
    Records of Track and Field Championships 1878–1909
  Montreal Bicycle club. Minute Book 1878–1882, 1885–1891; Letterbook
    1897–1903
  Montreal Toboggan and Lacrosse Club. Minute Books and Letterbooks
Montreal Caledonia Curling Club Papers
Royal Caledonian Curling Club Papers. Letterbooks 1869–1880

Woodstock Museum

Alex Matheson Sutherland Notebook
Frank Hyde Papers. "Old Time Sports." Unpublished manuscript. "The Sal-
  vation of True Amateur Hockey." Unpublished manuscript. "Sport is an
  Universal Institution. International in it's Scope" [*sic*]. Unpublished manu-
  script. "Why Sport is Organized." Unpublished manuscript
George A. Gray Diaries, 1857–1878
Photograph Collection
Testimonial to E.W. Nesbitt, 26 November 1879
Woodstock Amateur Athletic Association. *Constitution and Consolidated
  Bylaws, 1908.* Woodstock: Sentinel-Review Co. Printers, 1908
– *Programme Spring Championship Meet Victoria Day 24 May 1910*
– *Programme of the 4ᵗʰ Annual Meet and Races. Queen's Birthday 24 May
  1887*
Woodstock Fire Insurance Maps, 1899/1913

Local History Room, Oxford County Library, Woodstock Branch

Conway, Robert. "Memoirs of the 1880s." Unpublished manuscript
"A Cricket Sheaf." Uncataloged newspaper clipping, n.d.
Oxford County Name Index
Edwin Seaborn Collection
Leonard Keeler Coles Collection
Woodstock North Women's Institute Tweedsmuir History

Other Collections

Byron Jenvy Scrapbooks. Ingersoll Public Library

Ingersoll Amateur Athletic Association. *Constitution and Bylaws.* Ingersoll,
    1889. Ingersoll Cheese Factory Museum Archives
Ingersoll and Woodstock Fraternal Order Membership Lists, compiled and
    held in Christopher Anstead Private Collection
Ingersoll Scrapbooks. Ingersoll Public Library
Interview #1. Interview by author. Woodstock, Ontario, August 1989
Scrapbooks. London Public Library
Sports Memorabilia. Ingersoll Cheese Factory Museum Archives
Thomas Wells Diaries, 1854–1861. Public Archives of Ontario
W. Bettridge Papers. Ontario Archives
William Walker Diary, 1873. Norwich County Archives

GOVERNMENT SOURCES

Canada

Canada. *Census Report of Canada.* 1871, 1881, 1891
Canada. *Manuscript Census of Canada.* Ingersoll and Woodstock, 1871,
    1881, 1891 (microfilm)
Canada. *Report of the Royal Commission of the Relations of Labour and
    Capital in Canada.* 1889
Canada. *Royal Commission in Racing Inquiry* 10 George V 67 1920

Province of Canada

Census Report of the Canadas, 1851, 1861
Manuscript Census. Ingersoll and Woodstock, 1851, 1861 (microfilm)
Legislative Assembly. *Appendices to the Journals of the Legislative Assembly.*
    1844–1859
Legislative Assembly. *Journals of the Legislative Assembly.* 1842–1866
Legislative Assembly. *Sessional Papers.* 1860–1866

Province of Ontario

Ontario. *Annual Reports* (titles vary): Bureau of Industries, 1886, 1888,
    1890; Inspectors of Factories, 1888–1900; Schools, 1868, 1869, 1872–3,
    1878, 1883, 1888, 1893
Ontario. *Report of the Commissioners Appointed to enquire into the
    Prison and Reformatory System* Sessional papers v XXIII, part IV (18)
    1891
Ontario. *Twenty-third Annual Report of the Inspector of Prisons and Public
    Charities* Sessional Papers v XIII, part III (7) 1891

PERIODICALS AND NEWSPAPERS ON MICROFILM

Athletic Life (Canadian), 1885–1896
British American (Woodstock), 1848–1853
Canadian Cricket Field, 1880s
Canadian Gentleman's Journal and Sporting Times, 1875–1877
Canadian Wheelman, 1883–1887
Daily Chronicle (Ingersoll), 1879–1895
Daily Sentinel (Woodstock), 1886–1890
Herald and Brock District General Advertiser (Woodstock), 1840–1848
Journal-Argus (St Mary's), 1857–1897
Monarch (Woodstock), 1842–1845
New York Clipper, 1853–1870
Oxford Star and Woodstock Advertiser, 1848–1849
Sentinel-Review (Woodstock) The Garden of Ontario Special Edition, May 1897
Sentinel-Review Diamond Jubilee Edition, 25 October 1947
Sentinel-Review Express Industrial Number, February 1906
Sentinel-Review 50th Anniversary Edition, 11 September 1936
Sentinel-Review Inaugural Edition, 1901
Spirit of the Times (Woodstock), 1855
Sporting Life (Philadelphia), 1883–1887
Sun (Ingersoll) Industrial Ingersoll Illustrated, 25th Anniversary Souvenir Edition, February 1907
Tribune (Ingersoll), 1876–1879
Weekly Beacon (Stratford), 1855–1869
Weekly Chronicle and Canadian Dairyman (Ingersoll), 1853–1895
Weekly Review (Woodstock), 1869–1878
Weekly Sentinel (Woodstock), 1858–1869
Weekly Sentinel-Review (Woodstock), 1870–1895

PRINTED SOURCES

Abbott, Frank. "Cold Cash and Ice Palaces: The Quebec Winter Carnival of 1894." *Canadian Historical Review* 69 (2) (June 1988):167–202.
Adelman, Melvin L. *A Sporting Time: New York City and the Rise of Modern Athletics 1820–1870*. Urbana: University of Illinois Press, 1986.
Anstead, Christopher J. "Fraternalism in Victorian Ontario: Secret Societies and Cultural Hegemony." Ph.D. dissertation, University of Western Ontario, 1992.
– "Patriotism and Camaraderie: Workingmen in a Peacetime Militia Regiment." *Histoire Sociale/Social History* 26 (52) (November 1993):247–63.
Anstead, Christopher J. and Nancy B. Bouchier. "The 'Tombstone Affair,'

1845: Woodstock Tories and Cultural Change." *Ontario History* 86 (4) (December, 1994):363–81.

Armstrong, Christopher. *The Revenge of the Methodist Bicycle Company: Sunday Streetcars and Municipal Reform in Toronto, 1888–1897.* Toronto: P. Martin Associates, 1977.

Armstrong, F.H. "The Oligarchy of the Western District of Upper Canada, 1788–1841." *Canadian Historical Association Historical Papers,* (1977), 87–102.

Artibise, Alan F.J. "In Pursuit of Growth: Municipal Boosterism and Urban Development in the Canadian Prairie West, 1971–1913." In Gilbert A. Stelter and Alan F.J. Artibise. *Shaping the Urban Landscape: Aspects of the Canadian City-Building Process.* 116–47. Ottawa: Carleton University Press, 1982.

Athol, B. "How I Gained My Popularity on Queen's Birthday." *New Dominion Monthly* (May 1875):267–72.

Bailey, Peter. *Leisure and Class in Victorian England: Rational Recreation and the Contest for Control, 1830–1885.* Toronto: University of Toronto Press, 1978.

– " 'A Mingled Mass of Perfectly Legitimate Pleasures': The Victorian Middle Class and the Problem of Leisure." *Victorian Studies* 21 (2) (Winter 1978):7–28.

Baldwin, Maurice S. *Old St. Paul's Church 90th Anniversary, 1834–1924.* Woodstock: J. Rae Printer, 1924.

Bale, John. *Sport, Space and the City.* London: Routledge, 1993.

Ballem, C. *Abegweit Dynasty, 1899–1954: The Story of the Abegweit Amateur Athletic Association.* Charlottetown: Prince Edward Island Museum and Heritage Foundation, 1986.

Barman, Jean. "Sports and the Development of Character." In Morris Mott, ed., *Sports in Canada: Historical Readings.* 234–66. Toronto: Copp Clark Pitman, 1989.

Beamish, Rob. "Sport and the Logic of Capitalism." In Hart Cantelon, ed. *Sport, Culture, and the Modern State.* 141–97. Toronto: University of Toronto Press, 1982.

Becker, Carl M. and Richard H. Grigsby. "Baseball in the Small Ohio Community, 1865 to 1900." In Donald Spivey, ed. *Sport in America.* 277–94. Connecticut: Greenwood Press, 1985.

Beers, W.G. "Canadian Sports." *Century Magazine* 14 (May–October 1879):506–27.

– *Lacrosse the National Game of Canada.* Montreal: Dawson Brothers, 1869.

– "A Rival to Cricket." *Chambers Journal* 18 (December, 1862):366–8.

Berger, Carl. *The Sense of Power: Studies in the Ideas of Canadian Imperialism, 1867–1914.* Toronto: University of Toronto Press, 1970.

– "True North Strong and Free." In Peter Russell, ed. *Nationalism in Cana-da*. 3–26. Toronto: University of Toronto Press, 1966.

Bernard, David L. "The Guelph Maple Leafs: A Cultural Indicator of South-ern Ontario." *Ontario History* 84 (3) (September 1992):211–23.

Berryman, Jack W. "From Cradle to the Playing Field: America's Emphasis on Highly Organized Competitive Sports for PreAdolescent Boys." *Journal of Sport History* 2 (2) (Fall 1975):33–61.

Betke, Carl. "Sports Promotion in the Western Canadian City: The Example of Early Edmonton." *Urban History Review* 12 (2) (1983):47–56.

Betts, John Rickards. "Sporting Journalism in Nineteenth Century America." *American Quarterly* 5 (1) (1953):39–52.

Bledstein, Burton J. *The Culture of Professionalism*. New York: Norton, 1976.

Bloomfield, Elizabeth. "Boards of Trade and Canadian Urban Development." *Urban History Review* 12 (2) (October 1983):77–97.

– "Industry in Ontario Urban Centres, 1870." *Urban History Review* 15 (3) (February 1987): 279–83.

– "Municipal Bonusing of Industry: The Legislative Framework in Ontario to 1930." *Urban History Review* 9 (3) (1981):59–76.

Bloomfield, Elizabeth, G.T. Bloomfield, and Peter McCaskell. *Urban Growth and Local Services. The Development of Ontario Municipalities to 1981*. Guelph: University of Guelph, 1983.

Blumin, Stuart M. *The Emergence of the Middle Class. Social Experience in the American City, 1760–1900*. Cambridge: Cambridge University Press, 1989.

Blunderbus, *A History of Brighton. Being the story of a Woodstock settle-ment from the early thirties*. Reprinted from the *Express* 20, 29 December 1900, 5, 12 January 1901, and 1, 16 February 1901. Oxford Museum Bul-letin No. 7.

Bonney-James, Timothy Damian. "More Than a Game: The Interaction of Sport and Community in Guelph." M.A. thesis, University of Guelph, 1997.

Booth, Bernard F. and John S. Batts, "The Political Significance of Organized Sport in Upper Canada, 1825–1867." *Proceedings of the VII HISPA Inter-national Congress*. 399–416. Paris, 1978.

Bouchard, Gerard and Christian Pouyez. "Les Categories Socio-Profes-sionelles: Une Nouveau Grille de Classement." *Le Travail/Labour* (15) (Spring 1985):145–63.

Bouchier, Nancy B. and Robert K. Barney. "A Critical Examination of a Source on Early Ontario Baseball: The Reminiscences of Adam E. Ford." *Journal of Sport History* 15 (1) (Spring 1988): 75–90.

Bouchier, Nancy B. and Ken Cruikshank. "The War on the Squatters: Hamil-ton's Boathouse Community and the Re-Creation of Recreation on Burlington Bay, 1870–1940." *Labour/Le Travail* (forthcoming).

Bowen, Rowland. *Cricket: A History of its Growth and Development Throughout the World.* London: Eyre and Spottiswoode, 1970.

Brown, D. [David W.] "Athleticism in Selected Canadian Private Schools for Boys to 1918." Ph.D. dissertation, University of Alberta, 1984.

- "Canadian Imperialism and Sporting Exchanges: The Nineteenth Century Cultural Experience of Cricket and Lacrosse." *Canadian Journal of History of Sport* 18 (1) (May 1987):55–66.

- "The Northern Character Theme and Sport in Nineteenth Century Canada." *Canadian Journal of History of Sport* 20 (1) (May 1989):47–56.

- "Sport, Darwinism and Canadian Private Schooling to 1918." *Canadian Journal of History of Sport and Physical Education* 16 (1) (May 1985):27–37.

Brown, Doug. "Thoroughbred Horse-Racing Receives an Imperialist Nod: The Parliamentary Debate on Legalizing Gambling in Canada, 1910." *International Journal of the History of Sport* 11 (2) (August 1994):252–69.

Bryce's 1876 Canadian Baseball Guide. London, Ontario, 1876.

Bull, William Perkins. *From Rattlesnake Hunt to Hockey: The History of Sports in Canada and of the Sportsmen of Peel 1798 to 1934.* Toronto: George J. McLeod Ltd., 1934.

Burley, David G. *A Particular Condition in Life: Self Employment and Social Mobility in Mid Victorian Brantford, Ontario.* Kingston and Montreal: McGill-Queen's University Press, 1994.

Burns, Robert. "The First Elite of Toronto: An Examination of the Genesis, Consolidation, and Formation of Power in an Emerging Colonial Society." Ph.D. dissertation, University of Western Ontario, 1975.

Burr, Christine A. "The Process of Evolution of Competitive Sport: A Study of Senior Lacrosse in Canada 1844 to 1914." M.A. thesis, University of Western Ontario, 1986.

Canfield, Ethel. "Canon Bettridge." Woodstock Public Library, n.d.

- *Vice Admiral Henry Vansittart.* Oxford Historical Society, 1934.

Cannadine, David. "The Theory and Practice of the English Leisure Classes." *Historical Journal* 21 (June 1978):445–76.

Cantelon, Hart. *Sport, Culture and the Modern State.* Toronto: University of Toronto Press, 1982.

Cantelon, Hart and Robert Hollands, eds. *Leisure, Sport and Working class Cultures.* Toronto: Garamond Press, 1988.

Careless, J.M.S. *Frontier and Metropolis: Regions in Canada before 1914.* Toronto: University of Toronto Press, 1989.

- "Some Aspects of Urbanization in Nineteenth Century Ontario." In F.H. Armstrong, H.A. Stevenson, and J.D. Wilson eds. *Aspects of Nineteenth Century Ontario.* 65–79. Toronto: University of Toronto Press, 1974.

Cartwright, Donald G. "Cheese Production in Southwestern Ontario." M.A. thesis, University of Western Ontario, 1964.

Cavallo, Dom. *Muscles and Morals: Organized Play and Urban Reform, 1880–1920.* Philadelphia: University of Pennsylvania Press, 1981.

Chadwick, Henry, ed. *Beadle's Dime Base-Ball Player.* New York: Beadle, 1860.

Chapman, L.J. and D.F. Putnam. *The Physiography of Southern Ontario.* Toronto: University of Toronto Press, 1966.

Christie, Howard Angus. "The Function of the Tavern in Toronto, 1834–1875 with Special Reference to Sport." M.A. thesis, University of Windsor, 1973.

Clawson, M.A. *Constructing Brotherhood: Class, Gender and Fraternalism.* Princeton: Princeton University Press, 1989.

Consolidated Bylaws of the Town of Ingersoll. Ingersoll, January 1886.

Consolidated Bylaws of the Town of Woodstock. Woodstock: Times Job Printing, 1896.

Cooper, David Bernard. "Canadians Declare 'It Isn't Cricket': A Colonial Reflection of the Imperial Game." M.A. thesis, University of Toronto, 1996.

– "Canadians Declare 'It Isn't Cricket': A Century of Rejection of the Imperial Game." *Journal of Sport History* 26(1) (Spring 1999):51–81.

Costa, D. Margaret and Sharon R. Guthrie, eds. *Women and Sport: Interdisciplinary Perspectives.* Champaign, IL: Human Kinetics Press, 1994.

Cox, Allan E. "A History of Sport in Canada, 1868–1900." Ph.D. dissertation, University of Alberta, 1969.

Craig, Gerald M. *Upper Canada The Formative Years 1784–1841.* Toronto: McClelland & Stewart, 1979.

Crawford, Irene. "Captain Andrew Drew." Woodstock: Oxford Historical Society, 1981.

Crepeau, Richard C. "Urban and Rural Images in Baseball." *Journal of Popular Culture* 9 (1975):315–24.

Cropp, Marjorie E. "Beachville the Birthplace of Oxford." *Western Ontario Historical Nuggets* No. 14. Reprint Beachville Centennial Committee, 1967.

Cross, Harold. *One Hundred Years of Service with Youth: The Story of the Montreal YMCA.* Montreal: Southam Press, 1951.

Culin, Stewart. "Games of the North American Indians." *Twenty-fourth Annual Report of the Bureau of American Ethnology.* Washington: Government Printing Office, 1907.

Cunningham, Hugh. *Leisure in the Industrial Revolution, 1870–1880.* Surrey: Croom Helm, 1980.

Darroch, A. Gordon and Michael D. Ornstein. "Ethnicity and Occupational Structure in Canada in 1871: The Vertical Mosaic in Historical Perspective." *Canadian Historical Review* 61 (1980):305–33.

Davidson, S.A. "A History of Sports and Games in Eastern Canada Prior to World War I." Ph.D. dissertation, Columbia University, 1951.

Davis, Susan G. *Parades and Power: Street Theatre in Nineteenth Century Philadelphia*. Philadelphia: Temple University Press, 1986.

Dawe, Brian. *Old Oxford is Wide Awake! Pioneer Settlers and Politicians in Oxford County, 1973–1853*. John Deyell Co., 1980.

Day, Robert. "The British Army and Sport in Canada: Case Studies of the Garrisons at Montreal, Halifax, and Kingston." Ph.D. dissertation, University of Alberta, 1981.

– "The British Garrison at Halifax: Its Contribution to the Development of Sport in the Community." In Morris Mott, ed. *Sports in Canada: Historical Readings*. 28–36. Toronto: Copp Clark Pitman, Ltd., 1989.

– "Impulse to Addiction: Sport in Chatham, Ontario 1790–1895." M.A. thesis, University of Western Ontario, 1979.

Deacon, William Arthur. *The Four Jameses*. Toronto: Macmillan, 1974.

DeLottinville, Peter. "Joe Beef of Montreal: Working Class Culture and the Tavern, 1869–1889." *Labour/Le Travail* 8/9 (1981–2), 9–40.

Directory of the Town of Woodstock, 1888. Woodstock: Patullo & Co., 1888.

Ditchfield, P.H. *Old English Sports Pastimes and Customs*. Methuen & Co., 1891; reprint E.P. Publishing Ltd: British Book Centre Inc., 1975.

Dodds, E. King. *Canadian Turf Recollections and Other Sketches*. Toronto, 1909.

Dommett, Alfred. *Canadian Journal, 1833–1835*. ed. E.A. Horsman and Lillian Rea Benson. London: University of Western Ontario, 1955.

Donnelly, Peter. "Sport as a Site for 'Popular' Resistance." In Richard Gruneau. *Popular Cultures and Political Practices*. 69–82. Toronto: Garamond Press, 1988.

Doolittle, P.E. "Cycling of Today." *Massey's Magazine* 1 (January-June 1896):406–7.

Doucet, Michael and J.C. Weaver. "Town Fathers and Urban Community: The Roots of Community Power and Physical Form in Hamilton, Upper Canada in the 1830's." *Urban History Review* 13 (October 1984): 75–90.

Dufresne, Sylvia. "Le Carnival d'hive de Montreal, 1803–1889." *Urban History Review* 11 (3) (February, 1983), 25–45.

Dunham, Aileen. *Political Unrest in Upper Canada, 1815–1836*. Toronto: McClelland & Stewart, 1963.

Dumenil, Lynn. *Freemasonry and American Culture, 1880–1930*. Princeton: Princeton University Press, 1984.

Earl, D.W.L. *The Family Compact: Aristocracy or Oligarchy?* Toronto: Copp-Clark, 1967.

Echenberg, Havi. "Sport as a Social Response to Urbanization: A Case Study

– London, Ontario 1850–1900." M.A. thesis, University of Western Ontario, 1979.

Emery, George N. "Adam Oliver, Ingersoll and Thunder Bay District." *Ontario History* 68 (1) (1976):25–44.

– *Noxons of Ingersoll, 1856–1918: The Family and the Firm in Canada's Agricultural Implements Industry.* Ingersoll: Ingersoll Historical Society, 2001.

– "Voluntary Association Records and the Study of Southwestern Ontario's Past." In *The Landon Project Annual Report, 1977.* 319–34. London, University of Western Ontario, 1977.

Emery, George and J.C. Herbert Emery. *A Young Man's Benefit: The Independent Order of Odd Fellows and Sickness Insurance in the United States and Canada, 1860–1929.* Montreal and Kingston: McGill-Queen's University Press, 1999.

Epstein, J. "Understanding the Cap of Liberty: Symbolic Practice and Social Conflict in Early Nineteenth-Century England." *Past and Present* (122) (February 1989):75–118.

Fabbro, Mary Margaret. "Baseball, Boosterism, and Temperance in Akron, Ohio 1868–1880." In Don Morrow, ed. *Proceedings of the 6th Canadian Symposium on the History of Sport and Physical Education.* 90–7. London: University of Western Ontario, 1989.

Farber, Carole. "High, Healthy and Happy: Ontario Mythology on Parade." In Frank Manning, ed. *The Celebration of Society.* 33–50. Ohio: Bowling Green University Popular Press, 1983.

Felix on the Bat; Being a Scientific Inquiry into the use of the Cricket Bat: Together with the History and use of the Catapulta. 3rd edition, London: Bailey Bros., 1860.

Fisher and Taylor. *Gazetteer and General Directory for the County of Oxford, 1874–1875.* Toronto: Fisher and Taylor, 1874.

Fitzgerald, R.A. *Wickets in the West or, The Twelve in America.* London: Tinsley Bros., 1873.

Freedman, Stephen. "The Baseball Fad in Chicago, 1865–1870: An Exploration of the Role of Sport in the Nineteenth Century City." *Journal of Sport History* 2 (Summer 1978): 42–64.

From Forest to City. Woodstock, its Rise Growth and Development in Photogravure. Souvenir of the City of Woodstock, 1901.

Gates, Lillian. *Land Policies in Upper Canada.* Toronto: University of Toronto Press, 1968.

Gelber, Steven. "Their Hands are all out Playing: Business and Amateur Baseball. 1845–1917." *Journal of Sport History* 11 (1) (Spring 1984):5–27.

– "Working at Playing: The Culture of the Workplace and the Rise of Baseball." *Journal of Social History* 16 (1983):3–22.

Geertz, C. *The Interpretation of Cultures.* New York: Basic Books, 1973.

Gidney, R. and W.P.J. Millar. *Inventing Secondary Education: The Rise of the High School in Nineteenth Century Ontario.* Montreal and Kingston: McGill-Queen's University Press, 1990.

Gilkeson, J.S. *Middle Class Providence, 1820–1940.* Princeton: Princeton University Press, 1986.

Gillespie, Greg. "Roderick McLennan, Professionalism, and the Emergence of the Athlete in Caledonian Games." *Sport History Review* 31(1) (2000):43–63.

– "Sport and 'Masculinities' in Early Nineteenth-Century Ontario: The British Travellers' Image." *Ontario History* 92 (2) (Autumn 2000):113–26.

– "Wickets in the West: Cricket, Culture, and Constructed Images of Nineteenth Century Canada." *Journal of Sport History* 27 (1) (Spring 2000):51–66.

Glassberg, David. "Public Ritual and Cultural Hierarchy: Philadelphia's Civic Celebration at the Turn of the Twentieth Century." *Pennsylvania Magazine of History and Biography* 107 (3) (July 1983):421–8.

Goal Keeper. *The Game of Lacrosse.* Montreal: Montreal Steam Press, 1860.

Goheen, Peter. "Negotiating Access to Public Space in Mid-Nineteenth Century Toronto." *Journal of Historical Geography* 20 (4) (1994):430–49.

– "The Ritual of the Streets in Mid-Nineteenth Century Toronto." *Environment and Planning D: Society and Space* 11 (1993):127–45.

– "Symbols in the Streets: Parades in Victorian Urban Canada." *Urban History Review* 18 (3) (February 1990):237–43.

Gray, R.Q. "Styles of Life, the 'Labour Aristocracy' and Class Relations in Later Victorian Edinburgh." *International Review of Social History* 18 (1973):428–52.

Greenhill, Pauline. "Welcome and Unwelcome Visitors: Shivarees and the Political Economy of Rural/Urban Literature in Southwestern Ontario." *Journal of Ritual Studies* 23 (1) (Winter 1989):45–68.

Greer, Alan. "From Folklore to Revolution: Chivaris and the Lower Canadian Rebellion." *Social History* 15 (1) (January 1990):25–44.

Griffen, Scott. "A chat about lawn tennis." *Massey's Magazine* 2 (July-December 1896):58–60.

Gruneau, Richard. *Class, Sports and Social Development.* Amherst: University of Massachusetts Press, 1983.

– "Modernization or Hegemony: Two Views on Sport and Social Development." In Jean Harvey and Hart Cantelon, eds. *Not Just A Game: Essays in Canadian Sports Sociology.* 9–32. Ottawa: University of Ottawa Press, 1988.

Gruneau, Richard and David Whitson, *Hockey Night in Canada: Sport, Identities and Cultural Politics.* Toronto: Garamond Press, 1993.

Guillet, Edwin C. *Pioneer Days in Upper Canada.* Toronto: University of Toronto Press, 1979.

Guttmann, Allen. *From Ritual to Record: The Nature of Modern Sports.*
New York: Columbia University Press, 1978.
– *A Whole New Ball Game: An Interpretation of American Sports.* Chapel
Hill: University of North Carolina Press, 1988.
"Gymnastica." *Canadian Illustrated News.* 11 December 1875.
Haley, Bruce. *The Healthy Body and Victorian Culture.* Cambridge: Harvard
University Press, 1978.
– "Sports and the Victorian World." *Western Humanities Review* 22 (Spring
1968):115–25.
Hall, J.E. "Upper Canada College Cricket Club." In George Dickson and G.
Mercer Adam. *A History of Upper Canada College, 1829–1892.* 275–8.
Toronto: Rowsell & Hutchison, 1893.
Hall, J.E. and R.H. McCullough. *Sixty Years of Canadian Cricket.* Toronto:
Bryant Publishing Co., 1895.
Hall, M. [Margaret] Ann. *Feminism and Sporting Bodies: Essays on Theory
and Practice.* Champaign, IL: Human Kinetics, 1996.
– *The Girl and the Game: A History of Women's Sport in Canada.* Broad-
view Press, 2002.
– "Rarely Have We Asked Why: Reflections on Canadian Women's Experi-
ence in Sport." *Atlantis* 6 (1):51–60.
Hall, M. Ann and Dorothy A. Richardson. *Fair Ball: Towards Sex Equality
in Canadian Sport.* Ottawa: Canadian Advisory Committee on the Status
of Women, 1982.
Hardy, Stephen. "The City and the Rise of American Sport." *Exercise and
Sport Sciences Reivews* 9 (1981):183–219.
– "Entrepreneurs, Organizations and the Sport Marketplace." *Journal of
Sport History* 13 (1) (Spring 1986):14–33.
– *How Boston Played: Sport, Recreation, and Community, 1865–1915.*
Boston: Northeastern University Press, 1982.
– "Sport in Urbanizing America: A Historical Review." *Journal of Urban
History* 23 (6) (September 1997):675–708.
Hareven, Tamara K. *Free Time and Industrial Time: The Relationship
Between the Family and Work in a New England Industrial Community.*
Cambridge: Cambridge University Press, 1982.
Hargreaves, Jennifer. "Playing Like Gentlemen While Behaving like Ladies:
Contradictory Features of Women's Sport." *British Journal of Sport Histo-
ry* 2 (1) (May 1985):40–52.
– ed., *Sport, Culture and Ideology.* London: Routlege and Kegan Paul, 1982.
– *Sporting Females: Critical Issues in the History and Sociology of Women's
Sport.* London: Routledge, 1994.
Hargreaves, John. *Sport, Power, and Culture: A Social and Historical Analy-
sis of Popular Sports in Britain.* Cambridge: Polity Press, 1986.

Harvey, Jean and Hart Cantelon, eds. *Not Just A Game: Essays in Canadian Sport Sociology*. Ottawa: University of Ottawa Press, 1988.

Hedley, James. "Curling in Canada." *Dominion Illustrated Monthly* 1 (3) (April 1892):173.

Heine, Michael K. and Kevin B. Wamsley, "'Kickfest at Dawson City': Native Peoples and the Sports of the Klondike Gold Rush." *Sport History Review* 27 (1996):72–86.

Henderson, Robert W. *Ball, Bat and Bishop*. New York: Rockfort Press, 1947.

Heron, Craig and Steve Penfold. "The Craftsmen's Spectacle: Labour Day Parades in Canada, the Early Years." *Histoire Sociale/Social History* 29 (58) (November 1996):357–90.

Hershberg, Theodore and Robert Dockhorn. "Occupational Classification." *Historical Methods Newsletter* 9 (2–3) (March/June 1976):59–90.

Hobsbawm, Eric and Terrence Ranger, eds. *The Invention of Tradition*. Cambridge: Cambridge University Press, 1983.

Holman, Andrew C. *A Sense of Their Duty: Middle-Class Formation in Victorian Ontario Towns*. Kingston and Montreal: McGill-Queen's University Press, 2000.

Holt, R. "Cricket and Englishness: The Batsman as Hero." *International Journal of History of Sport* 13 (1) (March 1996):48–70

Homel, Gene Howard. "Sliders and Backsliders: Toronto's Sunday Tobogganing Controversy of 1912." *Urban History Review* 10 (2) (October 1981):25–34.

Hopkins, C. Howard. *History of the Y.M.C.A. in North America*. New York: Association Press, 1951.

Houston, Susan E. "Politics, Schools, and Social Change in Upper Canada." *Canadian Historical Review* 53 (September 1972):249–71.

– "Victorian Origins of Juvenile Delinquency: A Canadian Experience." *History of Education Quarterly* 20 (Fall 1972):254–80.

Houston, Susan E. and Alison L. Prentice. *Schools and Scholars in Nineteenth Century Ontario*. Toronto: University of Toronto Press, 1988.

Howell, Colin [D]. "Baseball, Class and Community in the Maritime Provinces, 1870–1910." *Histoire Sociale/Social History* 44 (November 1989):265–86.

– *Blood, Sweat, and Cheers: Sport and the Making of Modern Canada*. Toronto: University of Toronto Press, 2000.

– *Northern Sandlots: A Social History of Maritime Baseball*. Toronto: University of Toronto Press, 1996.

Howell, David and Peter Lindsay. "The Social Gospel and the Young Boy Problem, 1895–1925." *Canadian Journal of History of Sport* 17 (1) (May 1986):75–87.

Howell, Maxwell and Nancy Howell. *Sport and Games in Canadian Life: 1700 to the Present.* Toronto: Macmillan, 1969.

Huggins, Mike. "Culture, Class and Respectability: Racing and the English Middle Classes in the Nineteenth Century." *International Journal of the History of Sport* 11 (1) (April 1994):19–41.

– "Second-Class Citizens? English Middle-Class Culture and Sport 1850–1910: A Reconsideration." *International Journal of the History of Sport* 17 (1) (March 2000):1–35.

Humber, William. *Cheering for the Home Team: The Story of Baseball in Canada.* Erin, Ontario: Boston Mills Press, 1983.

– *Diamonds of the North: A Concise History of Baseball in Canada.* Toronto: University of Toronto Press, 1995.

– *Freewheeling: The Story of Bicycling in Canada.* Erin, Ontario: Boston Mills Press, 1986.

Huskins, Bonnie [L]. "The Ceremonial Space of Women: Public Processions in Victorian Saint John and Halifax." In Janet Guildford and Suzanne Morton, eds. *Separate Spheres: Women's Worlds in the Nineteenth Century Maritimes.* 145–60. Fredericton: Acadiensis Press, 1994.

– "Public Celebrations in Victorian Saint John and Halifax." Ph.D dissertation, Dalhousie University, 1991.

– "'A Tale of Two Cities': Boosterism and the Imagination of Community during the Visit of the Prince of Wales to Saint John and Halifax in 1860." *Urban History Review* 28 (1) (October 1999):31–46.

Ireland, John [pseud.]. "Andrew Drew and the Founding of Woodstock." *Ontario History* 60 (1968):231–3.

– "Andrew Drew, the Man Who Burned the Caroline." *Ontario History* 59 (1967):136–56.

Ingersoll Directory, 1894–1895. Ingersoll: Union Public Co., 1895.

Insurance Map of the City of Ingersoll, 1876, revised 1882. Charles E. Goad.

Insurance Map of the City of Ingersoll, 1885, revised 1905. Charles E. Goad.

Insurance Plan of the City of Woodstock, 1899, revised 1913. Underwriter's Survey Bureau, Ltd.

Jameson, Anna. *Winter Studies and Summer Rambles in Canada.* Vol. 2, London: Saunders and Otley, 1838; reprint Toronto: Coles Canadiana, 1972. .

Jobling, Ian F. "Sport in Nineteenth Century Canada: The Effects of Technology on its Development." Ph.D. dissertation, University of Alberta, 1970.

Johnson, J.K. *Becoming Prominent: Regional Leadership in Upper Canada, 1791–1841.* Kingston and Montreal: McGill-Queen's University Press, 1989.

Jones, Kevin G. "Developments in Amateurism and Professionalism in Early Twentieth Canadian Sport." *Journal of Sport History* 2 (1) (Spring 1975):29–40.

- "A History of Sport in Canada 1900–1920." Ph.D. dissertation, University of Alberta, 1970.
- "The Myth of Canada's National Sport." *CAPHER Journal* (September-October 1974):33–6.

Jones, Kevin G. and T. George Vellahottam. "Bagattawa to Boxla." *Proceedings of the 3rd Canadian Symposium on the History of Sport and Physical Education.* Halifax: Dalhousie University, 1974.

Jones, Robert Leslie. *History of Agriculture in Ontario, 1613–1880.* Toronto: University of Toronto Press, 1977.

Joyce, C. [Charles] Anthony [Tony]. "At Close of Play: the Evolution of Cricket in London, Ontario 1836–1902." M.A. thesis, University of Western Ontario, 1988.
- "Canadian Sport and State Control: Toronto, 1845–86." *International Journal of the History of Sport* 16 (1) (March 1999):22–37.
- "From Left Field: Sport and Class in Toronto, 1845–1886." Ph.D. dissertation, Queen's University, 1997.
- "Sport and the Cash Nexus in Nineteenth Century Toronto." *Sport History Review* 30 (2) (November 1999):140–167

Katz, Michael B. "Occupational Classification in History." *Journal of Interdisciplinary History* 3 (Summer 1972):63–88.
- *The People of Hamilton, Canada West: Family and Class in a Mid-Nineteenth Century City.* Cambridge: Harvard University Press, 1975.

Kealey, Gregory S., ed. *Canada Investigates Industrialism: The Royal Commission on Relations of Labor and Capital, 1889 (abridged).* Toronto: University of Toronto Press, 1973.
- *Toronto Workers Respond to Industrial Capitalism, 1867–1892.* Toronto: University of Toronto Press, 1980.

Kett, Joseph F. *Rites of Passage: Adolescence in America, 1790 to the Present.* New York, 1977.

Kidd, Bruce. *The Struggle for Canadian Sport.* Toronto: University of Toronto Press, 1996.

Kirsch, George B. *The Creation of American Team Sports: Baseball and Cricket 1838–1872.* Urbana: University of Illinois Press, 1989.

Kirshner, Don S. "The Perils of Pleasure: Commercial Recreation, Social Disorder and Moral Reform in the Progressive Era." *American Studies* 21 (Fall 1980):27–42.

Ladd, Tony and James A. Mathison. *Muscular Christianity: Evangelical Protestants and the Development of Amateur Sport.* Grand Rapids, MI: Baker Books, 1999.

Landon, Fred. *Western Ontario and the American Frontier.* Toronto: McClelland & Stewart, 1967.

Lansley, Keith. "The Amateur Athletic Union of Canada and Changing

Concepts of Amateurism." Ph.D. dissertation, University of Alberta,
   1971.
Lavell, W. Stewart. *100 Years Young: Woodstock Board of Trade and Cham-
   ber of Commerce, 1877–1977*. Woodstock: Board of Directors Centennial
   Committee, 1977.
Lears, T.J. Jackson. "The Concept of Cultural Hegemony: Problems and Pos-
   sibilities." *American Historical Review* 90 (3) (June 1985):567–93.
Lenskyj, Helen. "Femininity First, Sport and Physical Education for Ontario
   Girls 1890–1930." *Canadian Journal of History of Sport* 13 (2) (December
   1982):4–17.
– *Out of Bounds: Women, Sport and Sexuality*. Toronto: Women's Press,
   1986.
Lewis, Guy. "The Muscular Christianity Movement." *Journal of Health
   Physical Education and Recreation* (May 1966):27–30.
Lewis, Robert M. "Cricket and the Beginnings of Organized Baseball in New
   York City." *International Journal of the History of Sport* 4 (3) (December
   1987):315–32.
Lillywhite, Fred. *The English Cricketers Trip to Canada and the United
   States*. London: John Such Printer, 1860.
Lindsay, G.G.S. "College Cricket." In George Dickson and G. Mercer Adam,
   A History of Upper Canada College, 1829–1892. 263–70. Toronto:
   Rowsell & Hutchinson, 1893.
– "Cricket in Canada." *Dominion Illustrated* 1 (7) (August 1892):432–44;
   1 (8) (September 1892):495–508; 1 (10) (November 1892):609–19; 1 (12)
   (January 1893):228–43.
Lindsay, Peter [L]. "George Beers and the National Game Concept. A Behav-
   ioural Approach." *Proceedings of the 2nd Canadian Symposium on the
   History of Sport and Physical Education*. 27–44. Windsor: University of
   Windsor, 1972.
– "A History of Sport in Canada, 1807–1867." Ph.D. dissertation, Universi-
   ty of Alberta, 1969.
– "The Impact of the Military Garrisons on the Development of Sport in
   British North America." *Canadian Journal of History of Sport and Physi-
   cal Education* (1) (May 1970):33–44
Lorenz, Stacy L. "A Lively Interest on the Prairies: Western Canada, the
   Mass Media, and a World of Sport, 1870–1939." *Journal of Sport History*
   27 (2) (Summer 2000):195–228.
– "Local Teams in a 'World of Sport': Sports Coverage and Community
   Identity in Canadian Daily Newspapers, 1850–1900." Paper presented to
   the North American Society for Sport History, Banff Alberta, May 2000.
Lovell, James. *Lovell's Province of Ontario Directory for 1871*. Montreal:
   John Lovell, 1871.
Lowerson, John. "Middle Class Sport 1870–1914." In R.W. Cox, ed. *Aspects*

of the Sociology of Nineteenth Century Sport: Proceedings of the British Society for Sports History. Liverpool: University of Liverpool, March 1982.

– "Sport and the Victorian Sunday: The Beginnings of Middle-class Apostasy." *British Journal of Sport History* 1 (2) (September 1984):202–20.

MacKenzie, H.G. "History of Lawn Tennis in Canada." *Athletic Life* (January 1895):16–21.

MacLeod, David I. "Act Your Age: Boyhood, Adolescence and the Rise of Boy Scouts in America." *Journal of Social History* 16 (1982–83):3–20.

– *Building Character in the American Boy: The Boy Scouts, Y.M.C.A., and Their Forerunners, 1870–1920.* Wisconsin: University of Wisconsin Press, 1983.

– "A Live Vaccine: The Y.M.C.A. and Male Adolescence in the United States and Canada, 1870–1920." *Social History/Histoire Sociale* 11 (21) (1978):5–24.

Maguire, Joseph. "Images of Manliness and Competing Ways of Living in Late Victorian and Edwardian Britain." *British Journal of Sports History* 3 (3) (December 1986):265–87.

Malcolmson, Robert W. *Popular Recreations in English Society, 1700–1850.* Cambridge: Cambridge University Press, 1973.

– "Sports in Society: A Historical Perspective." *British Journal of Sport History* 1 (1) (May 1984):60–72.

Mandle, W.F. "W.G. Grace as Victorian Hero." *Historical Studies* 9 (April 1981):353–68.

Mangan, J.A. *Athleticism in the Victorian and Edwardian Public School: The Emergence and Consolidation of an Educational Ideology.* Cambridge: Cambridge University Press, 1981.

– *The Games Ethic and Imperialism: Aspects of the Diffusion of an Ideal.* London: Viking, 1986.

– ed. *Making Imperial Mentalities: Socialisation and British Imperialism.* Manchester: Manchester University Press, 1990.

– *Pleasure, Profit, Proselytism: British Culture and Sport at Home and Abroad, 1700–1914.* London: Frank Cass, 1988.

Mangan, J.A. and Roberta J. Park, eds. *From Fair Sex to Feminism: Sport and the Socialization of Women in the Industrial and Post-Industrial Eras.* London: Frank Cass, 1987.

Mangan, J.A. and James Walvin, eds. *Manliness and Morality: Middle Class Masculinity in Britain and America, 1800–1940.* Manchester: Manchester University Press, 1987.

Manning, Frank E. "Carnival in Canada: The Politics of Celebration." In Brian Sutton-Smith and Diana Kelly-Byrne, eds. *The Masks of Play.* 23–33. New York: Leisure Press, 1984.

– *The Celebration of Society.* Ohio: Bowling Green University Press, 1983.

Marks, Lynne. *Revivals and Roller Rinks: Religion, Leisure, and Identity in Late Nineteenth-Century Small-Town Ontario.* Toronto: University of Toronto Press, 1996.

Martin, W.H. "History of Woodstock's Early Bicycling Days." *Sentinel-Review* 3 May 1919.

Mathews, Mitford M. *A Dictionary of Americanisms. On Historical Principles.* Chicago: University of Chicago Press, 1956.

McCleneghan, Alexander and Arthur Riggs. *Aristocratic Woodstock 1834–1850.* 1909; reprint Oxford Historical Society, 1987.

McCrone, Kathleen. *Sport and the Physical Emancipation of English Women, 1870–1914.* Kentucky: University of Kentucky Press, 1988.

McDonald, Robert A.J. "'Holy Retreat' or 'Practical Breathing Spot'?: Class Perceptions of Vancouver's Stanley Park, 1910–1913." *Canadian Historical Review* 65 (2) (1984):127–53.

McFarlane, Elsie. *The Development of Public Recreation in Canada.* Canadian Parks and Recreation Association, 1970.

McIntosh, Peter. *Sport in Society.* London: C.A. Watts, 1963.

McIntyre, James. *Musings on the Banks of the Canadian Thames.* Ingersoll: Chronicle Press, 1884.

McLuhan, Marshall. "Baseball is Culture." In William Humber and John St James. *All I Thought About was Baseball: Writings on a Canadian Pastime.* 209–14. Toronto: University of Toronto Press, 1996.

McNaught, W.K. *Lacrosse and how to play it.* Toronto: Robert Marshall, 1873.

Meller, Helen E. *Leisure and the Changing City, 1870–1914.* Boston: Routlege and Kegan Paul, 1976.

Melville, Tom. "From Ethnic Tradition to Community Institution: Nineteenth-Century Cricket in Small Town Wisconsin and a Note on the Enigma of a Sporting Discontinuity." *International Journal of the History of Sport* 11(2) (August 1994), 281–4.

Mennil, David C. "A Regional Study of the Economy of Ingersoll." B.A. thesis, University of Western Ontario, 1963.

Metcalfe, Alan. "The Anatomy of Power in Amateur Sport in Ontario." *Canadian Journal of History of Sport* 12 (2) (December 1991):47–67.

– *Canada Learns to Play: The Emergence of Organized Sport 1807–1914.* Toronto: McClelland & Stewart, 1987.

– "The Growth of Organized Sport and the Development of Amateurism in Canada 1807–1914." In Jean Harvey and Hart Cantelon, eds. *Not Just A Game: Essays in Canadian Sport Sociology.* 33–50. Ottawa: University of Ottawa Press, 1988.

– "The Meaning of Amateurism: A Case Study of Canadian Sport, 1883–1970." *Canadian Journal of History of Sport* 16 (2) (December 1995):33–48.

- "Organized Sport and Social Stratification in Montreal, 1840–1891." In Richard S. Gruneau and J.G. Albinson, *Canadian Sport: Sociological Perspectives.* 77–101. Don Mills: Addison-Wesley, 1976.
- "Sport and Athletics: A Case Study of Lacrosse in Canada, 1840–1889." *Journal of Sport History* 3 (1) (Spring 1976):1–19.

Mills, David. *The Idea of Loyalty in Upper Canada, 1784–1850.* Kingston and Montreal: McGill-Queen's University Press, 1988.

Mitcheson, Wendy. "The Y.M.C.A. and Reform in the Nineteenth Century." *Social History/Histoire Sociale* 12 (24) (1979):368–84.

Mitchison, W. *The Nature of their Bodies: Women and Their Doctors in Victorian Canada.* Toronto: University of Toronto Press, 1991.

Morgan, Cecilia. "'In Search of the Phantom Misnamed Honour': Duelling in Upper Canada." *Canadian Historical Review* 76(4) (December 1995):529–62.

Morrow, Don. "The Canadian Image Abroad: The Great Lacrosse Tours of 1876 and 1883." *Proceedings of the 5th Canadian Symposium on the History of Sport and Physical Education.* 11–23. Toronto: University of Toronto, 1982.
- "A Case Study in Amateur Conflict: The Athletic War in Canada, 1906–1908." *British Journal of Sport History* 3 (2) (September 1986):173–90.
- "The Institutionalization of Sport: A Case Study of Canadian Lacrosse." *International Journal of History of Sport* 9 (2) (August 1992):236–51.
- "The Powerhouse of Canadian Sport: The Montreal Amateur Athletic Association, Inception to 1909." *Journal of Sport History* 8 (3) (Winter 1981):20–39.
- *A Sporting Evolution: The Montreal Amateur Athletic Association 1881–1981.* Montreal: Montreal Amateur Athletic Association, 1981.

Morrow, Don, Mary Keyes, Wayne Simpson, Frank Cosentino, and Ron Lappage. *A Concise History of Sport in Canada.* Toronto: Oxford University Press, 1989.

Mott, Morris. "The British Protestant Pioneers and the Establishment of Manly Sports in Manitoba 1870–1886." *Journal of Sport History* 7 (3) (Winter 1980):25–37.
- "Flawed Games, Splendid Ceremonies: The Hockey Matches of the Winnipeg Vics, 1890–1903." *Prairie Forum* 10 (1) (Spring 1985):169–87.
- "Manly Sports and Manitobans: Settlement Days to World War One." Ph.D. dissertation, Queen's University, 1980.
- "One Solution to the Urban Crisis: Manly Sports and Winnipeggers, 1900–1914." *Urban History Review* 12 (2) (October 1983):57–70.
- "One Town's Team: Souris and its Lacrosse Club: 1887–1906." *Manitoba History* 1 (1) (1980):10–16.
- ed. *Sports in Canada: Historical Readings.* Toronto: Copp-Clark, 1989.

Mrozek, Donald J. *Sport and American Mentality, 1880–1910.* Knoxville: University of Tennessee Press, 1983.

Neely, Wayne Caldwell. *The Agricultural Fair.* New York, 1935.

Neutel, Walter. "From 'Southern' Concept to Canada Southern Railway 1835–1873." M.A. thesis, University of Western Ontario, 1968.

Noel, Jan. *Canada Dry: Temperance Crusades Before Confederation.* Toronto: University of Toronto Press, 1995.

Northam, Janet A. and Jack Berryman. "Sport and Urban Boosterism in the Pacific Northwest: Seattle's Alaska-Yukon-Pacific Exhibition." *Journal of the West* 17 (1978):53–60.

Ontario Curling Association. *Annual Reports.* 1876–1896.

Oriard, Michael. *Sporting with the Gods: The Rhetoric of Play and Game in American Culture.* Cambridge: Cambridge University Press, 1991.

Oxendine, Joseph B. *American Indian Sports Heritage.* Champaign, Ill.: Human Kinetics, 1988.

Oxford and Norfolk Gazetteer and General Business Directory, 1867. Woodstock: Sutherland & Co., 1867.

Oxford County Directory, 1881. Ingersoll: Crotty and Dart, 1881.

Oxford Gazetteer and General Business Directory, 1870–1871. Toronto: Hunter and Rose, 1870.

Page and Smith. *Historical Atlas of Oxford and Brant Counties, 1875–1875.* Toronto: Page & Smith, 1876; reprint Owen Sound: Richardson, Bond and Wright, 1972.

Palmer, Bryan. *A Culture in Conflict: Skilled Workers and Industrial Capitalism in Hamilton, Ontario 1860–1914.* Kingston and Montreal: McGill-Queen's University Press, 1979.

– "Discordant Music: Charivaris and Whitecapping in Nineteenth Century North America." *Labour/Le Travail* 3 (1978):5–62.

"The Passing of Woodstock's Amateur Athletic Association Grounds." *Sentinel-Review* 22 November 1913.

[Patteson] T.C. "The Recent Cricket Match and Some of its Lessons." *Canadian Monthly and National Review* 1 (November 1878):608–15.

Paxson, Fredric L. "The Rise of Sport." *Mississippi Valley Historical Review* 4 (2) (September 1917):143–68.

"Petition to Messrs. Hay & Co., from Employees." *Sentinel-Review* 28 December 1887.

Phillips, T.D. *Canadian Cricketer's Guide and Review of the Past Season, 1876.* Ottawa: Free Press, 1876.

Pinto, Barbara S. "Ain't Misbehavin': The Montreal Shamrock Lacrosse Club Fans, 1868 to 1884." M.A. thesis, University of Western Ontario, 1990.

– "Ain't Misbehavin': The Montreal Shamrock Lacrosse Club Fans 1868 to 1884." Paper presented to the North American Society for Sport History, Banff, Alberta, 1990.

Pope, S.W. "Amateurism and American Sports Culture: The Invention of an Athletic Tradition in the United States, 1870–1900." *International Journal of the History of Sport* 13 (3) (December 1996):290–309.

Poulter, Gillian. "Playing the Game: The Transformation of Indigenous Cultural Activities and the Creation of National Identity in Victorian Canada." Paper presented to the Canadian Historical Association, 1997.

Pred, Allan R. *Urban Growth and the Circulation of Information: The United States System of Cities, 1790–1840.* Cambridge: Harvard University Press, 1973.

Prentice, Alison L. *The School Promoters: Education and Social Class in Mid-Nineteenth Century Upper Canada.* Toronto: McClelland & Stewart, 1977.

Rader, Benjamin. *American Sports: From the Age of Folk Games to the Age of Spectators.* New Jersey: Prentice-Hall, 1983.

Read, Colin. *The Rising in Western Upper Canada 1837–1838: The Duncombe Revolt and After.* Toronto: University of Toronto Press, 1982.

Redlich, Fritz. "Leisure-Time Activities: A Historical, Sociological, and Economic Analysis." *Explorations in Entrepreneurial History* 3 (1965–66):3–24.

Redmond, Gerald. *The Caledonian Games in Nineteenth Century America.* Cranbury, New Jersey: Associated Universities Press, 1971.

– "The First Tom Brown's Schooldays and Others: Origins of Muscular Christianity in Children's Literature, 1762–1855." *Quest* 30 (Summer 1978):4–18.

– "Some Aspects of Organized Sport and Leisure in Nineteenth Century Canada." *Society and Leisure* 2 (1) (April 1979):73–100.

– *The Sporting Scots of Nineteenth Century Canada.* Toronto: Fairleigh Dickinson University Press, 1982.

Riess, Steven A. *City Games: The Evolution of American Urban Society and the Rise of Sports.* Urbana: University of Illinois Press, 1989.

– "From Pitch to Putt: Sport and Class in Anglo-American Sport." *Journal of Sport History* 21 (2) (Summer 1994):138–84.

– "Sport and the Redefinition of Middle Class Masculinity." *International Journal of the History of Sport* 8 (1) (May 1991):5–27.

– *Sport in Industrial America, 1850–1920.* Wheeling, IL: Harlan Davidson, 1995.

Robinson, Alby [as told to Frank Hyde]. "Professional Sport a Half Century Ago." *Sentinel-Review* Anniversary Edition 11 September 1936.

Roll of Pupils of Upper Canada College from 1829 to 1898. Toronto, 1898.

Rosenzweig, Roy. *Eight Hours for What We Will: Workers and Leisure in an Industrial City, 1870–1920.* New York: Cambridge University Press, 1983.

– "Middle Class Parks and Working Class Play: The Struggle over

Recreational Space in Worcester Massachusetts, 1870–1910." *Radical History Review* 21 (Fall 1979):31–46.

– "The Parks and the People. Social History and Urban Parks." *Journal of Social History* 18 (1984–85):289–95.

Ross, Murray G. *The Y.M.C.A. in Canada: The Chronicle of a Century.* Toronto: Ryerson Press, 1951.

Rotundo, E. Anthony. "Body and Soul: Changing Ideals of American Middle Class Manhood." *Journal of Social History* 14 (1983):23–38.

Roxborough, Henry. *One Hundred Not Out: The Story of Nineteenth Century Canadian Sport.* Toronto: Ryerson Press, 1966.

Ryan, Mary P. "The American Parade: Representations of the Nineteenth Century Social Order." In Lynn Hunt, ed. *The New Cultural History.* 131–53. Berkeley: University of California Press, 1989.

Salter, Michael A. "The Effects of Acculturation on the Game of Lacrosse on its Role as an Agent of Indian Survival." *Canadian Journal of History of Sport and Physical Education* 3 (1) (May 1972):28–43.

Sandiford, Keith A.P. "Cricket and Victorian Society." *Journal of Social History* 17(1983–84):303–17.

– "The Victorians at Play: Problems in Historiographical Methodology." *Journal of Social History* (1981):271–88.

Sangster, Joan. "The Softball Solution: Female Workers, Male Managers, and the Operation of Paternalism at Westclox, 1923–1960." *Labour/Le Travail* 32 (Fall 1993):167–99.

Saunders, Robert E. "What Was the Family Compact?" *Ontario History* 49 (1957):165–78.

Sawtell, R.W. "The Woodstock of Days that are Gone." *Woodstock Express* Industrial Number. February 1906.

Schrodt, Barbara. "Sabbatarianism and Sport in Canadian Society." *Journal of Sport History* 4 (1) (Spring 1977):22–33.

Scott, James C. *Domination and the Arts of Resistance: Hidden Transcripts.* New Haven: Yale University Press, 1990.

Seymour, Harold. *Baseball: The Early Years.* New York: Oxford University Press, 1960.

Shenston, Thomas. *The Oxford Gazetteer, 1852.* Chatterton and Helliwell, 1852; reprint Woodstock: Commercial Print-Craft, 1968.

Shier, Ronald Adair. "Some Aspects of the Historical Geography of the Town of Ingersoll." B.A. thesis, University of Western Ontario, 1967.

Simpson, Robert Wayne. "The Elite and Sport Club Membership in Toronto, 1827–1881." Ph.D. dissertation, University of Alberta, 1987.

Smith, Michael. "Graceful Athleticism or Robust Womanhood: The Sporting Culture of Women in Victorian Nova Scotia, 1870–1914." *Journal of Canadian Studies* 12 (1&2) (Spring/Summer 1988):120–37.

Smith, Robert A. *A Social History of the Bicycle: Its Early Life and Times in America*. New York: American Heritage, 1972.

Smith, W.H. *Smith's Canadian Gazetteer*. Toronto: H & W Rowsell, 1846; reprint Toronto: Coles Canadiana Collection, 1972.

Somers, Dale A. *The Rise of Sports in New Orleans, 1850–1900*. Baton-Rouge: Louisiana State University Press, 1972.

Spaulding, A.G. *America's National Game*. New York: American Sports Publishing Co., 1911.

Spelt, J. *Urban Development in South-Central Ontario*. Toronto: McClelland & Stewart, 1972.

Spence, F.S. *The Facts of the Case: A Summary of the Most Important Evidence and Arguments Presented in the Royal Commission on the Liquor Traffic*. Toronto: Newton & Treloar, 1896; reprint Toronto: Coles Publishing Co., 1973.

"Sport in Literature." *The Canadian Magazine* 8 (5) (March 1897):449–50.

St Catherine's Cricket Club. *The Canadian Cricketer's Guide*. St Catherine's Ontario: Constitutional Office, 1858.

Start, Susan. *Fair Play, Woodstock's Agricultural Society, 1836–1936*. Woodstock: Woodstock Agricultural Society, 1986.

Steadman-Jones, Gareth. *Languages of Class*. Cambridge: Cambridge University Press, 1982.

Stearns, Peter. *Be a Man! Males and Masculinity in Modern Society*. New York: Holmes Meier, 1979.

Strutt, Joseph. *Sports and Pastimes of the People of England (1801)*.London: Methuen & Co., 1903; reprint Detroit: Singing Tree Press, 1968.

Sumner, Jim L. "The State Fair and the Development of Modern Sports in Late Nineteenth Century North Carolina." *Journal of Sport History* 15 (2) (Summer 1988):139–141.

Sutherland, James. *County of Oxford Gazetteer and General Business Directory for 1862–1863*. Ingersoll: James Sutherland, 1862.

Sutton-Smith, Brian. "Games of Order and Disorder." *The Association for the Anthropological Study of Play Newsletter* 4 (2) (1977):19–26.

– "The Study of Games: An Anthropological Approach." *Proceedings of HISPA*. 5–15. Leuven, Belgium, 1976.

Talman, J.J. "The Impact of the Railway on a Pioneer Community." *Canadian Historical Association Papers and Records* (1955): 1–12.

– "The Development of the Railway Network of Southwestern Ontario to 1876." *Canadian Historical Association Annual Report 1953*.

Tewaarathon (Lacrosse): Akwesasne's Story of Our National Game. North American Indian Traveling College, 1978.

"That Aristocratic Neighborhood of Woodstock." *Globe* 24 May 1878; reprinted *Globe and Mail* 24 July 1967.

Thomas, Keith. "Work and Leisure." *Past and Present* (December 1964):50–62.

– "Work and Leisure in Industrial Society." *Past and Present* 30 (1965):96–103.

Thompson, E.P. "Time, Work Discipline, and Industrial Capitalism." *Past and Present* 38 (December 1967):56–97.

Thompson, F.M.L. *The Rise of Respectable Society: A Social History of Victorian Britain, 1830–1900.* Cambridge: Cambridge University Press, 1988.

Tomlinson, Alan. "Shifting Patterns of Working Class Leisure: The Case of Knur-and-Spell." *Sociology of Sport Journal* 9 (1992):192–206.

"Town of Ingersoll." *Chronicle* 13 December 1894.

"Town of Ingersoll." *Globe* 28 May 1892.

Tozer, M.D.W. "Sport and the Mid-Victorian Ideal of Manliness." In J.A. Mangan, *Proceedings of the XI HISPA International Congress.* 101–4. Glasgow: Jordanhill College, 1985.

Turner, Victor, ed. *Celebration: Studies in Festivity and Ritual.* Washington: Smithsonian Institution Press, 1982.

– *The Ritual Process. Structure and Anti-Structure.* Ithaca, New York: Cornell University Press, 1969.

Tyrrell, Ian. "The Emergence of Modern American Baseball, c.1850–1880." In Richard Cashman and Michael McKernan, eds. *Sport in History: The Making of Modern Sporting History.* 205–26. Queensland: University of Queensland Press, 1979.

Union Publishing Company's Farmers and Business Directory for the Counties of Brant, Norfolk, and Oxford, 1887. Union Publishing Co., 1887.

Union Publishing Company's Woodstock Directory for 1894. Ingersoll: Union Publishing Co., 1894.

Veblen, Thorstein. *The Theory of the Leisure Class.* New York: Macmillan, 1899.

Vellathottam, T. George and Kevin Jones. "Highlights in the Development of Canadian Lacrosse to 1931." *Canadian Journal of History of Sport and Physical Education* 2 (December 1974):31–47.

Vennum, Thomas Jr. *American Indian Lacrosse: Little Brother of War.* Washington: Smithsonian Institute Press, 1994.

Vertinsky, [Patricia A.]. *The Eternally Wounded Woman: Women, Exercise and Doctors in the late Nineteenth Century.* Manchester: University of Manchester Press, 1990.

– "Exercise, Physical Capability and Eternally Wounded Woman in Late Nineteenth Century North America." *Journal of Sport History* 14 (1) (Spring 1987):7–27.

– "God, Science and the Marketplace: The Bases for Exercise Prescriptions for Females in Nineteenth Century North America." *Canadian Journal of History of Sport* 17 (1) (May 1986):38–45.

Voigt, David Q. *American Baseball: From Gentleman's Sport to the Commissioner System*. Oklahoma: University of Oklahoma Press, 1966.

Voisey, Paul. *Vulcan: The Making of a Prairie Community*. Toronto: University of Toronto Press, 1988.

Walvin, James. *A Child's World. A Social History of English Childhood, 1800–1914*. Harmondsworth, England: Penguin Books, 1982.

– *Leisure and Society*. New York: Longman, 1979.

Wamsley, Kevin [B.], "Legislation and Leisure in 19th Century Canada." Ph.D dissertation, University of Alberta, 1992.

– "Nineteenth Century Sport Tours, State Formation, and Canadian Foreign Policy." *Sporting Traditions* 13 (2) (1997):73–89.

Wamsley, Kevin B. and Robert S. Kossuth. "Fighting it Out in Nineteenth Century Upper Canada/Canada West: Masculinities and Physical Challenges in the Tavern." *Journal of Sport History* 27 (3) (Fall 2000):405–30.

Waters, C. " 'All Sorts and Any Quantity of Outlandish Recreations': History, Sociology, and the Study of Leisure in England, 1820–1870." *Canadian Historical Association Historical Papers* (1981): 8–33.

Waters, Greg. "Operating on the Border: A History of the Commercial Promotion, Moral Suppression and State Regulation of the Thoroughbred Racing Industry in Windsor, Ontario, 1884 to 1936." M.A. thesis, University of Windsor, 1992.

Weiler, John. "The Idea of Sport in Late Victorian Canada." In Michael Cross, ed. *The Workingman in the Nineteenth Century*. 228–31. Toronto: University of Toronto Press, 1974.

Wells, J.E. "Canadian Culture." *Canadian Monthly and National Review* 8 (6) (December 1875):459–67.

Wetherell, Donald G. with Irene Kmet. *Useful Pleasures: The Shaping of Leisure in Alberta, 1896–1945*. Regina: Great Plains Research Center, 1990.

Weyand, Alexander M. and M.R. Roberts. *The Lacrosse Story*. Baltimore: H & A Herman, 1965.

Wiebe, Robert H. *The Search for Order, 1877–1920*. New York: Hill and Wong, 1967.

Williams, Art and Edward Baker. *Bits and Pieces – A Montage of Woodstock, Ontario in Text and Pictures*. Woodstock: Commercial Print Craft Ltd., 1967.

Williams, Raymond. *Culture*. Glasgow: Wm Collins Sons & Co., 1981.

Williams, Trevor. "Cheap Rates, Special Trains and Canadian Sport in the 1850's." *Canadian Journal of History of Sport* 12 (2) (December 1981):84–93.

Willis, Joe D. and Richard D. Whettan. "Social Stratification in New York City Athletic Clubs, 1865–1915." *Journal of Sport History* 3 (Spring 1976):45–63.

Willis, Paul. "Women in Sport Ideology." In Jennifer Hargreaves, ed. *Sport,
     Culture, and Ideology.* 116–35. London: Routledge and Kegan Paul, 1982.
Wilson, Catharine Anne. "Reciprocal Work Bees and the Meaning of Neigh-
     borhood." *Canadian Historical Review* 82 (3) (September 2001):431–64.
Wise, S.F. "Sport and Class Values in Old Ontario and Quebec." in W.H.
     Heick and Roger Graham, eds. *His Own Man: Essays in Honour of
     A.R.M. Lower.* 93–116. Montreal and Kingston: McGill-Queen's Universi-
     ty Press, 1974.
– "Upper Canada and the Conservative Tradition." in E.G. Firth, ed. *Profiles
     of a Province.* 20–33. Toronto: Ontario Historical Society, 1967.
Wise, S.F. and Douglas Fisher. *Canada's Sporting Heroes.* Don Mills: General
     Publishing Company Ltd., 1974.
Wood, J. David. *Making Ontario: Agricultural Colonization and Landscape
     Re-Creation Before the Railway.* Montreal and Kingston: McGill-Queen's
     University Press, 2000.
*Woodstock Old Boys and Girls Home Coming Reunion and Diamond
     Jubilee Celebration. Official Program and Souvenir Booklet.* Woodstock:
     Old Boys and Girls Reunion Association, 1927.
100th Anniversary 1834–1934, Old St Paul's Church. Woodstock, 1934.
Zahavi, Gerald. *Workers, Managers, and Welfare Capitalism: The Shoework-
     ers and Tanners of Endicott Johnson, 1890–1950.* Urbana: University of
     Illinois Press, 1988.

Index

Page numbers in italics indicate illustrations. A lowercase "t" following a page reference indicates a table.

Abegweit Amateur Athletic Association (PEI), 61
Active Base Ball Team, *41*
Adelman, Melvin, 48, 64, 74, 98, 103
alcohol and drunkenness: at baseball games, 107, 114, 116; at civic holiday celebrations, 33; and horseracing, 50; Royal Commission on the Liquor Traffic, 115, 154n50; temperance organizations, 28
Alert baseball club (London), 66
alternate sports. *See* traditional (alternate) games and sports
Amateur Athletic Association of Canada (AAA of C): and amateur status, 62, 63–4, 73; and local associations, 63, 73, 135–6; as regulating body, 63, 64, 67, 73
Amateur Athletic Associations (AAAs), 61–87; and AAA of C, 63, 73, 135–6; and alternate sports, 82–3; anti-

modern *vs* modern, 64; as business clubs, 73, 75–6; camaraderie of, 78, 79; and churches, 77; club managers, 76, 83; democratic appearance of, 73, 76–7, 133; exclusion of cricket, 98–9; exclusion of women, 66–7, 74; exclusion of working class, 69, 73, 74, 79, 114; facilities and equipment, 75–6, 79; links with civic government, 61, 157n4; members of, 64, 74; as national movement, 60–1; organizers of, 67–72, 159t; resistance to, 80–7, 116, 128–9, 136; role of middle class in, 68–9, 133; and Sabbatarian observance, 116; social role, 73–5, 76. *See also* Ingersoll Amateur Athletic Association (IAAA)
amateurism and amateur athletes, 60–87, 131–7; AAAs and amateur status, 63–4, 66, 73,

135–6, 160n56; Christian overtones of, 78; and middle class values, 132, 133; moral code for, 64; and social reform, 4, 5; and town–team link, 110–12, 125, 131–2; and urban boosterism, 136–7; *vs* professionalism, 131–2. *See also* professional athletes
Ancient Free and Accepted Masons, 28, 52, 70, 71, 72, 78
Ancient Order of United Workmen, 28, 52, 70, 72
Anglican church (Church of England), 15, 16–17, 90, 96
Anstead, Christopher, 17, 25, 38; on fraternal organizations, 69, 149n75; on respectability, 26, 28
Athletic Association de St Roche de Quebec, 61
Atlantic baseball team (Brooklyn), 108
August civic holiday, 86, 136

Bain, J.A., 114
Bain Wagon Company
  (Woodstock), 23, 24,
  114; baseball club, 41,
  113, 114, 115
Baldwin Act (1849), 17
Ball, A.S., 69–70, 72, 83,
  84
Barton, 104
Barwick, James, 17
baseball, 41, 100–16; and
  AAAS, 112; amateur vs
  professional, 110–12,
  114; compared to
  cricket, 97, 100, 101,
  103; compared to
  lacrosse, 117–18, 123,
  124, 125; as contested
  social territory, 133; as
  culture, 3; egalitarianism, 102, 103; equip-
  ment and clothing for,
  12, 100, 106; exhibi-
  tion games, 104;
  factory teams, 24,
  113–16, 136, 150n83;
  financing of, 109–10,
  112; and hotels, 103,
  160n48; informality of,
  100–1; inter urban
  matches, 104–10;
  junior teams, 111, 134,
  173t; as middle class
  game, 102; origins of,
  100; popularity of, 107,
  108; rules for, 12,
  102–3, 104, 109–10,
  134; semi-professional
  leagues, 113, 114;
  senior clubs, 173t; as
  social activity, 12, 103,
  108, 109; social values
  of, 102, 111; as spectator sport, 107; tagging
  base runners, 168n7;
  team members, 108,
  109; and urban boost-
  erism, 103–4, 105–6,
  113, 114; at work bees,
  11; as working-class
  game, 102, 113–16. See
  also specific clubs (Vic-

torias, Young Canadi-
  ans, etc.)
Beachville, 10, 48,
  164n14; baseball in,
  12, 101
Beachville road (Old Stage
  Road), 11, 12, 88, 90;
  for cyclists, 65; use for
  horseracing, 51
Beadle's Dime Base-Ball
  Player (Chadwick),
  102, 105
Beavers lacrosse club
  (Woodstock), 41, 125;
  matches, 66, 128,
  174n56; members and
  leaders, 68, 70, 71, 78,
  120, 122, 128;
  pennant, 121; and
  WAAA, 60, 125; and
  YMCA, 173n32
Beers, Dr W. George, 118,
  119, 121–2
Belleville, 43
Belmont Stakes, 52
Berlin, 66
betting and gambling: and
  alternate sports, 82, 83;
  and amateur sport,
  64–5; on baseball
  games, 107, 108–9,
  116; on horseraces, 50,
  51, 53–4, 156n96; on
  lacrosse games, 128; on
  running races, 82,
  84–6; in Woodstock,
  61–2
Bettridge, Rev. William,
  16–17
bicycles and cycling, 43–6;
  clothing and equipment
  for, 44, 46, 154n49;
  cycle parades, 42, 43–4,
  45; penny-farthing,
  42–3, 46, 68; races,
  67–8, 80, 134; role in
  local culture, 46;
  women cyclists, 44, 45,
  46, 133
Bittle (prizefighter), 82
blacks, 36, 113, 153n26
Blandford Township, 13

blindfold races, 48–9
blood sports, 5, 136
boards of trade, 22, 61,
  69
Bonney-James, Timothy,
  82, 108
boosterism. See urban
  boosterism
Bouchard, Gerard, 141
Boyd, Billy, 65, 81
Boyle, Charles, 52
Boyle, "Klondike Joe," 52
Brampton, 43
Brantford, 23, 43, 66, 128
Brants lacrosse club:
  Brantford, 128; Paris,
  66
Brazer, George, 113
Brink, Joshua, 163n1
Brock District, 10, 14
Brooklyn Atlantics base-
  ball team, 108
Brown, David, 93
Brown, Doug, 54
Brown, James, 108–9
Brown, Thomas, 37
Brown foundry (Ingersoll),
  19
Brown's Carriage Works
  (Ingersoll), 114
Bryce's 1876 Canadian
  Baseball Guide, 109
Buchanan, M.T., 40
Buchanan Company
  (Ingersoll), 40
Buffalo (New York), 56
Bull, William Perkins, 51,
  54
Burley, David, 6

Caister House (Wood-
  stock), 52, 73
Caledonian Games, 47,
  55–9, 154n59; com-
  pared to team sports,
  55–6; itinerant profes-
  sional athletes, 56,
  57–8; prize money, 56,
  57; vs AAA events,
  58–9, 62
Caledonian Society, 39,
  55, 56, 58–9, 61, 72

callathumpians, 32, 33–4, 35–6, 47, 152n10
Canadian Association of Amateur Base Ball Players (CAABBP), 110
Canadian Association of Base Ball Players (CABBP), 104, 109–10, 134, 135
Canadian Baseball Championship. See Silver Ball
Canadian Cricketer's Guide (Phillips), 92, 93
Canadian Cricket Field, 92
Canadian Gentleman's Journal and Sporting Times, 52
Canadian Lacrosse Association (CLA), 123, 124, 125, 126, 135
Canadian Monthly and National Review, 95
Canadian Order of Foresters, 71
Canadian Wheelmen's Association (CWA), 71, 134, 135; Woodstock meet (1885), 43, 63, 135
capitalism: and baseball, 114–15; corporate capitalist system of sport, 3
Careless, J.M.S., 27–8
Caroline, 16
Carroll, Henry, 88
Cartwright, Alexander, 102
Casey (prizefighter), 82
census records, 22, 139, 140–1
Central Hotel (Woodstock), 83
Central Park (Woodstock), 66
Chadwick, Henry: Beadle's Dime Base-Ball Player, 102, 105
character development, moral, 4, 49, 121, 158n24
charivaris, 34

Charlottetown, 61
Chatham, 113, 114
children and youth: exclusion from holiday parades, 36; junior baseball for, 111; lacrosse for, 118–19; young boy problem, 119–20
Chipperfield, William, 24
churches and religion: clergy reserves, 16; opposition to cockfighting, 83; opposition to horseracing, 50; in pioneer communities, 11; Protestant, 26, 77, 96, 120, 123; Sabbatarian observance, 11, 53, 79, 116, 172n80; support of AAAS, 77–8. See also specific churches (Anglican, Methodist, etc.)
Church of England. See Anglican church
Church of Scotland, 16
civic government: control by Tory elite, 11; links with AAAs, 61, 157n4; middle-class control of, 17; political patronage, 13–14
civic holiday celebrations, 23, 31–59; AAA control of, 58, 60, 61, 65–6, 136, 157n6; August civic holiday, 86, 136; baseball matches, 102, 105, 112; Dominion Day, 39, 60, 65; games and sports, 33; gender-specific events, 48, 132; horseracing events at, 53; Labour Day, 39; lacrosse matches, 117, 125, 126; organizing committees for, 31–2, 65; parades, 32–3, 36–46; and private enterprise, 57–8; in public parks, 29–30;

Queen's Birthday (24 May), 31, 32–3, 60, 65; respectability vs rowdiness, 33–5; social role of, 31; typical scenario for, 32–3
civic voluntarism, 18
Clarke, Herb, 67, 68, 85
Claxton, James T., 121
Claxton Flags lacrosse competition, 121
clothing. See equipment and clothing
cockfighting, 12, 81, 82–3, 136, 162n102
Colborne, Sir John, 13, 16
Coleman, Kit, 46
Commercial Hotel (Woodstock), 62, 134
Commission Appointed to Enquire into the Prison and Reformatory System, 119
Cornwall, 57, 131
corporate capitalist system of sport, 3
Coyne (runner), 81
Credit Valley Railway (CVR), 19, 21, 24, 148n72
cricket, 72, 88–99; compared to baseball, 97, 100, 101, 103; compared to lacrosse, 97; decline of, 97–8; district system, 96; in eastern Canada, 98; egalitarian aspects of, 92, 165n25; as elite sport, 15, 90–2, 101; exclusion from AAA, 98–9; grounds and equipment for, 92, 95, 96; link with England, 89, 90, 92, 93, 97, 98; as middle-class sport, 93, 94–5, 96; moral and physical values of, 93, 96–7, 165n32; in private schools, 93, 165n32; social culture of, 88, 90

Cricketer's Hotel, 164n14
Cromwell, Jim, 80
Cromwell, Samson, 80
cycling. See bicycles and cycling

Davis, Susan, 33
Dawe, Brian, 12
de Blaquiere, Peter Boyle, 14, 16
Deedes, Edmund, 15, 88–9, 90, 92, 163n1, 164n11
Detroit (Michigan), 10, 113, 114
Diamonds of the North (Humber), 113
disorder or inversion, games of. See traditional (alternate) games and sports
Dodds, E.K., 52, 61
dogfighting, 81
Dolson, "Old" Ned, 48, 154n57
Dominion Alliance Pioneer, 71
Dominion Day. See civic holiday celebrations
Donnelly, Peter, 81
Doubleday, Abner, 100
Drew, Andrew, 13, 14
Driving Park Association (Woodstock), 51–2, 60
duelling, 14
Dufferin lacrosse club (Ingersoll), 65, 72, 124, 125, 126
Duncombe revolt, 16
Dundas, 104, 105; Mechanics baseball club, 43, 107
Dunkin Act (1864), 72

Eastwood estate (Woodstock), 52, 82, 95
Eastwood foundry (Ingersoll), 19
Elder, A.N., 160n56
Elgin, James Bruce, 8th earl of, 15

Ellis Furniture Company (Ingersoll), 24, 114
Embro, 56
Embro Courier, 129
Emery, George, 141
equipment and clothing: for baseball, 12, 100, 106; for cricket, 90, 95, 96; for cyclists, 44, 46, 154n49
Evans Brothers piano factory (Ingersoll), 22

factories, 22–5; baseball teams, 24, 113–16, 136, 150n83; cycle clubs, 44–5; early closing, 23; wages in, 24, 45, 154n50; working conditions in, 23–5
fancy men, 82, 83
Farrell, Billy, 73, 83, 113, 136, 160n56
Farrell, Patrick, 103, 160n48
Farthing, Rev. Dr J.C., 77
fat mens' race, 33, 49
Finkle, Alexander, 135
firefighters, 38–9, 153n37
fires, 21, 39, 80
fireworks, 33
Firs Stables (Woodstock), 52
fixing: of baseball games, 108–9; at Caledonian games, 57; of lacrosse games, 128; of running races, 62–3, 84–6
Flamborough, 104
football, 3; Canadian Football League, 3; Tigers (Tiger Cats) team (Hamilton), 3, 114
Forbes, John, 52, 62, 134
Ford, Adam E., 12, 101, 102
Foresters. See Independent Order of Foresters
Francis, A.W., 81

fraternal orders and societies, 52, 69, 149n75; sporting freemasonary, 122. See also specific orders (Independent Order of Odd Fellows, Royal Arcanum, etc.)

Galloway, Bill "Hippo," 113
Galt, 112
gambling. See betting and gambling
Geertz, Clifford, 7
Gentlemen of the Province, 93, 99
Gibson, Joseph, 44, 71–2, 74, 94, 98
Gilkeson, J.S., 74
Gillespie, William, 117
Glengarry, 56
Governor's Road, 11, 12
Grace, W.G., 94
Graham, Philip, 13, 16, 17
Grand Trunk Railway (GTR), 25, 71, 104
Grant, J.L., 40
Grant's Pork Packing and Cheese Exporting Company (Ingersoll), 40
Gray, George, 126
greased pig, 33, 49
Great Western Railway (GWR), 18, 19, 21, 104, 106
Gruneau, Richard, 93, 107, 111
Guelph, 140; baseball matches, 104, 105, 107, 109, 110, 112, 134; Maple Leaf baseball club, 105, 107, 109, 132, 161n56
Guelph Evening Mercury, 107
Guillet, Edwin, 50
Gurnett, G.F., 81
Guttmann, Allen, 48

Hamilton, 18, 23, 56, 61, 66, 140; baseball

matches, 104, 105, 109, 113, 114; cricket matches, 91; Maple Leaf baseball club, 103, 105; Tigers (Tiger Cats), 3, 114
Hamilton, Peter, 91
Harris, James, 19, 20
Harriston: Brown Baseball club, 110
Hault Furniture Company (Ingersoll), 22, 114
Hay, J.G., 66, 114
Hay's Furniture Factory (Woodstock), 83, 114; baseball club, 41, 114
Head, Sir Edmund, 15
Hearn, William, 106
Hearn's hotel (Ingersoll), 103, 160n48
Heron, Craig, 35
Highland games. See Caledonian Games
Hincks, Francis, 18, 147n61
hockey, 41, 52, 131; National Hockey League, 3; Ontario Hockey Association, 131, 135, 158n22; Woodstock Hockey Club, 41
Hodge, A.G., 56, 62, 63, 156n105
Holman, Andrew, 6
Holmes, David, 117
horseracing, 12, 49–55, 134, 135; on civic holidays, 47; and gambling, 50, 51, 53–4; and horse breeding, 50–1; respectability vs rowdiness, 51, 53–5; role of inns and taverns, 12, 50, 51; and sports reform, 49–50, 51–3, 54–5; in Woodstock, 50–3
Howell, Colin, 98, 103
Howell, David, 119
Huggins, Mike, 51
Hughes, Thomas, 4

Humber, William, 105, 110; Diamonds of the North, 113
hunting (riding to the hunt), 15, 50, 90
Huskins, Bonnie, 34
Hyde, Frank, 135, 158n22

Independent Order of Foresters, 28, 39, 71
Independent Order of Good Templars, 28, 39
Independent Order of Odd Fellows, 28, 37, 39, 52
Indians, North American, 118, 126–7, 174n56
industrial development, 19–25, 148t
Ingersoll: baseball clubs, 173t (See also Victorias); Beehive factory, 80; bird's-eye view of, 26; board of trade, 22; Caledonian Games, 55–9; compared to Woodstock, 20–2, 134–7; cricket club, 94; Dominion Day parade, 39; early history, 10–11; fire (1872), 21, 39; industrial development in, 19–21, 22–3, 148t; lacrosse clubs, 173t; Dufferin lacrosse club, 65, 72, 124, 125, 126; Shamrock lacrosse club (Ingersoll), 117, 129; Mammoth Cheese, 19, 20, 29; naming of, 10; newspapers, 140; parklands, 29–30; pole vaulters, 49; "pond monster" prank, 34; population, 22, 148t, 149t; railway connections to, 18, 19, 21; rivalry with Woodstock, 47, 61–3, 65, 129; road connections to, 11, 12; and Silver Ball championship, 106; skating club, 80;

urban growth and services, 147t; Victoria Park, 37, 159n31
Ingersoll, Charles, 145n36
Ingersoll, James, 14, 78, 162n83
Ingersoll, James Beverly, 78–9, 84, 99
Ingersoll, James Hamilton, 145n36
Ingersoll, Thomas, 10, 144n8, 162n83
Ingersoll Amateur Athletic Association (IAAA): Dominion Day trades parade, 39; facilities and equipment, 75; founding of, 61, 65; 112, 134–5; members of, 76–7; organizers of, 71–2, 159t. See also Amateur Athletic Associations (AAAs)
Ingersoll Chronicle, 81; on Caledonian Games, 58; on cricket, 96–7; on IAAA, 74, 75; on lacrosse, 117, 124, 129; on public parks, 29; on skating club fire, 80; on workers' recreation, 23
Ingersoll family, 10–11
Ingersoll Fish and Game Association, 76
Ingersoll Sun, 24
Innkeepers Purse event, 12, 51
inns and taverns: and baseball, 103, 160n48; and horseracing, 12, 50, 51; social gatherings at, 12; and sparring matches, 62, 162n102
International Order of Odd Fellows, 72
inversion, games of. See traditional (alternate) games and sports

Jameson, Anna, 11, 90, 92

Jarvis Hall (Ingersoll),
   103, 160n48
Joyce, Tony, 81, 82, 86

Karn, D.W., 27, 66, 71,
   114–15
Karn, W.A., 25, 71, 72,
   135
Karn Drugstore (Wood-
   stock), 25, 71
Karn Organ factory
   (Woodstock), 24, 25;
   baseball club, 24, 114;
   cycle club, 44–5, 45;
   workers wages, 154n50
Kelly, Patrick, 128
Kennedy, Ed, 128
Kidd, Bruce, 3, 6, 133
Kincardine, 56
Kingsley, Charles, 4
Kingston, 56
Kintrea, James, 17
Kirsch, George, 103
Knights of Labor, 24, 26,
   40, 41, 86

Labour Day, 39
labour unrest, 24–5, 41
lacrosse, 117–30; amateur
   vs professional, 128;
   club members, 123–4;
   club organizers, 123;
   club structure of, 124;
   compared to baseball,
   117–18, 123, 124, 125;
   compared to cricket,
   97; as egalitarian, 123;
   exhibition matches,
   126; fan rowdiness,
   128; inter urban
   matches, 125, 126;
   junior clubs, 123, 124,
   173t; Native Indian
   roots of, 118, 126–7,
   174n56; player vio-
   lence, 128–9; prizes,
   121, 125–6; rules for,
   118, 121–2, 124; senior
   clubs and leagues, 123,
   124, 125–30, 173t;
   social agenda of,
   122–3; social values of,

118–20; as spectator
   sport, 125; teams, 41;
   as working class sport,
   123; and YMCA,
   173n32. See also spe-
   cific clubs (Beavers,
   Dufferins, etc.)
Lacrosse the National
   Game of Canada
   (Beers), 118
Ladies Benevolent Society
   (Woodstock), 121
Laird, Ed, 128
Light, Alexander Whalley,
   13, 14, 16, 17
Lindsay, Peter, 119
Littler piano factory
   (Ingersoll), 22
London, 18, 41, 56, 66,
   140; Alert baseball
   club, 66; baseball
   matches, 105, 109;
   cricket matches, 91;
   Tecumseh baseball club,
   102, 106, 108–9
Lorenz, Stacy, 5
Love's Hotel (Oxford
   County), 91
Lucknow, 56

McColl, Evans, 56
Macdonald, Sir John A.,
   72
McIntyre, James, 37–8,
   42; "A Civic Holiday
   Trip," 156n105; "Ode
   to a Mammoth
   Cheese," 29; "Our
   Firemen," 153n37
McIvor race, 82
McKay, W., 107
McKee, T.W., 120
Mackenzie, William Lyon,
   16
McLennan, Roderick "Big
   Rory," 57
MacLeod, David, 119
McLuhan, Marshall, 3, 6,
   133, 137
McMurray, William,
   162n88
McQueen, Fred, 93

McRobie, W. Ormie, 56
McWhinnie, Robert, 103
Mammoth Cheese, 19, 20,
   29
manliness: and baseball,
   111; and cricket, 96;
   and lacrosse, 118, 119,
   120–1; and muscular
   Christianity, 4, 78; and
   organized sport, 132
Maple Leaf baseball club:
   Guelph, 105, 107, 132,
   161n56, and Silver Ball,
   109; Hamilton, 103,
   105
Marks, Lynne, 6, 24, 25,
   38; Revivals and Roller
   Rinks, 120
Marsden Pond, 76
Martin, W. Henry, 83
Marylebone Cricket Club,
   89, 96
Mason and Company
   (Ingersoll), 126
masturbation, 120–1
Mechanics baseball club
   (Dundas), 43, 107
Merritt, William Hamil-
   ton, 145n36
Metcalfe, Alan, 110, 129,
   158n24
Methodist church, 11, 72,
   96
middle classes, Victorian:
   in Caledonian Society,
   55; and lacrosse, 123;
   power and resources of,
   17, 27–8; proportion of
   population, 27; rise of,
   9–10, 17–18; role in
   AAAS, 68–9; role in civic
   holiday celebrations,
   26, 31–2, 65, 132; role
   in representative sport,
   131–3; view of
   respectability, 26–31
military officers, retired:
   sporting activities of,
   15, 50, 89, 155n64; in
   Woodstock, 13, 88–9
militia, 12, 38
Mills, David, 9

Mills, Walter, 93
Mitchell Carriage
Company (Ingersoll), 40
Montreal, 56, 61, 129
Montreal Amateur Athletic Association
(MAAA), 60–1, 135, 157n6, 161n72
Morgan, Cecilia, 14
Morrow Screw and Nut
Company (Ingersoll), 22, 23
Mott, Morris, 4, 55
Mount Elgin Brass Band, 40
Muir Block (Woodstock), 75
Murphy, Rev. Arthur, 77
muscular Christianity, 4, 5, 54, 78, 99, 121, 132, 165n32
musical events: at Caledonian Games, 56; at civic holiday celebrations, 66

National Association of
Base Ball Players
(NABBP), 104
National Lacrosse Association (NLA), 118, 124, 125; Claxton Flags, 121
Native Peoples, 118, 126–7, 174n56
Nesbitt, Edward W., 122–3, 126, 135
Newcastle, 105
newspapers: biased reporting, 47, 107, 129; in Oxford County, 15, 140, 165n21; sports coverage, 5, 48, 81–2, 136, 140; support of AAAs, 81; and urban boosterism, 28–9. See also individual newspapers (Ingersoll Chronicle, Woodstock Sentinel, etc.)
New York Athletic Club, 157n6

New York Clipper, 75; on cricket and baseball, 100, 103; on Young Canadians, 101, 105, 108
New York Ladies Handicap, 52
New York Scotsman, 56
Niagara, 18, 108
Nichol, Rev. Dr, 120
Nissouri, 56
North American United
Caledonian Association, 56
North Oxford township, 101
Norwich, 12, 94, 125
Noxon Brothers Agricultural Works (Ingersoll), 19, 24–5, 40; baseball club, 114

Odd Fellows. See Independent Order of Odd Fellows
Old Stage Road. See Beachville road
Olympic games, 137
O'Neill, Charley, 113
O'Neill, Edward "Tip," 112, 170n70
O'Neill, James, 103, 160n48
Ontario Hockey Association, 131, 135, 158n22
Ontario Jockey Club, 52, 82, 96
Order of Fraternal
Guardians, 28, 71
Order of Scottish Clans, 28, 70
Ottawa, 43
Otters lacrosse team (Woodstock), 67, 68, 71
Oxford County: baseball in, 100; land registry office, 14, 162n83; newspapers, 15, 140, 165n21; roads, 10
Oxford Hotel (Woodstock), 83

Oxford-on-the-Thames, 10
Oxford Rifles, 70, 78, 79
Oxford Village, 10, 162n83

Page, George, 24
Palmer, Bryan, 34, 114
parades, 32–2, 36–46; bicycle, 42, 43–4, 45; callathumpian, 33–4; political elements of, 36; and respectability, 35–6; routes of, 36, 38; sports teams in, 41–6, 66; trades processions, 39
Paris, 94, 160n48; Brants lacrosse club, 66
parklands, public, 29–30; role in representative sport, 29–30, 95; use as pastures, 29; use by AAAs, 79–80, 84
Patterson factory (Woodstock), 128
Patteson, Thomas Charles, 52, 82, 155n84, 167n53; on cricket, 95–6
Pattullo, Andrew, 81, 135
Penfold, Steve, 35
Pinto, Barbara, 129
pioneer communities, 11–12
pole-vaulting, 49
political patronage, 13–14
political reform movement, 12–13, 17
Pope, Steve, 6
Port Dover, 86
Port Dover and Lake
Huron Railway, 19, 21
Port Stanley, 86
Poulter, Gillian, 123
Pouyez, Christian, 141
pre-modern sport, 48
Princeton, 94
prizefighting, 81–2
prizes: cash, 56, 57, 125; symbolic, 64, 126
professional athletes: and amateur events, 63, 73;

on baseball teams,
110–11; itinerant, 56,
57–8, 62, 63, 81–2;
local attitudes to,
112–13, 158n22. *See
also* amateurism and
amateur athletes
pugilism, 12
Pyne, Charles, 76, 80, 83,
134, 161n72

Quakers (Society of
Friends), 12
Quebec City, 61
Queen's Birthday (24
May). *See* civic holiday
celebrations
Queen's Plate, 52, 53, 135

racism, 36, 153n26
railways. *See* transportation
Rebellion Losses Bill, 15
records (of AAA events), 67
Redmond, Gerald, 4
representative sport: athletes or teams as surro-
gates, 3–4, 42, 67, 137;
contradictions in,
136–7; and imported
players, 110, 131–2; as
invented athletic tradi-
tion, 6; local *vs*
national, 6, 135, 139;
and mass media, 5; and
middle-class values,
131–3; model of, 3–5;
and public parklands,
29–30; resistance to, 5;
town-team link, 125,
126–7; and urban boos-
terism, 103–4, 105–6,
107, 132
respectability, 26–31,
131–7; and ama-
teurism, 133; meaning
of, 26; and urban boos-
terism, 28–9, 107; *vs*
rowdiness, 33–5, 51,
53–5, 107, 129,
158n24
responsible government, 17

Revivals and Roller Rinks
(Marks), 120
Richardson, H., 126
Richards Soap Factory
(Woodstock), 114
Riess, Steven, 119
rivalry, inter town, 47,
61–3, 65, 107, 127
roads. *See* transportation
Robertson, Jessie, 56
Robinson, Alby, 57, 62,
64, 84, 85
Roman Catholic church,
123, 132
Ross, Alex, 113
rowdiness: in horseracing,
51, 53–5; of spectators,
81, 107, 128, 129; *vs*
respectability, 33–5, 35,
51, 53–5, 107, 129,
158n24
Royal Arcanum, 28, 52,
70
Royal Arch Masons, 28
Royal Hotel (Woodstock),
83, 104, 134
Royal Hotel Block (Inger-
soll), 75
rules: for baseball, 12,
102–3, 104, 109–10,
121, 134; for lacrosse,
118, 121–2, 124; for
traditional games and
sport, 48

Sabbatarian observance,
116, 172n80; and base-
ball, 116; and horserac-
ing, 53; and leisure
sports, 79; in pioneer
communities, 11
sack races, 33, 48, 154n59
St Catharines, 61
St James Anglican Church
(Ingersoll), 77
St James Hotel (Toronto),
56
St Mary's, 57, 140
St Mary's *Journal-Argus,*
57
St Paul's Anglican Church
(Woodstock), 15, 16,

77, 78, 90; tombstone
affair (1845), 17
St Thomas, 21, 40, 41, 66,
94
Salvation Army, 26
Sandiford, Keith A.P., 89
Sarnia, 18
Sawtell, R.W., 92
Scarff Carriage Shops
(Woodstock), 114
Scott Act, 36
Scottish American Journal,
58
Secord, Laura, 144n5
secret societies, 28, 39
Shamrock lacrosse club
(Ingersoll), 117, 129
Shenston, T.S., 17
Silver Ball (Canadian Base-
ball Championship),
43, 44, 107, 121, 135;
creation of, 70, 101,
104, 134, 135; rules of,
104–5, 121; Victorias'
winning of, 44, 72,
105, 106, 107, 118;
Woodstock's loss of,
109, 134
Simcoe, 66, 94, 128
Simcoe, John Graves, 10,
12, 144n8
Sinclair, James, 35
skating club (Ingersoll), 80
Sleeman, George, 110,
132, 161n56, 170n64
Snelgrove cabinetmakers,
92
Sons of England, 28, 97
Sons of Scotland, 37
sparring matches, 62,
162n102
spectator-oriented sports:
AAA events, 67; Cale-
donian Games, 56, 57;
fan rowdiness, 81, 107,
128; and importance of
winning, 108–9; popu-
larity of baseball, 107,
108; track and field,
67; and violence, 129
sporting freemasonary,
122

Sporting Life, 75, 101
sporting parades, 41–6
sport reformers: and
  amateur ideology,
  136–7; and baseball,
  100; and cricket, 99;
  and lacrosse, 118, 123,
  125, 128; methods of,
  73; national influence
  of, 60–1; resistance to,
  80–7, 128–9; support
  of AAAs, 62; and town-
  team link, 106, 110,
  125, 126–7, 136–7; and
  traditional games, 47,
  49, 62
sports, "illegitimate" or
  illegal, 81–2
steeplechases, 15, 50, 90,
  146n47, 155n64
Stewart Stove Company
  (Woodstock), 23
Stratford, 43, 66, 131,
  140; baseball matches,
  112, 113, 114
Stratford *Herald,* 62
strikes, 24–5
Sutherland, Alex Mathe-
  son, 11
Sutherland, James, 82

teams and team sport: and
  character development,
  4, 121; imported
  players, 110, 131–2; in
  parades, 41–6; as surrogates, 3–4, 42
Tecumseh baseball club
  (London), 102, 106,
  108–9
temperance legislation, 36
temperance movement, 72
temperance organizations,
  28
Templars. *See* Independent
  Order of Good Tem-
  plars
tennis, 133; Western
  Ontario Lawn Tennis
  Association, 135
Thackeray, William, 122
Thames River, 10, 51

Thomas Organ Factory
  (Woodstock), 23, 114
Thompson, J.E., 103,
  160n48
three-legged races, 33, 48
Tigers (Tiger Cats) foot-
  ball team (Hamilton),
  3, 114
Tillsonburg, 94, 95
Tillsonburg *Liberal,* 129
Tom Brown's Schooldays
  (Hughes), 4
tombstone affair (Wood-
  stock, 1845), 17
Toronto, 18, 21, 56, 61,
  66, 140; baseball
  matches, 109, 113, 114
Toronto Blue Jays, 3
Toronto *Globe,* 81–2, 90
Toronto *Mail,* 46, 52, 82
Toronto *Telegram,* 131
Tory elite, 9, 13–17; exclusivity of, 15, 90, 133;
  as leisure class, 15,
  89–90; political patronage, 13–14
Totten, Warren, 93, 98–9
track and field: for female
  athletes, 159n38;
  gender and age specific,
  48, 132; lacrosse
  running competitions,
  126; regulation of, 63,
  66–7; roots in tradi-
  tional games, 48
trades processions, 39
traditional (alternate)
  games and sports, 5,
  80–7; at civic holiday
  celebrations, 33, 47;
  games of disorder or
  inversion, 48–9, 67,
  136; illegal, 81–2; *vs*
  organized sport, 47, 67,
  136
transportation: early
  roads, 10, 11, 12,
  91–2; inns and taverns,
  12; railways, 18–20,
  25, 134; for sporting
  events, 91–2, 94, 95,
  104, 107, 134

Turquand, Dr John, 126
Two Years Ago (Kinglsey),
  4

uniforms. *See* equipment
  and clothing
Upper Canada Club
  (Toronto), 14
Upper Canada College
  (Toronto), 78, 93, 99
Upper Canadian rebellion,
  16, 90
urban boosterism, 18; and
  baseball, 103–4, 105,
  113, 114; and civic
  holiday celebrations,
  31, 36–7; and fan row-
  diness, 81; and Inger-
  soll-Woodstock rivalry,
  61–3, 65; and lacrosse,
  129–30; and represen-
  tative sport teams,
  103–4, 105–6, 107,
  136–7; and respectabil-
  ity, 28–9, 107; role of
  AAAs, 60; role of orga-
  nized sport in, 47; and
  spectator sports, 81;
  view of amateur sport,
  5–6

Vance, C.L., 135
Vance, James, 126
Vansittart, Henry, 13, 14
Vansittart, John George,
  15, 17, 147n61,
  165n21
Victoria Park (Ingersoll),
  37, 159n31
Victorias baseball team
  (Ingersoll), 43; forma-
  tion of, 102; inter
  urban matches, 103–4;
  in lacrosse match, 117,
  121; members of, 102,
  109, 168n10; name of,
  168n8; as Silver Ball
  champions, 44, 72,
  105, 106, 107, 118
violence: of spectators,
  107, 129; of team
  players, 128–9

voluntary societies and organizations, 28, 38, 39

Waites, William, 83
Walker House Hotel (Toronto), 109
Walsh, Michael, 135
Waters, Greg, 54
Weeks, Alf, 113
Weeks, George, 113
Welford, Dr A. Beverly, 70–1, 72
Wells, Thomas, 103
Western Ontario Lawn Tennis Association, 135
Westward Ho! (Kingsley), 4
wheelbarrow races, 48, 154n59
Whitson, David, 107, 111
Wilson, Catherine Anne, 11
Wilson, William, 17
Windsor, 18
winning, importance of, 136–7; in baseball, 108–9; in lacrosse, 128
women: as athletes, 132–3, 159n38; as callathumpians, 34; as cyclists, 44, 45, 46, 133; exclusion from AAA, 66–7, 74; exclusion from baseball, 102; exclusion from holiday parades, 36; influence on male children, 119
Wood, C.L., 103, 104, 135, 160n48
Woodbine Race Track (Toronto), 53
Woodcock, Ralph, 106
Woodroofe, Samuel, 126, 135
Woodstock: as aristocratic, 29, 90, 134; as baseball centre, 106; baseball clubs, 41, 114, 136, 173t (*See also* Woodstocks; Young Canadi-

ans); bird's-eye view of, 27; board of trade, 22; Central Park, 83; city status of, 125; as cock-fighting centre, 162n102; compared to Ingersoll, 20–2, 134–7; Dundas Street, 21, 25, 75; early history of, 12–15; first election in, 17; as gambling centre, 60–1; as horseracing centre, 50–3; as industrial centre, 23, 29, 135, 148t; lacrosse clubs, 41, 173t (*see also* Beavers; Otters); leadership in sport, 134–5; military presence in, 13, 88–9, 90; newspapers, 140; parklands, 29–30; population, 22, 148t, 149t; railway connections to, 18, 19, 21, 148n72; rivalry with Ingersoll, 47, 61–3, 65, 129; road connections to, 11, 12; urban growth and services, 147t
Woodstock Amateur Athletic Association (WAAA): affiliation with AAA of C, 73, 135–6; and alternate sports, 73; and civic holiday sports, 58, 157n6; club managers, 76; and factory baseball clubs, 113, 114; financing of, 157n6; founding of, 58, 60, 112, 134; grounds, facilities and equipment, 75–6, 161n68; hill overlooking grounds, 84, 136; organizers of, 67–71, 159t; resistance to, 84. *See also* Amateur Athletic Associations (AAAS)
Woodstock Cricket Club, 88–9, 90–2, 101, 163n1

Woodstock Cycle Club, 42–3, 71
Woodstock *Herald,* 50
Woodstock Hockey Club, 41
Woodstock Old Boys Reunion, 70, 71
Woodstock Opera House, 98
Woodstock rules (baseball), 104, 109, 134
Woodstocks baseball team (Woodstock), 66, 111, 112
Woodstock *Sentinel,* 81; on AAA, 77; on alternate sports, 81; on baseball, 112; on civic holidays, 35–6, 66; on gambling, 65; on Ingersoll, 47; on labour unrest, 25; on lacrosse, 118, 124, 128; on prizefighting, 82; on Pyne, 83; on Silver Ball championship, 118
Woodstock *Sentinel-Review,* 45, 76, 125, 127
Woodstock *Spirit of the Times,* 81, 82
Woodstock *Weekly Review,* 94, 97
work bees, 11
working class: and alchohol, 116; August civic holiday activities, 86, 136; and baseball, 102, 113–16; conditions in factories, 23–5; and cricket, 92; in cycle clubs, 44–6; exclusion from AAAS, 69, 73, 74, 79; exclusion from cricket, 96; exclusion from representative sport, 132; itinerant workers, 25; job-related injury, 24, 150n83; juvenile crime, 119; labour unrest, 24–5, 41; and lacrosse, 123; leisure time and activi-

ties, 79, 86, 115, 116, 132, 172n80; in militia, 38; population of, 149t; Protestant church organizations, 26; role in holiday parades, 36, 38, 39–41; trades processions, 39; and traditional (alternate) sports, 62, 83; wages, 24, 45, 154n50

wrestling, 12, 86
Wright, Rev. P., 120

young boy problem, 119–20
Young Canadians baseball team (Woodstock), 21, 41, 43, 101; formation of, 102; inter urban matches, 103–4, 106, 107; members of,

102, 108, 109, 168n10; and Silver Ball championship, 44, 70, 101, 104–5, 107
Young Men's Christian Association (YMCA), 120, 121, 173n32

Zingari cricket tour, 94
Zorra, 56, 101, 102

SI